Almighty God,
Father of our Lord Jesus Christ,
grant, we pray,
that we might be grounded and settled
in your truth
by the coming of your Holy Spirit
into our hearts.

What we do not know,
reveal to us;
what is lacking within us,
make complete;
that which we do know,
confirm in us;
and keep us blameless in your service,
through Jesus Christ our Lord.

Amen.

IMMERSE™
—— The Reading Bible ——

CHRONICLES

Tyndale House Publishers, Inc.
Carol Stream, Illinois

CREATED IN ALLIANCE WITH

INSTITUTE FOR
BIBLE READING

Visit Tyndale online at www.immerseBible.com, www.newlivingtranslation.com, and www.tyndale.com.

Visit the Institute for Bible Reading at www.instituteforbiblereading.org.

For information about special discounts for bulk purchases, please contact Tyndale House Publishers at csresponse@tyndale.com, or call 1-800-323-9400.

Library of Congress Cataloging-in-Publication Data

Names: Tyndale House Publishers.
Title: Chronicles.
Other titles: Bible. Chronicles. English. New Living Translation. 2017. |
  Bible. Ezra. English. New Living Translation. 2017. | Bible. Nehemiah.
  English. New Living Translation. 2017. | Bible. Esther. English. New
  Living Translation. 2017. | Bible. Daniel. English. New Living
  Translation. 2017.
Description: Carol Stream, Illinois : Tyndale House Publishers, Inc., 2017. |
  Series: Immerse: the reading Bible
Identifiers: LCCN 2017025336 | ISBN 9781496424198 (sc)
Classification: LCC BS195 .N394 2017 | DDC 222/.0520834—dc23 LC record available at
  https://lccn.loc.gov/2017025336

Printed in the United States of America

23 22 21 20 19 18 17
 7   6   5   4   3   2   1

CONTENTS

––––– *Welcome to* –––––

I M M E R S E
The Bible Reading Experience

The Bible is a great gift. The Creator of all things entered into our human story and spoke to us. He inspired people over many centuries to shape words into books that reveal his mind, bringing wisdom into our lives and light to our paths. But God's biggest intention for the Bible is to invite us into its Story. What God wants for us, more than anything else, is that we make the Bible's great drama of restoration and new life the story of our lives, too.

The appropriate way to receive a gift like this is to come to know the Bible deeply, to lose ourselves in it precisely so that we can find ourselves in it. In other words, we need to immerse ourselves in it—to read God's words at length and without distraction, to read with deeper historical and literary perspective, and to read through the Bible with friends in a regular three-year rhythm. *Immerse: The Bible Reading Experience* has been specially designed for this purpose.

Immerse: The Reading Bible presents each book of the Bible without the distractions of chapter and verse markers, subject headers, or footnotes—all later historical additions to the text. The *Holy Bible*, New Living Translation, is presented in a single-column format with easy-to-read type. To provide meaningful perspective, book introductions give historical and literary context, and the books are often reordered chronologically or grouped with books that share similar ancient audiences. Every feature in this unique Bible enhances the opportunity for readers to engage with God's words in simple clarity.

A more complete explanation of this unique Bible presentation can be found in the articles that begin on page 183 at the back of this volume.

—— *Introduction to* ——

CHRONICLES

WE BEGAN OUR JOURNEY into the Bible's First Testament with a comprehensive telling of Israel's history, from the creation story to Israel's exile from the Land of Promise. Then we heard the prophets delivering the word of the LORD to Israel, intervening as the people wandered again and again from their allegiance to God. We joined with Israel in singing songs of both lament and praise, entering into the worship of God in a way that acknowledges a full range of human emotions. We listened in as Israel's wisdom teachers taught the good way of life meant for all the Creator's people.

This final part of the *Immerse* First Testament contains its three remaining books. This last collection focuses once again on telling stories. The Hebrew expression translated as *Chronicles* means "words or events of the days." That is, it's a record of day-to-day events, much like a diary or journal. The stories in this volume are all "chronicles" that tell how the people of God lived out their faith after his covenants with Noah, Abraham, Moses, and David were established.

First comes the book of Chronicles–Ezra–Nehemiah. This unique telling of Israel's history is presented in most Bibles as four separate books, although it was originally a unified work. (Notice that the ending of 2 Chronicles overlaps with the beginning of Ezra.) This book of Chronicles–Ezra–Nehemiah emphasizes the importance of the true worship of God. The shorter books in this volume, Esther and Daniel, show God's people facing extreme challenges in foreign lands. Whether in their careful day-to-day observance of God's Law or in their willingness to suffer death through persecution, faithful and courageous men and women demonstrate an unfailing loyalty to God.

All three works presented here were written after the Jewish people were conquered by foreign empires and scattered among the other nations. These books tell stories that carry on the grand Story of God's covenants into later centuries. It is important to read these final books of the First Testament with the overall development of the Bible's story in mind.

God created the world to be his temple, the place where he would dwell in fellowship with humanity. After sin entered the world, God chose Abraham and his family, the people of Israel, as those who would bring blessing and life back into the world. But most of the story so far has been about Israel's struggle to live up to its divinely given vocation. God initiated covenants with humanity in order to move the story closer and closer to his intention for all of creation. But the goal has not been reached. God wants a people who worship him well so they can go out into the world to share his light and life.

The Exile had caused a crisis in Israel's story, leading many to question God's own faithfulness to the covenant as well as their status as his chosen people. God's vision for Israel and for the world could not be fulfilled as long as foreign powers controlled God's people and their land.

These books at the end of the First Testament were written to remind the people of their true story and their ultimate hope. The issues raised will continue into the period between the First Testament and the New Testament. As the years go by and Israel's struggles persist, the longing for God to keep his covenant promises will grow stronger and stronger. This is a story begging for its fitting conclusion.

IMMERSED IN CHRONICLES–EZRA–NEHEMIAH

IN 407 BC, leaders of the Jewish community on the Egyptian island fortress of Elephantine wrote to the Persian governor in Judea for help. They explained that their ancestors had built a temple to Yahu (Yahweh) there but that it had recently been destroyed by a mob incited by the priests of the Egyptian god Khnum. These Jewish leaders complained that they had requested assistance from the priests and elders in Jerusalem but had heard nothing back. In response, the Persian governor authorized them to rebuild their temple. But why hadn't their fellow Jews in Jerusalem been the first to help?

This request for the Jerusalem community to invest in a temple in Egypt illustrates why the writing of a grand, new history of Israel was necessary. These Jews in Egypt were worshiping "Yahu" alongside other gods in a mix of Jewish and pagan rituals. This newly written history repeatedly makes a vital claim: True worship of God will follow the instructions God gave in the Law of Moses and will occur in the place God has chosen—the Temple in Jerusalem.

This history comprises the books commonly known as 1 and 2 Chronicles, Ezra, and Nehemiah. It draws on accounts kept by prophets in earlier times, on the personal memoirs of Ezra and Nehemiah, and on community records. These materials were brought together into one large work to address the particular challenges of this time.

Israel's previously written history (from Genesis to Samuel–Kings) addressed the situation of Israel's exile and answered the question: *Why did the Exile happen?* Chronicles–Ezra–Nehemiah addresses the situation of the people after the Exile and answers the question: *Who are we now?*

This new telling of Israel's history begins with an elaborate genealogy (a list of ancestors) that goes all the way back to Adam and reveals the origins and development of the twelve tribes of Israel. Special attention is given to Judah (the tribe of King David) and Levi (the tribe of priests). This genealogy helps the current generation see that they are linked to Israel's most ancient people and stories. Thus, the lists begin the work of reminding them of who they are.

As the book changes to narrative, the reigns of David and Solomon come into the spotlight. The story alternates three times between accounts of David's wars and long descriptions of arrangements he made for true worship in the Temple. David is careful to ensure that God will be worshiped in the place and in the way that God himself has chosen. But since David is a man of bloodshed and war, God appoints his son Solomon to actually build the Temple. With its completion, the key sign of God's presence among his people is now in place.

The reigns of later kings are described more briefly, with the exceptions of Hezekiah and Josiah whose religious reforms restore the proper worship of the LORD after periods of idolatry. In contrast, most of the kings lead the people astray from God's ways. This unfaithfulness becomes chronic and widespread, and the people are ultimately punished with exile.

The story continues with the memoirs of Ezra and Nehemiah, describing the people's return to Judea from exile. Following God's instructions and with his help, they rebuild Jerusalem's Temple and walls. As the story reaches its conclusion, the returned exiles diligently restore their ancient worship and community practices. At a grand ceremony, the Book of the Law of Moses is read aloud to the entire community, leading first to weeping and confession and then to celebration, as the people understand and respond to God's words.

The Temple and the Law lie at the heart of the true worship of God. The Temple represents God's new world, and the Law reveals the path for the community to become his renewed people. This community, as the covenant people, are to resume their special role in God's plan. So it's vital for them to know and obey God's instructions, to protect their faith from being diluted and distorted, and to worship and honor God in his Holy Place.

CHRONICLES–EZRA–NEHEMIAH

———— ✠ ————

The descendants of Adam were Seth, Enosh, Kenan, Mahalalel, Jared, Enoch, Methuselah, Lamech, and Noah.

The sons of Noah were Shem, Ham, and Japheth.

The descendants of Japheth were Gomer, Magog, Madai, Javan, Tubal, Meshech, and Tiras.

The descendants of Gomer were Ashkenaz, Riphath, and Togarmah.

The descendants of Javan were Elishah, Tarshish, Kittim, and Rodanim.

The descendants of Ham were Cush, Mizraim, Put, and Canaan.

The descendants of Cush were Seba, Havilah, Sabtah, Raamah, and Sabteca. The descendants of Raamah were Sheba and Dedan. Cush was also the ancestor of Nimrod, who was the first heroic warrior on earth.

Mizraim was the ancestor of the Ludites, Anamites, Lehabites, Naphtuhites, Pathrusites, Casluhites, and the Caphtorites, from whom the Philistines came.

Canaan's oldest son was Sidon, the ancestor of the Sidonians. Canaan was also the ancestor of the Hittites, Jebusites, Amorites, Girgashites, Hivites, Arkites, Sinites, Arvadites, Zemarites, and Hamathites.

The descendants of Shem were Elam, Asshur, Arphaxad, Lud, and Aram.

The descendants of Aram were Uz, Hul, Gether, and Mash.

Arphaxad was the father of Shelah.

Shelah was the father of Eber.

Eber had two sons. The first was named Peleg (which means "division"), for during his lifetime the people of the world were divided into different language groups. His brother's name was Joktan.

Joktan was the ancestor of Almodad, Sheleph, Hazarmaveth, Jerah, Hadoram, Uzal, Diklah, Obal, Abimael, Sheba, Ophir, Havilah, and Jobab. All these were descendants of Joktan.

So this is the family line descended from Shem: Arphaxad, Shelah, Eber, Peleg, Reu, Serug, Nahor, Terah, and Abram, later known as Abraham.

+ + +

The sons of Abraham were Isaac and Ishmael. These are their genealogical records:

The sons of Ishmael were Nebaioth (the oldest), Kedar, Adbeel, Mibsam, Mishma, Dumah, Massa, Hadad, Tema, Jetur, Naphish, and Kedemah. These were the sons of Ishmael.

The sons of Keturah, Abraham's concubine, were Zimran, Jokshan, Medan, Midian, Ishbak, and Shuah.
The sons of Jokshan were Sheba and Dedan.
The sons of Midian were Ephah, Epher, Hanoch, Abida, and Eldaah.
All these were descendants of Abraham through his concubine Keturah.

Abraham was the father of Isaac. The sons of Isaac were Esau and Israel.

The sons of Esau were Eliphaz, Reuel, Jeush, Jalam, and Korah.
The descendants of Eliphaz were Teman, Omar, Zepho, Gatam, Kenaz, and Amalek, who was born to Timna.
The descendants of Reuel were Nahath, Zerah, Shammah, and Mizzah.

The descendants of Seir were Lotan, Shobal, Zibeon, Anah, Dishon, Ezer, and Dishan.
The descendants of Lotan were Hori and Hemam. Lotan's sister was named Timna.
The descendants of Shobal were Alvan, Manahath, Ebal, Shepho, and Onam.
The descendants of Zibeon were Aiah and Anah.
The son of Anah was Dishon.
The descendants of Dishon were Hemdan, Eshban, Ithran, and Keran.
The descendants of Ezer were Bilhan, Zaavan, and Akan.
The descendants of Dishan were Uz and Aran.

These are the kings who ruled in the land of Edom before any king ruled over the Israelites:

Bela son of Beor, who ruled from his city of Dinhabah.
When Bela died, Jobab son of Zerah from Bozrah became king in his place.
When Jobab died, Husham from the land of the Temanites became king in his place.
When Husham died, Hadad son of Bedad became king in his place

and ruled from the city of Avith. He was the one who destroyed the Midianite army in the land of Moab.

When Hadad died, Samlah from the city of Masrekah became king in his place.

When Samlah died, Shaul from the city of Rehoboth-on-the-River became king in his place.

When Shaul died, Baal-hanan son of Acbor became king in his place.

When Baal-hanan died, Hadad became king in his place and ruled from the city of Pau. His wife was Mehetabel, the daughter of Matred and granddaughter of Me-zahab. Then Hadad died.

The clan leaders of Edom were Timna, Alvah, Jetheth, Oholibamah, Elah, Pinon, Kenaz, Teman, Mibzar, Magdiel, and Iram. These are the clan leaders of Edom.

✦ ✦ ✦

The sons of Israel were Reuben, Simeon, Levi, Judah, Issachar, Zebulun, Dan, Joseph, Benjamin, Naphtali, Gad, and Asher.

✦

Judah had three sons from Bathshua, a Canaanite woman. Their names were Er, Onan, and Shelah. But the LORD saw that the oldest son, Er, was a wicked man, so he killed him. Later Judah had twin sons from Tamar, his widowed daughter-in-law. Their names were Perez and Zerah. So Judah had five sons in all.

The sons of Perez were Hezron and Hamul.

The sons of Zerah were Zimri, Ethan, Heman, Calcol, and Darda—five in all.

The son of Carmi (a descendant of Zimri) was Achan, who brought disaster on Israel by taking plunder that had been set apart for the LORD.

The son of Ethan was Azariah.

The sons of Hezron were Jerahmeel, Ram, and Caleb.

Ram was the father of Amminadab.

Amminadab was the father of Nahshon, a leader of Judah.

Nahshon was the father of Salmon.

Salmon was the father of Boaz.

Boaz was the father of Obed.

Obed was the father of Jesse.

Jesse's first son was Eliab, his second was Abinadab, his third was Shimea, his fourth was Nethanel, his fifth was Raddai, his sixth was Ozem, and his seventh was David.

Their sisters were named Zeruiah and Abigail. Zeruiah had three sons named Abishai, Joab, and Asahel. Abigail married a man named Jether, an Ishmaelite, and they had a son named Amasa.

Hezron's son Caleb had sons from his wife Azubah and from Jerioth. Her sons were named Jesher, Shobab, and Ardon. After Azubah died, Caleb married Ephrathah, and they had a son named Hur. Hur was the father of Uri. Uri was the father of Bezalel.

When Hezron was sixty years old, he married Gilead's sister, the daughter of Makir. They had a son named Segub. Segub was the father of Jair, who ruled twenty-three towns in the land of Gilead. (But Geshur and Aram captured the Towns of Jair and also took Kenath and its sixty surrounding villages.) All these were descendants of Makir, the father of Gilead.

Soon after Hezron died in the town of Caleb-ephrathah, his wife Abijah gave birth to a son named Ashhur (the father of Tekoa).

The sons of Jerahmeel, the oldest son of Hezron, were Ram (the firstborn), Bunah, Oren, Ozem, and Ahijah. Jerahmeel had a second wife named Atarah. She was the mother of Onam.

The sons of Ram, the oldest son of Jerahmeel, were Maaz, Jamin, and Eker.

The sons of Onam were Shammai and Jada.

The sons of Shammai were Nadab and Abishur.

The sons of Abishur and his wife Abihail were Ahban and Molid.

The sons of Nadab were Seled and Appaim. Seled died without children, but Appaim had a son named Ishi. The son of Ishi was Sheshan. Sheshan had a descendant named Ahlai.

The sons of Jada, Shammai's brother, were Jether and Jonathan. Jether died without children, but Jonathan had two sons named Peleth and Zaza.

These were all descendants of Jerahmeel.

Sheshan had no sons, though he did have daughters. He also had an Egyptian servant named Jarha. Sheshan gave one of his daughters to be the wife of Jarha, and they had a son named Attai.

Attai was the father of Nathan.

Nathan was the father of Zabad.

Zabad was the father of Ephlal.

Ephlal was the father of Obed.

Obed was the father of Jehu.

Jehu was the father of Azariah.

Azariah was the father of Helez.

Helez was the father of Eleasah.

Eleasah was the father of Sismai.
Sismai was the father of Shallum.
Shallum was the father of Jekamiah.
Jekamiah was the father of Elishama.

The descendants of Caleb, the brother of Jerahmeel, included Mesha
(the firstborn), who became the father of Ziph. Caleb's descendants
also included the sons of Mareshah, the father of Hebron.

The sons of Hebron were Korah, Tappuah, Rekem, and Shema. Shema
was the father of Raham. Raham was the father of Jorkeam. Rekem
was the father of Shammai. The son of Shammai was Maon. Maon was
the father of Beth-zur.

Caleb's concubine Ephah gave birth to Haran, Moza, and Gazez. Haran
was the father of Gazez.

The sons of Jahdai were Regem, Jotham, Geshan, Pelet, Ephah, and
Shaaph.

Another of Caleb's concubines, Maacah, gave birth to Sheber and
Tirhanah. She also gave birth to Shaaph (the father of Madmannah)
and Sheva (the father of Macbenah and Gibea). Caleb also had a
daughter named Acsah.

These were all descendants of Caleb.

The sons of Hur, the oldest son of Caleb's wife Ephrathah, were Shobal
(the founder of Kiriath-jearim), Salma (the founder of Bethlehem),
and Hareph (the founder of Beth-gader).

The descendants of Shobal (the founder of Kiriath-jearim) were Haroeh,
half the Manahathites, and the families of Kiriath-jearim—the Ithrites,
Puthites, Shumathites, and Mishraites, from whom came the people of
Zorah and Eshtaol.

The descendants of Salma were the people of Bethlehem, the
Netophathites, Atroth-beth-joab, the other half of the Manahathites,
the Zorites, and the families of scribes living at Jabez—the Tirathites,
Shimeathites, and Sucathites. All these were Kenites who descended
from Hammath, the father of the family of Recab.

These are the sons of David who were born in Hebron:

The oldest was Amnon, whose mother was Ahinoam from Jezreel.
The second was Daniel, whose mother was Abigail from Carmel.
The third was Absalom, whose mother was Maacah, the daughter
of Talmai, king of Geshur.
The fourth was Adonijah, whose mother was Haggith.
The fifth was Shephatiah, whose mother was Abital.

The sixth was Ithream, whose mother was Eglah, David's wife.
These six sons were born to David in Hebron, where he reigned seven and a half years.

Then David reigned another thirty-three years in Jerusalem. The sons born to David in Jerusalem included Shammua, Shobab, Nathan, and Solomon. Their mother was Bathsheba, the daughter of Ammiel. David also had nine other sons: Ibhar, Elishua, Elpelet, Nogah, Nepheg, Japhia, Elishama, Eliada, and Eliphelet.

These were the sons of David, not including his sons born to his concubines. Their sister was named Tamar.

The descendants of Solomon were Rehoboam, Abijah, Asa, Jehoshaphat, Jehoram, Ahaziah, Joash, Amaziah, Uzziah, Jotham, Ahaz, Hezekiah, Manasseh, Amon, and Josiah.

The sons of Josiah were Johanan (the oldest), Jehoiakim (the second), Zedekiah (the third), and Jehoahaz (the fourth).

The successors of Jehoiakim were his son Jehoiachin and his brother Zedekiah.

The sons of Jehoiachin, who was taken prisoner by the Babylonians, were Shealtiel, Malkiram, Pedaiah, Shenazzar, Jekamiah, Hoshama, and Nedabiah.

The sons of Pedaiah were Zerubbabel and Shimei.

The sons of Zerubbabel were Meshullam and Hananiah. (Their sister was Shelomith.) His five other sons were Hashubah, Ohel, Berekiah, Hasadiah, and Jushab-hesed.

The sons of Hananiah were Pelatiah and Jeshaiah. Jeshaiah's son was Rephaiah. Rephaiah's son was Arnan. Arnan's son was Obadiah. Obadiah's son was Shecaniah.

The descendants of Shecaniah were Shemaiah and his sons, Hattush, Igal, Bariah, Neariah, and Shaphat—six in all.

The sons of Neariah were Elioenai, Hizkiah, and Azrikam—three in all.

The sons of Elioenai were Hodaviah, Eliashib, Pelaiah, Akkub, Johanan, Delaiah, and Anani—seven in all.

The descendants of Judah were Perez, Hezron, Carmi, Hur, and Shobal.

Shobal's son Reaiah was the father of Jahath. Jahath was the father of Ahumai and Lahad. These were the families of the Zorathites.

The descendants of Etam were Jezreel, Ishma, Idbash, their sister Hazzelelponi, Penuel (the father of Gedor), and Ezer (the father of Hushah). These were the descendants of Hur (the firstborn of Ephrathah), the ancestor of Bethlehem.

Ashhur (the father of Tekoa) had two wives, named Helah and Naarah. Naarah gave birth to Ahuzzam, Hepher, Temeni, and Haahashtari. Helah gave birth to Zereth, Izhar, Ethnan, and Koz, who became the ancestor of Anub, Zobebah, and all the families of Aharhel son of Harum.

There was a man named Jabez who was more honorable than any of his brothers. His mother named him Jabez because his birth had been so painful. He was the one who prayed to the God of Israel, "Oh, that you would bless me and expand my territory! Please be with me in all that I do, and keep me from all trouble and pain!" And God granted him his request.

Kelub (the brother of Shuhah) was the father of Mehir. Mehir was the father of Eshton. Eshton was the father of Beth-rapha, Paseah, and Tehinnah. Tehinnah was the father of Ir-nahash. These were the descendants of Recah.

The sons of Kenaz were Othniel and Seraiah. Othniel's sons were Hathath and Meonothai. Meonothai was the father of Ophrah. Seraiah was the father of Joab, the founder of the Valley of Craftsmen, so called because they were craftsmen.

The sons of Caleb son of Jephunneh were Iru, Elah, and Naam. The son of Elah was Kenaz.

The sons of Jehallelel were Ziph, Ziphah, Tiria, and Asarel.

The sons of Ezrah were Jether, Mered, Epher, and Jalon. One of Mered's wives became the mother of Miriam, Shammai, and Ishbah (the father of Eshtemoa). He married a woman from Judah, who became the mother of Jered (the father of Gedor), Heber (the father of Soco), and Jekuthiel (the father of Zanoah). Mered also married Bithia, a daughter of Pharaoh, and she bore him children.

Hodiah's wife was the sister of Naham. One of her sons was the father of Keilah the Garmite, and another was the father of Eshtemoa the Maacathite.

The sons of Shimon were Amnon, Rinnah, Ben-hanan, and Tilon. The descendants of Ishi were Zoheth and Ben-zoheth.

Shelah was one of Judah's sons. The descendants of Shelah were Er (the father of Lecah); Laadah (the father of Mareshah); the families of linen workers at Beth-ashbea; Jokim; the men of Cozeba; and Joash and Saraph, who ruled over Moab and Jashubi-lehem. These names all come from ancient records. They were the pottery makers who lived in Netaim and Gederah. They lived there and worked for the king.

+

The sons of Simeon were Jemuel, Jamin, Jarib, Zohar, and Shaul.
The descendants of Shaul were Shallum, Mibsam, and Mishma.
The descendants of Mishma were Hammuel, Zaccur, and Shimei.
Shimei had sixteen sons and six daughters, but none of his brothers had
   large families. So Simeon's tribe never grew as large as the tribe of Judah.
They lived in Beersheba, Moladah, Hazar-shual, Bilhah, Ezem, Tolad,
   Bethuel, Hormah, Ziklag, Beth-marcaboth, Hazar-susim, Beth-biri,
   and Shaaraim. These towns were under their control until the time
   of King David. Their descendants also lived in Etam, Ain, Rimmon,
   Token, and Ashan—five towns and their surrounding villages as far
   away as Baalath. This was their territory, and these names are listed in
   their genealogical records.
Other descendants of Simeon included Meshobab, Jamlech, Joshah son
   of Amaziah, Joel, Jehu son of Joshibiah, son of Seraiah, son of Asiel,
   Elioenai, Jaakobah, Jeshohaiah, Asaiah, Adiel, Jesimiel, Benaiah, and
   Ziza son of Shiphi, son of Allon, son of Jedaiah, son of Shimri, son of
   Shemaiah.

These were the names of some of the leaders of Simeon's wealthy clans.
Their families grew, and they traveled to the region of Gerar, in the east
part of the valley, seeking pastureland for their flocks. They found lush
pastures there, and the land was spacious, quiet, and peaceful.

Some of Ham's descendants had been living in that region. But during
the reign of King Hezekiah of Judah, these leaders of Simeon invaded the
region and completely destroyed the homes of the descendants of Ham
and of the Meunites. No trace of them remains today. They killed everyone who lived there and took the land for themselves, because they wanted
its good pastureland for their flocks. Five hundred of these invaders from
the tribe of Simeon went to Mount Seir, led by Pelatiah, Neariah, Rephaiah, and Uzziel—all sons of Ishi. They destroyed the few Amalekites who
had survived, and they have lived there ever since.

+

The oldest son of Israel was Reuben. But since he dishonored his father
by sleeping with one of his father's concubines, his birthright was given
to the sons of his brother Joseph. For this reason, Reuben is not listed in
the genealogical records as the firstborn son. The descendants of Judah
became the most powerful tribe and provided a ruler for the nation, but
the birthright belonged to Joseph.

The sons of Reuben, the oldest son of Israel, were Hanoch, Pallu,
   Hezron, and Carmi.

The descendants of Joel were Shemaiah, Gog, Shimei, Micah, Reaiah, Baal, and Beerah. Beerah was the leader of the Reubenites when they were taken into captivity by King Tiglath-pileser of Assyria.

Beerah's relatives are listed in their genealogical records by their clans: Jeiel (the leader), Zechariah, and Bela son of Azaz, son of Shema, son of Joel.

The Reubenites lived in the area that stretches from Aroer to Nebo and Baal-meon. And since they had so many livestock in the land of Gilead, they spread east toward the edge of the desert that stretches to the Euphrates River.

During the reign of Saul, the Reubenites defeated the Hagrites in battle. Then they moved into the Hagrite settlements all along the eastern edge of Gilead.

+

Next to the Reubenites, the descendants of Gad lived in the land of Bashan as far east as Salecah. Joel was the leader in the land of Bashan, and Shapham was second-in-command, followed by Janai and Shaphat.

Their relatives, the leaders of seven other clans, were Michael, Meshullam, Sheba, Jorai, Jacan, Zia, and Eber. These were all descendants of Abihail son of Huri, son of Jaroah, son of Gilead, son of Michael, son of Jeshishai, son of Jahdo, son of Buz. Ahi son of Abdiel, son of Guni, was the leader of their clans.

The Gadites lived in the land of Gilead, in Bashan and its villages, and throughout all the pasturelands of Sharon. All of these were listed in the genealogical records during the days of King Jotham of Judah and King Jeroboam of Israel.

There were 44,760 capable warriors in the armies of Reuben, Gad, and the half-tribe of Manasseh. They were all skilled in combat and armed with shields, swords, and bows. They waged war against the Hagrites, the Jeturites, the Naphishites, and the Nodabites. They cried out to God during the battle, and he answered their prayer because they trusted in him. So the Hagrites and all their allies were defeated. The plunder taken from the Hagrites included 50,000 camels, 250,000 sheep and goats, 2,000 donkeys, and 100,000 captives. Many of the Hagrites were killed in the battle because God was fighting against them. The people of Reuben, Gad, and Manasseh lived in their land until they were taken into exile.

The half-tribe of Manasseh was very large and spread through the land from Bashan to Baal-hermon, Senir, and Mount Hermon. These were the leaders of their clans: Epher, Ishi, Eliel, Azriel, Jeremiah, Hodaviah, and Jahdiel. These men had a great reputation as mighty warriors and leaders of their clans.

But these tribes were unfaithful to the God of their ancestors. They worshiped the gods of the nations that God had destroyed. So the God of Israel caused King Pul of Assyria (also known as Tiglath-pileser) to invade the land and take away the people of Reuben, Gad, and the half-tribe of Manasseh as captives. The Assyrians exiled them to Halah, Habor, Hara, and the Gozan River, where they remain to this day.

+

The sons of Levi were Gershon, Kohath, and Merari.
The descendants of Kohath included Amram, Izhar, Hebron, and Uzziel.
The children of Amram were Aaron, Moses, and Miriam.
The sons of Aaron were Nadab, Abihu, Eleazar, and Ithamar.
    Eleazar was the father of Phinehas.
    Phinehas was the father of Abishua.
    Abishua was the father of Bukki.
    Bukki was the father of Uzzi.
    Uzzi was the father of Zerahiah.
    Zerahiah was the father of Meraioth.
    Meraioth was the father of Amariah.
    Amariah was the father of Ahitub.
    Ahitub was the father of Zadok.
    Zadok was the father of Ahimaaz.
    Ahimaaz was the father of Azariah.
    Azariah was the father of Johanan.
    Johanan was the father of Azariah, the high priest at the Temple built
       by Solomon in Jerusalem.
    Azariah was the father of Amariah.
    Amariah was the father of Ahitub.
    Ahitub was the father of Zadok.
    Zadok was the father of Shallum.
    Shallum was the father of Hilkiah.
    Hilkiah was the father of Azariah.
    Azariah was the father of Seraiah.
    Seraiah was the father of Jehozadak, who went into exile when the
       LORD sent the people of Judah and Jerusalem into captivity under
       Nebuchadnezzar.

The sons of Levi were Gershon, Kohath, and Merari.
The descendants of Gershon included Libni and Shimei.

The descendants of Kohath included Amram, Izhar, Hebron, and Uzziel. The descendants of Merari included Mahli and Mushi.

The following were the Levite clans, listed according to their ancestral descent:

The descendants of Gershon included Libni, Jahath, Zimmah, Joah, Iddo, Zerah, and Jeatherai.
The descendants of Kohath included Amminadab, Korah, Assir, Elkanah, Abiasaph, Assir, Tahath, Uriel, Uzziah, and Shaul.
The descendants of Elkanah included Amasai, Ahimoth, Elkanah, Zophai, Nahath, Eliab, Jeroham, Elkanah, and Samuel.
The sons of Samuel were Joel (the older) and Abijah (the second).
The descendants of Merari included Mahli, Libni, Shimei, Uzzah, Shimea, Haggiah, and Asaiah.

David assigned the following men to lead the music at the house of the LORD after the Ark was placed there. They ministered with music at the Tabernacle until Solomon built the Temple of the LORD in Jerusalem. They carried out their work, following all the regulations handed down to them. These are the men who served, along with their sons:

Heman the musician was from the clan of Kohath. His genealogy was traced back through Joel, Samuel, Elkanah, Jeroham, Eliel, Toah, Zuph, Elkanah, Mahath, Amasai, Elkanah, Joel, Azariah, Zephaniah, Tahath, Assir, Abiasaph, Korah, Izhar, Kohath, Levi, and Israel.
Heman's first assistant was Asaph from the clan of Gershon. Asaph's genealogy was traced back through Berekiah, Shimea, Michael, Baaseiah, Malkijah, Ethni, Zerah, Adaiah, Ethan, Zimmah, Shimei, Jahath, Gershon, and Levi.
Heman's second assistant was Ethan from the clan of Merari. Ethan's genealogy was traced back through Kishi, Abdi, Malluch, Hashabiah, Amaziah, Hilkiah, Amzi, Bani, Shemer, Mahli, Mushi, Merari, and Levi.

Their fellow Levites were appointed to various other tasks in the Tabernacle, the house of God.

Only Aaron and his descendants served as priests. They presented the offerings on the altar of burnt offering and the altar of incense, and they performed all the other duties related to the Most Holy Place. They made atonement for Israel by doing everything that Moses, the servant of God, had commanded them.

The descendants of Aaron were Eleazar, Phinehas, Abishua, Bukki, Uzzi, Zerahiah, Meraioth, Amariah, Ahitub, Zadok, and Ahimaaz.

This is a record of the towns and territory assigned by means of sacred lots to the descendants of Aaron, who were from the clan of Kohath. This territory included Hebron and its surrounding pasturelands in Judah, but the fields and outlying areas belonging to the city were given to Caleb son of Jephunneh. So the descendants of Aaron were given the following towns, each with its pasturelands: Hebron (a city of refuge), Libnah, Jattir, Eshtemoa, Holon, Debir, Ain, Juttah, and Beth-shemesh. And from the territory of Benjamin they were given Gibeon, Geba, Alemeth, and Anathoth, each with its pasturelands. So thirteen towns were given to the descendants of Aaron. The remaining descendants of Kohath received ten towns from the territory of the half-tribe of Manasseh by means of sacred lots.

The descendants of Gershon received by sacred lots thirteen towns from the territories of Issachar, Asher, Naphtali, and from the Bashan area of Manasseh, east of the Jordan.

The descendants of Merari received by sacred lots twelve towns from the territories of Reuben, Gad, and Zebulun.

So the people of Israel assigned all these towns and pasturelands to the Levites. The towns in the territories of Judah, Simeon, and Benjamin, mentioned above, were assigned to them by means of sacred lots.

The descendants of Kohath were given the following towns from the territory of Ephraim, each with its pasturelands: Shechem (a city of refuge in the hill country of Ephraim), Gezer, Jokmeam, Beth-horon, Aijalon, and Gath-rimmon. The remaining descendants of Kohath were assigned the towns of Aner and Bileam from the territory of the half-tribe of Manasseh, each with its pasturelands.

The descendants of Gershon received the towns of Golan (in Bashan) and Ashtaroth from the territory of the half-tribe of Manasseh, each with its pasturelands. From the territory of Issachar, they were given Kedesh, Daberath, Ramoth, and Anem, each with its pasturelands. From the territory of Asher, they received Mashal, Abdon, Hukok, and Rehob, each with its pasturelands. From the territory of Naphtali, they were given Kedesh in Galilee, Hammon, and Kiriathaim, each with its pasturelands.

The remaining descendants of Merari received the towns of Jokneam, Kartah, Rimmon, and Tabor from the territory of Zebulun, each with its pasturelands. From the territory of Reuben, east of the Jordan River opposite Jericho, they received Bezer (a desert town), Jahaz, Kedemoth, and Mephaath, each with its pasturelands. And from the territory of Gad, they received Ramoth in Gilead, Mahanaim, Heshbon, and Jazer, each with its pasturelands.

+

The four sons of Issachar were Tola, Puah, Jashub, and Shimron.
The sons of Tola were Uzzi, Rephaiah, Jeriel, Jahmai, Ibsam, and
  Shemuel. Each of them was the leader of an ancestral clan. At the
  time of King David, the total number of mighty warriors listed in the
  records of these clans was 22,600.
The son of Uzzi was Izrahiah. The sons of Izrahiah were Michael,
  Obadiah, Joel, and Isshiah. These five became the leaders of clans.
  All of them had many wives and many sons, so the total number
  of men available for military service among their descendants was
  36,000.
The total number of mighty warriors from all the clans of the tribe of
  Issachar was 87,000. All of them were listed in their genealogical records.

+

Three of Benjamin's sons were Bela, Beker, and Jediael.
The five sons of Bela were Ezbon, Uzzi, Uzziel, Jerimoth, and Iri. Each of
  them was the leader of an ancestral clan. The total number of mighty
  warriors from these clans was 22,034, as listed in their genealogical
  records.
The sons of Beker were Zemirah, Joash, Eliezer, Elioenai, Omri,
  Jeremoth, Abijah, Anathoth, and Alemeth. Each of them was the
  leader of an ancestral clan. The total number of mighty warriors and
  leaders from these clans was 20,200, as listed in their genealogical
  records.
The son of Jediael was Bilhan. The sons of Bilhan were Jeush, Benjamin,
  Ehud, Kenaanah, Zethan, Tarshish, and Ahishahar. Each of them was
  the leader of an ancestral clan. From these clans the total number of
  mighty warriors ready for war was 17,200.
The sons of Ir were Shuppim and Huppim. Hushim was the son of Aher.

+

The sons of Naphtali were Jahzeel, Guni, Jezer, and Shillem. They were
  all descendants of Jacob's concubine Bilhah.

+

The descendants of Manasseh through his Aramean concubine included
  Asriel. She also bore Makir, the father of Gilead. Makir found wives
  for Huppim and Shuppim. Makir had a sister named Maacah. One of
  his descendants was Zelophehad, who had only daughters.

Makir's wife, Maacah, gave birth to a son whom she named Peresh.
His brother's name was Sheresh. The sons of Peresh were Ulam
and Rakem. The son of Ulam was Bedan. All these were considered
Gileadites, descendants of Makir son of Manasseh.
Makir's sister Hammoleketh gave birth to Ishhod, Abiezer, and Mahlah.
The sons of Shemida were Ahian, Shechem, Likhi, and Aniam.

+

The descendants of Ephraim were Shuthelah, Bered, Tahath, Eleadah,
Tahath, Zabad, Shuthelah, Ezer, and Elead. These two were killed
trying to steal livestock from the local farmers near Gath. Their father,
Ephraim, mourned for them a long time, and his relatives came to
comfort him. Afterward Ephraim slept with his wife, and she became
pregnant and gave birth to a son. Ephraim named him Beriah because
of the tragedy his family had suffered. He had a daughter named
Sheerah. She built the towns of Lower and Upper Beth-horon and
Uzzen-sheerah.
The descendants of Ephraim included Rephah, Resheph, Telah, Tahan,
Ladan, Ammihud, Elishama, Nun, and Joshua.

The descendants of Ephraim lived in the territory that included Bethel
and its surrounding towns to the south, Naaran to the east, Gezer and
its villages to the west, and Shechem and its surrounding villages to the
north as far as Ayyah and its towns. Along the border of Manasseh were
the towns of Beth-shan, Taanach, Megiddo, Dor, and their surrounding
villages. The descendants of Joseph son of Israel lived in these towns.

+

The sons of Asher were Imnah, Ishvah, Ishvi, and Beriah. They had a
sister named Serah.
The sons of Beriah were Heber and Malkiel (the father of Birzaith).
The sons of Heber were Japhlet, Shomer, and Hotham. They had a sister
named Shua.
The sons of Japhlet were Pasach, Bimhal, and Ashvath.
The sons of Shomer were Ahi, Rohgah, Hubbah, and Aram.
The sons of his brother Helem were Zophah, Imna, Shelesh, and Amal.
The sons of Zophah were Suah, Harnepher, Shual, Beri, Imrah, Bezer,
Hod, Shamma, Shilshah, Ithran, and Beera.
The sons of Jether were Jephunneh, Pispah, and Ara.
The sons of Ulla were Arah, Hanniel, and Rizia.

Each of these descendants of Asher was the head of an ancestral clan. They were all select men—mighty warriors and outstanding leaders. The total number of men available for military service was 26,000, as listed in their genealogical records.

+

Benjamin's first son was Bela, the second was Ashbel, the third was Aharah, the fourth was Nohah, and the fifth was Rapha.

The sons of Bela were Addar, Gera, Abihud, Abishua, Naaman, Ahoah, Gera, Shephuphan, and Huram.

The sons of Ehud, leaders of the clans living at Geba, were exiled to Manahath. Ehud's sons were Naaman, Ahijah, and Gera. Gera, who led them into exile, was the father of Uzza and Ahihud.

After Shaharaim divorced his wives Hushim and Baara, he had children in the land of Moab. His wife Hodesh gave birth to Jobab, Zibia, Mesha, Malcam, Jeuz, Sakia, and Mirmah. These sons all became the leaders of clans.

Shaharaim's wife Hushim had already given birth to Abitub and Elpaal. The sons of Elpaal were Eber, Misham, Shemed (who built the towns of Ono and Lod and their nearby villages), Beriah, and Shema. They were the leaders of the clans living in Aijalon, and they drove out the inhabitants of Gath.

Ahio, Shashak, Jeremoth, Zebadiah, Arad, Eder, Michael, Ishpah, and Joha were the sons of Beriah.

Zebadiah, Meshullam, Hizki, Heber, Ishmerai, Izliah, and Jobab were the sons of Elpaal.

Jakim, Zicri, Zabdi, Elienai, Zillethai, Eliel, Adaiah, Beraiah, and Shimrath were the sons of Shimei.

Ishpan, Eber, Eliel, Abdon, Zicri, Hanan, Hananiah, Elam, Anthothijah, Iphdeiah, and Penuel were the sons of Shashak.

Shamsherai, Shehariah, Athaliah, Jaareshiah, Elijah, and Zicri were the sons of Jeroham.

These were the leaders of the ancestral clans; they were listed in their genealogical records, and they all lived in Jerusalem.

Jeiel (the father of Gibeon) lived in the town of Gibeon. His wife's name was Maacah, and his oldest son was named Abdon. Jeiel's other sons were Zur, Kish, Baal, Ner, Nadab, Gedor, Ahio, Zechariah, and Mikloth, who was the father of Shimeam. All these families lived near each other in Jerusalem.

Ner was the father of Kish.

Kish was the father of Saul.

Saul was the father of Jonathan, Malkishua, Abinadab, and Esh-baal.
Jonathan was the father of Merib-baal.
Merib-baal was the father of Micah.
Micah was the father of Pithon, Melech, Tahrea, and Ahaz.
Ahaz was the father of Jadah.
Jadah was the father of Alemeth, Azmaveth, and Zimri.
Zimri was the father of Moza.
Moza was the father of Binea.
Binea was the father of Rephaiah.
Rephaiah was the father of Eleasah.
Eleasah was the father of Azel.
Azel had six sons: Azrikam, Bokeru, Ishmael, Sheariah, Obadiah, and
Hanan. These were the sons of Azel.
Azel's brother Eshek had three sons: the first was Ulam, the second
was Jeush, and the third was Eliphelet. Ulam's sons were all
mighty warriors and expert archers. They had many sons and
grandsons—150 in all.

All these were descendants of Benjamin.

So all Israel was listed in the genealogical records in *The Book of the Kings
of Israel.*

+ + +

The people of Judah were exiled to Babylon because they were unfaithful to the LORD. The first of the exiles to return to their property in their
former towns were priests, Levites, Temple servants, and other Israelites.
Some of the people from the tribes of Judah, Benjamin, Ephraim, and
Manasseh came and settled in Jerusalem.

One family that returned was that of Uthai son of Ammihud, son of
Omri, son of Imri, son of Bani, a descendant of Perez son of Judah.
Others returned from the Shilonite clan, including Asaiah (the oldest)
and his sons.
From the Zerahite clan, Jeuel returned with his relatives.
In all, 690 families from the tribe of Judah returned.

From the tribe of Benjamin came Sallu son of Meshullam, son of
Hodaviah, son of Hassenuah; Ibneiah son of Jeroham; Elah son of
Uzzi, son of Micri; and Meshullam son of Shephatiah, son of Reuel,
son of Ibnijah.
These men were all leaders of clans, and they were listed in their genea-
logical records. In all, 956 families from the tribe of Benjamin returned.

Among the priests who returned were Jedaiah, Jehoiarib, Jakin, Azariah son of Hilkiah, son of Meshullam, son of Zadok, son of Meraioth, son of Ahitub. Azariah was the chief officer of the house of God.

Other returning priests were Adaiah son of Jeroham, son of Pashhur, son of Malkijah, and Maasai son of Adiel, son of Jahzerah, son of Meshullam, son of Meshillemith, son of Immer.

In all, 1,760 priests returned. They were heads of clans and very able men. They were responsible for ministering at the house of God.

The Levites who returned were Shemaiah son of Hasshub, son of Azrikam, son of Hashabiah, a descendant of Merari; Bakbakkar; Heresh; Galal; Mattaniah son of Mica, son of Zicri, son of Asaph; Obadiah son of Shemaiah, son of Galal, son of Jeduthun; and Berekiah son of Asa, son of Elkanah, who lived in the area of Netophah.

The gatekeepers who returned were Shallum, Akkub, Talmon, Ahiman, and their relatives. Shallum was the chief gatekeeper. Prior to this time, they were responsible for the King's Gate on the east side. These men served as gatekeepers for the camps of the Levites. Shallum was the son of Kore, a descendant of Abiasaph, from the clan of Korah. He and his relatives, the Korahites, were responsible for guarding the entrance to the sanctuary, just as their ancestors had guarded the Tabernacle in the camp of the LORD.

Phinehas son of Eleazar had been in charge of the gatekeepers in earlier times, and the LORD had been with him. And later Zechariah son of Meshelemiah was responsible for guarding the entrance to the Tabernacle.

In all, there were 212 gatekeepers in those days, and they were listed according to the genealogies in their villages. David and Samuel the seer had appointed their ancestors because they were reliable men. These gatekeepers and their descendants, by their divisions, were responsible for guarding the entrance to the house of the LORD when that house was a tent. The gatekeepers were stationed on all four sides—east, west, north, and south. Their relatives in the villages came regularly to share their duties for seven-day periods.

The four chief gatekeepers, all Levites, were trusted officials, for they were responsible for the rooms and treasuries at the house of God. They would spend the night around the house of God, since it was their duty to guard it and to open the gates every morning.

Some of the gatekeepers were assigned to care for the various articles used in worship. They checked them in and out to avoid any loss. Others were responsible for the furnishings, the items in the sanctuary, and the supplies, such as choice flour, wine, olive oil, frankincense, and spices. But it was the priests who blended the spices. Mattithiah, a Levite and the oldest son of Shallum the Korahite, was entrusted with baking the bread used in the offerings. And some members of the clan of Kohath were in charge of preparing the bread to be set on the table each Sabbath day.

The musicians, all prominent Levites, lived at the Temple. They were exempt from other responsibilities since they were on duty at all hours. All these men lived in Jerusalem. They were the heads of Levite families and were listed as prominent leaders in their genealogical records.

+ + +

Jeiel (the father of Gibeon) lived in the town of Gibeon. His wife's name was Maacah, and his oldest son was named Abdon. Jeiel's other sons were Zur, Kish, Baal, Ner, Nadab, Gedor, Ahio, Zechariah, and Mikloth. Mikloth was the father of Shimeam. All these families lived near each other in Jerusalem.

Ner was the father of Kish.

Kish was the father of Saul.

Saul was the father of Jonathan, Malkishua, Abinadab, and Esh-baal.

Jonathan was the father of Merib-baal.

Merib-baal was the father of Micah.

The sons of Micah were Pithon, Melech, Tahrea, and Ahaz.

Ahaz was the father of Jadah.

Jadah was the father of Alemeth, Azmaveth, and Zimri.

Zimri was the father of Moza.

Moza was the father of Binea.

Binea's son was Rephaiah.

Rephaiah's son was Eleasah.

Eleasah's son was Azel.

Azel had six sons, whose names were Azrikam, Bokeru, Ishmael, Sheariah, Obadiah, and Hanan. These were the sons of Azel.

NOW THE PHILISTINES attacked Israel, and the men of Israel fled before them. Many were slaughtered on the slopes of Mount Gilboa. The Philistines closed in on Saul and his sons, and they killed three of his sons—Jonathan, Abinadab, and Malkishua. The fighting grew very fierce around Saul, and the Philistine archers caught up with him and wounded him.

Saul groaned to his armor bearer, "Take your sword and kill me before these pagan Philistines come to taunt and torture me."

But his armor bearer was afraid and would not do it. So Saul took his own sword and fell on it. When his armor bearer realized that Saul was dead, he fell on his own sword and died. So Saul and his three sons died there together, bringing his dynasty to an end.

When all the Israelites in the Jezreel Valley saw that their army had fled and that Saul and his sons were dead, they abandoned their towns and fled. So the Philistines moved in and occupied their towns.

The next day, when the Philistines went out to strip the dead, they found the bodies of Saul and his sons on Mount Gilboa. So they stripped off Saul's armor and cut off his head. Then they proclaimed the good news of Saul's death before their idols and to the people throughout the land of Philistia. They placed his armor in the temple of their gods, and they fastened his head to the temple of Dagon.

But when everyone in Jabesh-gilead heard about everything the Philistines had done to Saul, all their mighty warriors brought the bodies of Saul and his sons back to Jabesh. Then they buried their bones beneath the great tree at Jabesh, and they fasted for seven days.

So Saul died because he was unfaithful to the LORD. He failed to obey the LORD's command, and he even consulted a medium instead of asking the LORD for guidance. So the LORD killed him and turned the kingdom over to David son of Jesse.

+ + +

Then all Israel gathered before David at Hebron and told him, "We are your own flesh and blood. In the past, even when Saul was king, you were the one who really led the forces of Israel. And the LORD your God told you, 'You will be the shepherd of my people Israel. You will be the leader of my people Israel.'"

So there at Hebron, David made a covenant before the LORD with all the elders of Israel. And they anointed him king of Israel, just as the LORD had promised through Samuel.

Then David and all Israel went to Jerusalem (or Jebus, as it used to be called), where the Jebusites, the original inhabitants of the land, were living. The people of Jebus taunted David, saying, "You'll never get in here!" But David captured the fortress of Zion, which is now called the City of David.

David had said to his troops, "Whoever is first to attack the Jebusites will become the commander of my armies!" And Joab, the son of David's sister Zeruiah, was first to attack, so he became the commander of David's armies.

David made the fortress his home, and that is why it is called the City of David. He extended the city from the supporting terraces to the surrounding area, while Joab rebuilt the rest of Jerusalem. And David became more and more powerful, because the LORD of Heaven's Armies was with him.

+

These are the leaders of David's mighty warriors. Together with all Israel, they decided to make David their king, just as the LORD had promised concerning Israel.

Here is the record of David's mightiest warriors: The first was Jashobeam the Hacmonite, who was leader of the Three—the mightiest warriors among David's men. He once used his spear to kill 300 enemy warriors in a single battle.

Next in rank among the Three was Eleazar son of Dodai, a descendant of Ahoah. He was with David when the Philistines gathered for battle at Pas-dammim and attacked the Israelites in a field full of barley. The Israelite army fled, but Eleazar and David held their ground in the middle of the field and beat back the Philistines. So the LORD saved them by giving them a great victory.

Once when David was at the rock near the cave of Adullam, the Philistine army was camped in the valley of Rephaim. The Three (who were among the Thirty—an elite group among David's fighting men) went down to meet him there. David was staying in the stronghold at the time, and a Philistine detachment had occupied the town of Bethlehem.

David remarked longingly to his men, "Oh, how I would love some of that good water from the well by the gate in Bethlehem." So the Three broke through the Philistine lines, drew some water from the well by the gate in Bethlehem, and brought it back to David. But David refused to drink it. Instead, he poured it out as an offering to the LORD. "God forbid that I should drink this!" he exclaimed. "This water is as precious as the blood of these men who risked their lives to bring it to me." So David did not drink it. These are examples of the exploits of the Three.

Abishai, the brother of Joab, was the leader of the Thirty. He once used his spear to kill 300 enemy warriors in a single battle. It was by such feats that he became as famous as the Three. Abishai was the most famous of the Thirty and was their commander, though he was not one of the Three.

There was also Benaiah son of Jehoiada, a valiant warrior from Kabzeel. He did many heroic deeds, which included killing two champions of Moab. Another time, on a snowy day, he chased a lion down into a pit and killed it. Once, armed only with a club, he killed an Egyptian warrior who was 7½ feet tall and who was armed with a spear as thick as a weaver's beam. Benaiah wrenched the spear from the Egyptian's hand and killed him with it. Deeds like these made Benaiah as famous as the three mightiest warriors. He was more honored than the other members of the Thirty, though he was not one of the Three. And David made him captain of his bodyguard.

David's mighty warriors also included:

Asahel, Joab's brother;
Elhanan son of Dodo from Bethlehem;
Shammah from Harod;
Helez from Pelon;
Ira son of Ikkesh from Tekoa;
Abiezer from Anathoth;
Sibbecai from Hushah;
Zalmon from Ahoah;
Maharai from Netophah;
Heled son of Baanah from Netophah;
Ithai son of Ribai from Gibeah (in the land of Benjamin);
Benaiah from Pirathon;
Hurai from near Nahale-gaash;
Abi-albon from Arabah;
Azmaveth from Bahurim;
Eliahba from Shaalbon;
the sons of Jashen from Gizon;
Jonathan son of Shagee from Harar;
Ahiam son of Sharar from Harar;
Eliphal son of Ur;
Hepher from Mekerah;
Ahijah from Pelon;
Hezro from Carmel;
Paarai son of Ezbai;
Joel, the brother of Nathan;
Mibhar son of Hagri;
Zelek from Ammon;
Naharai from Beeroth, the armor bearer of Joab son of Zeruiah;
Ira from Jattir;
Gareb from Jattir;
Uriah the Hittite;
Zabad son of Ahlai;
Adina son of Shiza, the Reubenite leader who had thirty men with him;
Hanan son of Maacah;
Joshaphat from Mithna;
Uzzia from Ashtaroth;

Shama and Jeiel, the sons of Hotham, from Aroer;
Jediael son of Shimri;
Joha, his brother, from Tiz;
Eliel from Mahavah;
Jeribai and Joshaviah, the sons of Elnaam;
Ithmah from Moab;
Eliel and Obed;
Jaasiel from Zobah.

The following men joined David at Ziklag while he was hiding from Saul son of Kish. They were among the warriors who fought beside David in battle. All of them were expert archers, and they could shoot arrows or sling stones with their left hand as well as their right. They were all relatives of Saul from the tribe of Benjamin. Their leader was Ahiezer son of Shemaah from Gibeah; his brother Joash was second-in-command. These were the other warriors:

Jeziel and Pelet, sons of Azmaveth;
Beracah;
Jehu from Anathoth;
Ishmaiah from Gibeon, a famous warrior and leader among the
    Thirty;
Jeremiah, Jahaziel, Johanan, and Jozabad from Gederah;
Eluzai, Jerimoth, Bealiah, Shemariah, and Shephatiah from Haruph;
Elkanah, Isshiah, Azarel, Joezer, and Jashobeam, who were Korahites;
Joelah and Zebadiah, sons of Jeroham from Gedor.

Some brave and experienced warriors from the tribe of Gad also defected to David while he was at the stronghold in the wilderness. They were expert with both shield and spear, as fierce as lions and as swift as deer on the mountains.

Ezer was their leader.
Obadiah was second.
Eliab was third.
Mishmannah was fourth.
Jeremiah was fifth.
Attai was sixth.
Eliel was seventh.
Johanan was eighth.
Elzabad was ninth.
Jeremiah was tenth.
Macbannai was eleventh.

These warriors from Gad were army commanders. The weakest among them could take on a hundred regular troops, and the strongest could take on a thousand! These were the men who crossed the Jordan River during its seasonal flooding at the beginning of the year and drove out all the people living in the lowlands on both the east and west banks.

Others from Benjamin and Judah came to David at the stronghold. David went out to meet them and said, "If you have come in peace to help me, we are friends. But if you have come to betray me to my enemies when I am innocent, then may the God of our ancestors see it and punish you."

Then the Spirit came upon Amasai, the leader of the Thirty, and he said,

"We are yours, David!
     We are on your side, son of Jesse.
Peace and prosperity be with you,
     and success to all who help you,
     for your God is the one who helps you."

So David let them join him, and he made them officers over his troops.

Some men from Manasseh defected from the Israelite army and joined David when he set out with the Philistines to fight against Saul. But as it turned out, the Philistine rulers refused to let David and his men go with them. After much discussion, they sent them back, for they said, "It will cost us our heads if David switches loyalties to Saul and turns against us."

Here is a list of the men from Manasseh who defected to David as he was returning to Ziklag: Adnah, Jozabad, Jediael, Michael, Jozabad, Elihu, and Zillethai. Each commanded 1,000 troops from the tribe of Manasseh. They helped David chase down bands of raiders, for they were all brave and able warriors who became commanders in his army. Day after day more men joined David until he had a great army, like the army of God.

These are the numbers of armed warriors who joined David at Hebron. They were all eager to see David become king instead of Saul, just as the LORD had promised.

From the tribe of Judah, there were 6,800 warriors armed with shields and spears.

From the tribe of Simeon, there were 7,100 brave warriors.

From the tribe of Levi, there were 4,600 warriors. This included Jehoiada, leader of the family of Aaron, who had 3,700 under his command. This also included Zadok, a brave young warrior, with 22 members of his family who were all officers.

From the tribe of Benjamin, Saul's relatives, there were 3,000 warriors. Most of the men from Benjamin had remained loyal to Saul until this time.

From the tribe of Ephraim, there were 20,800 brave warriors, each highly
respected in his own clan.

From the half-tribe of Manasseh west of the Jordan, 18,000 men were
designated by name to help David become king.

From the tribe of Issachar, there were 200 leaders of the tribe with their
relatives. All these men understood the signs of the times and knew
the best course for Israel to take.

From the tribe of Zebulun, there were 50,000 skilled warriors. They
were fully armed and prepared for battle and completely loyal to
David.

From the tribe of Naphtali, there were 1,000 officers and 37,000
warriors armed with shields and spears.

From the tribe of Dan, there were 28,600 warriors, all prepared for
battle.

From the tribe of Asher, there were 40,000 trained warriors, all prepared
for battle.

From the east side of the Jordan River—where the tribes of Reuben and
Gad and the half-tribe of Manasseh lived—there were 120,000 troops
armed with every kind of weapon.

All these men came in battle array to Hebron with the single purpose of
making David the king over all Israel. In fact, everyone in Israel agreed that
David should be their king. They feasted and drank with David for three
days, for preparations had been made by their relatives for their arrival.
And people from as far away as Issachar, Zebulun, and Naphtali brought
food on donkeys, camels, mules, and oxen. Vast supplies of flour, fig cakes,
clusters of raisins, wine, olive oil, cattle, sheep, and goats were brought to
the celebration. There was great joy throughout the land of Israel.

+

David consulted with all his officials, including the generals and captains
of his army. Then he addressed the entire assembly of Israel as follows: "If
you approve and if it is the will of the LORD our God, let us send messages
to all the Israelites throughout the land, including the priests and Levites
in their towns and pasturelands. Let us invite them to come and join us.
It is time to bring back the Ark of our God, for we neglected it during the
reign of Saul."

The whole assembly agreed to this, for the people could see it was the
right thing to do. So David summoned all Israel, from the Shihor Brook of
Egypt in the south all the way to the town of Lebo-hamath in the north, to
join in bringing the Ark of God from Kiriath-jearim. Then David and all

Israel went to Baalah of Judah (also called Kiriath-jearim) to bring back the Ark of God, which bears the name of the LORD who is enthroned between the cherubim. They placed the Ark of God on a new cart and brought it from Abinadab's house. Uzzah and Ahio were guiding the cart. David and all Israel were celebrating before God with all their might, singing songs and playing all kinds of musical instruments—lyres, harps, tambourines, cymbals, and trumpets.

But when they arrived at the threshing floor of Nacon, the oxen stumbled, and Uzzah reached out his hand to steady the Ark. Then the LORD's anger was aroused against Uzzah, and he struck him dead because he had laid his hand on the Ark. So Uzzah died there in the presence of God.

David was angry because the LORD's anger had burst out against Uzzah. He named that place Perez-uzzah (which means "to burst out against Uzzah"), as it is still called today.

David was now afraid of God, and he asked, "How can I ever bring the Ark of God back into my care?" So David did not move the Ark into the City of David. Instead, he took it to the house of Obed-edom of Gath. The Ark of God remained there in Obed-edom's house for three months, and the LORD blessed the household of Obed-edom and everything he owned.

Then King Hiram of Tyre sent messengers to David, along with cedar timber, and stonemasons and carpenters to build him a palace. And David realized that the LORD had confirmed him as king over Israel and had greatly blessed his kingdom for the sake of his people Israel.

Then David married more wives in Jerusalem, and they had more sons and daughters. These are the names of David's sons who were born in Jerusalem: Shammua, Shobab, Nathan, Solomon, Ibhar, Elishua, Elpelet, Nogah, Nepheg, Japhia, Elishama, Eliada, and Eliphelet.

When the Philistines heard that David had been anointed king over all Israel, they mobilized all their forces to capture him. But David was told they were coming, so he marched out to meet them. The Philistines arrived and made a raid in the valley of Rephaim. So David asked God, "Should I go out to fight the Philistines? Will you hand them over to me?"

The LORD replied, "Yes, go ahead. I will hand them over to you."

So David and his troops went up to Baal-perazim and defeated the Philistines there. "God did it!" David exclaimed. "He used me to burst through my enemies like a raging flood!" So they named that place Baal-perazim (which means "the Lord who bursts through"). The Philistines had abandoned their gods there, so David gave orders to burn them.

But after a while the Philistines returned and raided the valley again. And once again David asked God what to do. "Do not attack them straight on," God replied. "Instead, circle around behind and attack them near the poplar trees. When you hear a sound like marching feet in the tops of the poplar trees, go out and attack! That will be the signal that God is moving ahead of you to strike down the Philistine army." So David did what God commanded, and they struck down the Philistine army all the way from Gibeon to Gezer.

So David's fame spread everywhere, and the LORD caused all the nations to fear David.

David now built several buildings for himself in the City of David. He also prepared a place for the Ark of God and set up a special tent for it. Then he commanded, "No one except the Levites may carry the Ark of God. The LORD has chosen them to carry the Ark of the LORD and to serve him forever."

Then David summoned all Israel to Jerusalem to bring the Ark of the LORD to the place he had prepared for it. This is the number of the descendants of Aaron (the priests) and the Levites who were called together:

From the clan of Kohath, 120, with Uriel as their leader.
From the clan of Merari, 220, with Asaiah as their leader.
From the clan of Gershon, 130, with Joel as their leader.
From the descendants of Elizaphan, 200, with Shemaiah as their leader.
From the descendants of Hebron, 80, with Eliel as their leader.
From the descendants of Uzziel, 112, with Amminadab as their leader.

Then David summoned the priests, Zadok and Abiathar, and these Levite leaders: Uriel, Asaiah, Joel, Shemaiah, Eliel, and Amminadab. He said to them, "You are the leaders of the Levite families. You must purify yourselves and all your fellow Levites, so you can bring the Ark of the LORD, the God of Israel, to the place I have prepared for it. Because you Levites did not carry the Ark the first time, the anger of the LORD our God burst out against us. We failed to ask God how to move it properly." So the priests and the Levites purified themselves in order to bring the Ark of the LORD, the God of Israel, to Jerusalem. Then the Levites carried the Ark of God on their shoulders with its carrying poles, just as the LORD had instructed Moses.

David also ordered the Levite leaders to appoint a choir of Levites who were singers and musicians to sing joyful songs to the accompaniment of harps, lyres, and cymbals. So the Levites appointed Heman son of Joel along with his fellow Levites: Asaph son of Berekiah, and Ethan son of Kushaiah from the clan of Merari. The following men were chosen as their assistants: Zechariah, Jaaziel, Shemiramoth, Jehiel, Unni, Eliab, Benaiah, Maaseiah, Mattithiah, Eliphelehu, Mikneiah, and the gatekeepers—Obed-edom and Jeiel.

The musicians Heman, Asaph, and Ethan were chosen to sound the bronze cymbals. Zechariah, Aziel, Shemiramoth, Jehiel, Unni, Eliab, Maaseiah, and Benaiah were chosen to play the harps. Mattithiah, Eliphelehu, Mikneiah, Obed-edom, Jeiel, and Azaziah were chosen to play the lyres. Kenaniah, the head Levite, was chosen as the choir leader because of his skill.

Berekiah and Elkanah were chosen to guard the Ark. Shebaniah, Joshaphat, Nethanel, Amasai, Zechariah, Benaiah, and Eliezer—all of whom were priests—were chosen to blow the trumpets as they marched in front of the Ark of God. Obed-edom and Jehiah were chosen to guard the Ark.

Then David and the elders of Israel and the generals of the army went to the house of Obed-edom to bring the Ark of the LORD's Covenant up to Jerusalem with a great celebration. And because God was clearly helping the Levites as they carried the Ark of the LORD's Covenant, they sacrificed seven bulls and seven rams.

David was dressed in a robe of fine linen, as were all the Levites who carried the Ark, and also the singers, and Kenaniah the choir leader. David was also wearing a priestly garment. So all Israel brought up the Ark of the LORD's Covenant with shouts of joy, the blowing of rams' horns and trumpets, the crashing of cymbals, and loud playing on harps and lyres.

But as the Ark of the LORD's Covenant entered the City of David, Michal, the daughter of Saul, looked down from her window. When she saw King David skipping about and laughing with joy, she was filled with contempt for him.

They brought the Ark of God and placed it inside the special tent David had prepared for it. And they presented burnt offerings and peace offerings to God. When he had finished his sacrifices, David blessed the people in the name of the LORD. Then he gave to every man and woman in all Israel a loaf of bread, a cake of dates, and a cake of raisins.

David appointed the following Levites to lead the people in worship before the Ark of the LORD—to invoke his blessings, to give thanks, and to praise the LORD, the God of Israel. Asaph, the leader of this group, sounded the cymbals. Second to him was Zechariah, followed by Jeiel, Shemiramoth, Jehiel, Mattithiah, Eliab, Benaiah, Obed-edom, and Jeiel. They played the harps and lyres. The priests, Benaiah and Jahaziel, played the trumpets regularly before the Ark of God's Covenant.

On that day David gave to Asaph and his fellow Levites this song of thanksgiving to the LORD:

Give thanks to the LORD and proclaim his greatness.
    Let the whole world know what he has done.
Sing to him; yes, sing his praises.
    Tell everyone about his wonderful deeds.
Exult in his holy name;
    rejoice, you who worship the LORD.
Search for the LORD and for his strength;
    continually seek him.
Remember the wonders he has performed,
    his miracles, and the rulings he has given,
you children of his servant Israel,
    you descendants of Jacob, his chosen ones.

He is the LORD our God.
    His justice is seen throughout the land.
Remember his covenant forever—
    the commitment he made to a thousand generations.
This is the covenant he made with Abraham
    and the oath he swore to Isaac.
He confirmed it to Jacob as a decree,
    and to the people of Israel as a never-ending covenant:
"I will give you the land of Canaan
    as your special possession."

He said this when you were few in number,
    a tiny group of strangers in Canaan.
They wandered from nation to nation,
    from one kingdom to another.
Yet he did not let anyone oppress them.
    He warned kings on their behalf:
"Do not touch my chosen people,
    and do not hurt my prophets."

Let the whole earth sing to the LORD!
    Each day proclaim the good news that he saves.
Publish his glorious deeds among the nations.
    Tell everyone about the amazing things he does.
Great is the LORD! He is most worthy of praise!
    He is to be feared above all gods.
The gods of other nations are mere idols,
    but the LORD made the heavens!
Honor and majesty surround him;
    strength and joy fill his dwelling.

O nations of the world, recognize the LORD,
   recognize that the LORD is glorious and strong.
Give to the LORD the glory he deserves!
   Bring your offering and come into his presence.
Worship the LORD in all his holy splendor.
   Let all the earth tremble before him.
   The world stands firm and cannot be shaken.

Let the heavens be glad, and the earth rejoice!
   Tell all the nations, "The LORD reigns!"
Let the sea and everything in it shout his praise!
   Let the fields and their crops burst out with joy!
Let the trees of the forest sing for joy before the LORD,
   for he is coming to judge the earth.

Give thanks to the LORD, for he is good!
   His faithful love endures forever.
Cry out, "Save us, O God of our salvation!
   Gather and rescue us from among the nations,
so we can thank your holy name
   and rejoice and praise you."

Praise the LORD, the God of Israel,
   who lives from everlasting to everlasting!

And all the people shouted "Amen!" and praised the LORD.

David arranged for Asaph and his fellow Levites to serve regularly before the Ark of the LORD's Covenant, doing whatever needed to be done each day. This group included Obed-edom (son of Jeduthun), Hosah, and sixty-eight other Levites as gatekeepers.

Meanwhile, David stationed Zadok the priest and his fellow priests at the Tabernacle of the LORD at the place of worship in Gibeon, where they continued to minister before the LORD. They sacrificed the regular burnt offerings to the LORD each morning and evening on the altar set aside for that purpose, obeying everything written in the Law of the LORD, as he had commanded Israel. David also appointed Heman, Jeduthun, and the others chosen by name to give thanks to the LORD, for "his faithful love endures forever." They used their trumpets, cymbals, and other instruments to accompany their songs of praise to God. And the sons of Jeduthun were appointed as gatekeepers.

Then all the people returned to their homes, and David turned and went home to bless his own family.

When David was settled in his palace, he summoned Nathan the prophet. "Look," David said, "I am living in a beautiful cedar palace, but the Ark of the Lord's Covenant is out there under a tent!"

Nathan replied to David, "Do whatever you have in mind, for God is with you."

But that same night God said to Nathan,

"Go and tell my servant David, 'This is what the Lord has declared: You are not the one to build a house for me to live in. I have never lived in a house, from the day I brought the Israelites out of Egypt until this very day. My home has always been a tent, moving from one place to another in a Tabernacle. Yet no matter where I have gone with the Israelites, I have never once complained to Israel's leaders, the shepherds of my people. I have never asked them, "Why haven't you built me a beautiful cedar house?"'

"Now go and say to my servant David, 'This is what the Lord of Heaven's Armies has declared: I took you from tending sheep in the pasture and selected you to be the leader of my people Israel. I have been with you wherever you have gone, and I have destroyed all your enemies before your eyes. Now I will make your name as famous as anyone who has ever lived on the earth! And I will provide a homeland for my people Israel, planting them in a secure place where they will never be disturbed. Evil nations won't oppress them as they've done in the past, starting from the time I appointed judges to rule my people Israel. And I will defeat all your enemies.

"'Furthermore, I declare that the Lord will build a house for you—a dynasty of kings! For when you die and join your ancestors, I will raise up one of your descendants, one of your sons, and I will make his kingdom strong. He is the one who will build a house—a temple—for me. And I will secure his throne forever. I will be his father, and he will be my son. I will never take my favor from him as I took it from the one who ruled before you. I will confirm him as king over my house and my kingdom for all time, and his throne will be secure forever.'"

So Nathan went back to David and told him everything the Lord had said in this vision.

Then King David went in and sat before the Lord and prayed,

"Who am I, O Lord God, and what is my family, that you have brought me this far? And now, O God, in addition to everything else, you speak of giving your servant a lasting dynasty! You speak as though I were someone very great, O Lord God!

"What more can I say to you about the way you have honored me? You know what your servant is really like. For the sake of your servant, O Lord, and according to your will, you have done all these great things and have made them known.

"O Lord, there is no one like you. We have never even heard of another God like you! What other nation on earth is like your people Israel? What other nation, O God, have you redeemed from slavery to be your own people? You made a great name for yourself when you redeemed your people from Egypt. You performed awesome miracles and drove out the nations that stood in their way. You chose Israel to be your very own people forever, and you, O Lord, became their God.

"And now, O Lord, I am your servant; do as you have promised concerning me and my family. May it be a promise that will last forever. And may your name be established and honored forever so that everyone will say, 'The Lord of Heaven's Armies, the God of Israel, is Israel's God!' And may the house of your servant David continue before you forever.

"O my God, I have been bold enough to pray to you because you have revealed to your servant that you will build a house for him—a dynasty of kings! For you are God, O Lord. And you have promised these good things to your servant. And now, it has pleased you to bless the house of your servant, so that it will continue forever before you. For when you grant a blessing, O Lord, it is an eternal blessing!"

+

After this, David defeated and subdued the Philistines by conquering Gath and its surrounding towns. David also conquered the land of Moab, and the Moabites who were spared became David's subjects and paid him tribute money.

David also destroyed the forces of Hadadezer, king of Zobah, as far as Hamath, when Hadadezer marched out to strengthen his control along the Euphrates River. David captured 1,000 chariots, 7,000 charioteers, and 20,000 foot soldiers. He crippled all the chariot horses except enough for 100 chariots.

When Arameans from Damascus arrived to help King Hadadezer, David killed 22,000 of them. Then he placed several army garrisons in Damascus, the Aramean capital, and the Arameans became David's subjects and paid him tribute money. So the Lord made David victorious wherever he went.

David brought the gold shields of Hadadezer's officers to Jerusalem, along with a large amount of bronze from Hadadezer's towns of Tebah and Cun. Later Solomon melted the bronze and molded it into the great bronze basin called the Sea, the pillars, and the various bronze articles used at the Temple.

When King Toi of Hamath heard that David had destroyed the entire army of King Hadadezer of Zobah, he sent his son Joram to congratulate King David for his successful campaign. Hadadezer and Toi had been enemies and were often at war. Joram presented David with many gifts of gold, silver, and bronze.

King David dedicated all these gifts to the LORD, along with the silver and gold he had taken from the other nations—from Edom, Moab, Ammon, Philistia, and Amalek.

Abishai son of Zeruiah destroyed 18,000 Edomites in the Valley of Salt. He placed army garrisons in Edom, and all the Edomites became David's subjects. In fact, the LORD made David victorious wherever he went.

So David reigned over all Israel and did what was just and right for all his people. Joab son of Zeruiah was commander of the army. Jehoshaphat son of Ahilud was the royal historian. Zadok son of Ahitub and Ahimelech son of Abiathar were the priests. Seraiah was the court secretary. Benaiah son of Jehoiada was captain of the king's bodyguard. And David's sons served as the king's chief assistants.

Some time after this, King Nahash of the Ammonites died, and his son Hanun became king. David said, "I am going to show loyalty to Hanun because his father, Nahash, was always loyal to me." So David sent messengers to express sympathy to Hanun about his father's death.

But when David's ambassadors arrived in the land of Ammon, the Ammonite commanders said to Hanun, "Do you really think these men are coming here to honor your father? No! David has sent them to spy out the land so they can come in and conquer it!" So Hanun seized David's ambassadors and shaved them, cut off their robes at the buttocks, and sent them back to David in shame.

When David heard what had happened to the men, he sent messengers to tell them, "Stay at Jericho until your beards grow out, and then come back." For they felt deep shame because of their appearance.

When the people of Ammon realized how seriously they had angered David, Hanun and the Ammonites sent 75,000 pounds of silver to hire chariots and charioteers from Aram-naharaim, Aram-maacah, and Zobah. They also hired 32,000 chariots and secured the support of the king of Maacah and his army. These forces camped at Medeba, where they were joined by the Ammonite troops that Hanun had recruited from his own towns. When David heard about this, he sent Joab and all his warriors to fight them. The Ammonite troops came out and drew up their battle lines at the entrance of the city, while the other kings positioned themselves to fight in the open fields.

When Joab saw that he would have to fight on both the front and the rear, he chose some of Israel's elite troops and placed them under his personal command to fight the Arameans in the fields. He left the rest of the army under the command of his brother Abishai, who was to attack the Ammonites. "If the Arameans are too strong for me, then come over and help me," Joab told his brother. "And if the Ammonites are too strong for you, I will help you. Be courageous! Let us fight bravely for our people and the cities of our God. May the LORD's will be done."

When Joab and his troops attacked, the Arameans began to run away. And when the Ammonites saw the Arameans running, they also ran from Abishai and retreated into the city. Then Joab returned to Jerusalem.

The Arameans now realized that they were no match for Israel, so they sent messengers and summoned additional Aramean troops from the other side of the Euphrates River. These troops were under the command of Shobach, the commander of Hadadezer's forces.

When David heard what was happening, he mobilized all Israel, crossed the Jordan River, and positioned his troops in battle formation. Then David engaged the Arameans in battle, and they fought against him. But again the Arameans fled from the Israelites. This time David's forces killed 7,000 charioteers and 40,000 foot soldiers, including Shobach, the commander of their army. When Hadadezer's allies saw that they had been defeated by Israel, they surrendered to David and became his subjects. After that, the Arameans were no longer willing to help the Ammonites.

In the spring of the year, when kings normally go out to war, Joab led the Israelite army in successful attacks against the land of the Ammonites. In the process he laid siege to the city of Rabbah, attacking and destroying it. However, David stayed behind in Jerusalem.

Then David went to Rabbah and removed the crown from the king's head, and it was placed on his own head. The crown was made of gold and set with gems, and he found that it weighed seventy-five pounds. David took a vast amount of plunder from the city. He also made slaves of the people of Rabbah and forced them to labor with saws, iron picks, and iron axes. That is how David dealt with the people of all the Ammonite towns. Then David and all the army returned to Jerusalem.

After this, war broke out with the Philistines at Gezer. As they fought, Sibbecai from Hushah killed Saph, a descendant of the giants, and so the Philistines were subdued.

During another battle with the Philistines, Elhanan son of Jair killed Lahmi, the brother of Goliath of Gath. The handle of Lahmi's spear was as thick as a weaver's beam!

In another battle with the Philistines at Gath, they encountered a huge man with six fingers on each hand and six toes on each foot, twenty-four in all, who was also a descendant of the giants. But when he defied and taunted Israel, he was killed by Jonathan, the son of David's brother Shimea.

These Philistines were descendants of the giants of Gath, but David and his warriors killed them.

+

Satan rose up against Israel and caused David to take a census of the people of Israel. So David said to Joab and the commanders of the army, "Take a census of all the people of Israel—from Beersheba in the south to Dan in the north—and bring me a report so I may know how many there are."

But Joab replied, "May the LORD increase the number of his people a hundred times over! But why, my lord the king, do you want to do this? Are they not all your servants? Why must you cause Israel to sin?"

But the king insisted that they take the census, so Joab traveled throughout all Israel to count the people. Then he returned to Jerusalem and reported the number of people to David. There were 1,100,000 warriors in all Israel who could handle a sword, and 470,000 in Judah. But Joab did not include the tribes of Levi and Benjamin in the census because he was so distressed at what the king had made him do.

God was very displeased with the census, and he punished Israel for it. Then David said to God, "I have sinned greatly by taking this census. Please forgive my guilt for doing this foolish thing."

Then the LORD spoke to Gad, David's seer. This was the message: "Go and say to David, 'This is what the LORD says: I will give you three choices. Choose one of these punishments, and I will inflict it on you.'"

So Gad came to David and said, "These are the choices the LORD has given you. You may choose three years of famine, three months of destruction by the sword of your enemies, or three days of severe plague as the angel of the LORD brings devastation throughout the land of Israel. Decide what answer I should give the LORD who sent me."

"I'm in a desperate situation!" David replied to Gad. "But let me fall into the hands of the LORD, for his mercy is very great. Do not let me fall into human hands."

So the LORD sent a plague upon Israel, and 70,000 people died as a result. And God sent an angel to destroy Jerusalem. But just as the angel was preparing to destroy it, the LORD relented and said to the death angel, "Stop! That is enough!" At that moment the angel of the LORD was standing by the threshing floor of Araunah the Jebusite.

David looked up and saw the angel of the LORD standing between heaven and earth with his sword drawn, reaching out over Jerusalem. So David and the leaders of Israel put on burlap to show their deep distress and fell face down on the ground. And David said to God, "I am the one who called for the census! I am the one who has sinned and done wrong! But these people are as innocent as sheep—what have they done? O LORD my God, let your anger fall against me and my family, but do not destroy your people."

Then the angel of the LORD told Gad to instruct David to go up and build an altar to the LORD on the threshing floor of Araunah the Jebusite. So David went up to do what the LORD had commanded him through Gad. Araunah, who was busy threshing wheat at the time, turned and saw the angel there. His four sons, who were with him, ran away and hid. When Araunah saw David approaching, he left his threshing floor and bowed before David with his face to the ground.

David said to Araunah, "Let me buy this threshing floor from you at its full price. Then I will build an altar to the LORD there, so that he will stop the plague."

"Take it, my lord the king, and use it as you wish," Araunah said to David. "I will give the oxen for the burnt offerings, and the threshing boards for wood to build a fire on the altar, and the wheat for the grain offering. I will give it all to you."

But King David replied to Araunah, "No, I insist on buying it for the full price. I will not take what is yours and give it to the LORD. I will not present burnt offerings that have cost me nothing!" So David gave Araunah 600 pieces of gold in payment for the threshing floor.

David built an altar there to the LORD and sacrificed burnt offerings and peace offerings. And when David prayed, the LORD answered him by sending fire from heaven to burn up the offering on the altar. Then the LORD spoke to the angel, who put the sword back into its sheath.

When David saw that the LORD had answered his prayer, he offered sacrifices there at Araunah's threshing floor. At that time the Tabernacle of the LORD and the altar of burnt offering that Moses had made in the wilderness were located at the place of worship in Gibeon. But David was not able to go there to inquire of God, because he was terrified by the drawn sword of the angel of the LORD.

Then David said, "This will be the location for the Temple of the LORD God and the place of the altar for Israel's burnt offerings!"

So David gave orders to call together the foreigners living in Israel, and he assigned them the task of preparing finished stone for building the Temple of God. David provided large amounts of iron for the nails that would be needed for the doors in the gates and for the clamps, and he gave more bronze than could be weighed. He also provided innumerable cedar logs, for the men of Tyre and Sidon had brought vast amounts of cedar to David.

David said, "My son Solomon is still young and inexperienced. And since the Temple to be built for the LORD must be a magnificent structure, famous and glorious throughout the world, I will begin making preparations for it now." So David collected vast amounts of building materials before his death.

Then David sent for his son Solomon and instructed him to build a Temple for the LORD, the God of Israel. "My son, I wanted to build a Temple to honor the name of the LORD my God," David told him. "But the LORD said to me, 'You have killed many men in the battles you have fought. And since you have shed so much blood in my sight, you will not be the one to build a Temple to honor my name. But you will have a son who will be a man of peace. I will give him peace with his enemies in all the surrounding lands. His name will be Solomon, and I will give peace and quiet to Israel during his reign. He is the one who will build a Temple to honor my name. He will be my son, and I will be his father. And I will secure the throne of his kingdom over Israel forever.'

"Now, my son, may the LORD be with you and give you success as you follow his directions in building the Temple of the LORD your God. And may the LORD give you wisdom and understanding, that you may obey the Law of the LORD your God as you rule over Israel. For you will be successful if you carefully obey the decrees and regulations that the LORD gave to Israel through Moses. Be strong and courageous; do not be afraid or lose heart!

"I have worked hard to provide materials for building the Temple of the LORD—nearly 4,000 tons of gold, 40,000 tons of silver, and so much iron and bronze that it cannot be weighed. I have also gathered timber and stone for the walls, though you may need to add more. You have a large number of skilled stonemasons and carpenters and craftsmen of every kind. You have expert goldsmiths and silversmiths and workers of bronze and iron. Now begin the work, and may the LORD be with you!"

Then David ordered all the leaders of Israel to assist Solomon in this project. "The LORD your God is with you," he declared. "He has given you peace with the surrounding nations. He has handed them over to me, and they are now subject to the LORD and his people. Now seek the LORD your God with all your heart and soul. Build the sanctuary of the LORD God so that you can bring the Ark of the LORD's Covenant and the holy vessels of God into the Temple built to honor the LORD's name."

When David was an old man, he appointed his son Solomon to be king over Israel. David summoned all the leaders of Israel, together with the priests and Levites. All the Levites who were thirty years old or older were counted, and the total came to 38,000. Then David said, "From all the Levites, 24,000 will supervise the work at the Temple of the LORD. Another 6,000 will serve as officials and judges. Another 4,000 will work as gatekeepers, and 4,000 will praise the LORD with the musical instruments I have made." Then David divided the Levites into divisions named after the clans descended from the three sons of Levi—Gershon, Kohath, and Merari.

The Gershonite family units were defined by their lines of descent from Libni and Shimei, the sons of Gershon. Three of the descendants of Libni were Jehiel (the family leader), Zetham, and Joel. These were the leaders of the family of Libni.
Three of the descendants of Shimei were Shelomoth, Haziel, and Haran. Four other descendants of Shimei were Jahath, Ziza, Jeush, and Beriah. Jahath was the family leader, and Ziza was next. Jeush and Beriah were counted as a single family because neither had many sons.

Four of the descendants of Kohath were Amram, Izhar, Hebron, and Uzziel.
The sons of Amram were Aaron and Moses. Aaron and his descendants were set apart to dedicate the most holy things, to offer sacrifices in the LORD's presence, to serve the LORD, and to pronounce blessings in his name forever.
   As for Moses, the man of God, his sons were included with the tribe of Levi. The sons of Moses were Gershom and Eliezer. The descendants of Gershom included Shebuel, the family leader. Eliezer had only one son, Rehabiah, the family leader. Rehabiah had numerous descendants.
The descendants of Izhar included Shelomith, the family leader.
The descendants of Hebron included Jeriah (the family leader), Amariah (the second), Jahaziel (the third), and Jekameam (the fourth).
The descendants of Uzziel included Micah (the family leader) and Isshiah (the second).

The descendants of Merari included Mahli and Mushi.
The sons of Mahli were Eleazar and Kish. Eleazar died with no sons, only daughters. His daughters married their cousins, the sons of Kish.
Three of the descendants of Mushi were Mahli, Eder, and Jerimoth.

These were the descendants of Levi by clans, the leaders of their family groups, registered carefully by name. Each had to be twenty years old or older to qualify for service in the house of the LORD. For David said, "The LORD, the God of Israel, has given us peace, and he will always live in Jerusalem. Now the Levites will no longer need to carry the Tabernacle and its furnishings from place to place." In accordance with David's final instructions, all the Levites twenty years old or older were registered for service.

The work of the Levites was to assist the priests, the descendants of Aaron, as they served at the house of the LORD. They also took care of the courtyards and side rooms, helped perform the ceremonies of purification, and served in many other ways in the house of God. They were in charge of the sacred bread that was set out on the table, the choice flour for the grain offerings, the wafers made without yeast, the cakes cooked in olive oil, and the other mixed breads. They were also responsible to check all the weights and measures. And each morning and evening they stood before the LORD to sing songs of thanks and praise to him. They assisted with the burnt offerings that were presented to the LORD on Sabbath days, at new moon celebrations, and at all the appointed festivals. The required number of Levites served in the LORD's presence at all times, following all the procedures they had been given.

And so, under the supervision of the priests, the Levites watched over the Tabernacle and the Temple and faithfully carried out their duties of service at the house of the LORD.

This is how Aaron's descendants, the priests, were divided into groups for service. The sons of Aaron were Nadab, Abihu, Eleazar, and Ithamar. But Nadab and Abihu died before their father, and they had no sons. So only Eleazar and Ithamar were left to carry on as priests.

With the help of Zadok, who was a descendant of Eleazar, and of Ahimelech, who was a descendant of Ithamar, David divided Aaron's descendants into groups according to their various duties. Eleazar's descendants were divided into sixteen groups and Ithamar's into eight, for there were more family leaders among the descendants of Eleazar.

All tasks were assigned to the various groups by means of sacred lots so that no preference would be shown, for there were many qualified officials serving God in the sanctuary from among the descendants of both Eleazar and Ithamar. Shemaiah son of Nethanel, a Levite, acted as secretary and wrote down the names and assignments in the presence of the king, the officials, Zadok the priest, Ahimelech son of Abiathar, and the family leaders of the priests and Levites. The descendants of Eleazar and Ithamar took turns casting lots.

The first lot fell to Jehoiarib.
The second lot fell to Jedaiah.
The third lot fell to Harim.
The fourth lot fell to Seorim.
The fifth lot fell to Malkijah.
The sixth lot fell to Mijamin.
The seventh lot fell to Hakkoz.
The eighth lot fell to Abijah.
The ninth lot fell to Jeshua.
The tenth lot fell to Shecaniah.
The eleventh lot fell to Eliashib.
The twelfth lot fell to Jakim.
The thirteenth lot fell to Huppah.
The fourteenth lot fell to Jeshebeab.
The fifteenth lot fell to Bilgah.
The sixteenth lot fell to Immer.
The seventeenth lot fell to Hezir.
The eighteenth lot fell to Happizzez.
The nineteenth lot fell to Pethahiah.
The twentieth lot fell to Jehezkel.
The twenty-first lot fell to Jakin.
The twenty-second lot fell to Gamul.
The twenty-third lot fell to Delaiah.
The twenty-fourth lot fell to Maaziah.

Each group carried out its appointed duties in the house of the LORD according to the procedures established by their ancestor Aaron in obedience to the commands of the LORD, the God of Israel.

These were the other family leaders descended from Levi:

From the descendants of Amram, the leader was Shebuel.
From the descendants of Shebuel, the leader was Jehdeiah.
From the descendants of Rehabiah, the leader was Isshiah.
From the descendants of Izhar, the leader was Shelomith.
From the descendants of Shelomith, the leader was Jahath.
From the descendants of Hebron, Jeriah was the leader, Amariah was second, Jahaziel was third, and Jekameam was fourth.
From the descendants of Uzziel, the leader was Micah.
From the descendants of Micah, the leader was Shamir, along with Isshiah, the brother of Micah.
From the descendants of Isshiah, the leader was Zechariah.
From the descendants of Merari, the leaders were Mahli and Mushi.

From the descendants of Jaaziah, the leader was Beno.

From the descendants of Merari through Jaaziah, the leaders were
Beno, Shoham, Zaccur, and Ibri.

From the descendants of Mahli, the leader was Eleazar, though he had
no sons.

From the descendants of Kish, the leader was Jerahmeel.

From the descendants of Mushi, the leaders were Mahli, Eder, and
Jerimoth.

These were the descendants of Levi in their various families. Like the
descendants of Aaron, they were assigned to their duties by means of sacred lots, without regard to age or rank. Lots were drawn in the presence
of King David, Zadok, Ahimelech, and the family leaders of the priests
and the Levites.

David and the army commanders then appointed men from the families
of Asaph, Heman, and Jeduthun to proclaim God's messages to the accompaniment of lyres, harps, and cymbals. Here is a list of their names
and their work:

From the sons of Asaph, there were Zaccur, Joseph, Nethaniah, and
Asarelah. They worked under the direction of their father, Asaph, who
proclaimed God's messages by the king's orders.

From the sons of Jeduthun, there were Gedaliah, Zeri, Jeshaiah, Shimei,
Hashabiah, and Mattithiah, six in all. They worked under the direction
of their father, Jeduthun, who proclaimed God's messages to the
accompaniment of the lyre, offering thanks and praise to the LORD.

From the sons of Heman, there were Bukkiah, Mattaniah, Uzziel,
Shubael, Jerimoth, Hananiah, Hanani, Eliathah, Giddalti, Romamti-
ezer, Joshbekashah, Mallothi, Hothir, and Mahazioth. All these were
the sons of Heman, the king's seer, for God had honored him with
fourteen sons and three daughters.

All these men were under the direction of their fathers as they made
music at the house of the LORD. Their responsibilities included the playing of cymbals, harps, and lyres at the house of God. Asaph, Jeduthun,
and Heman reported directly to the king. They and their families were
all trained in making music before the LORD, and each of them—288 in
all—was an accomplished musician. The musicians were appointed to
their term of service by means of sacred lots, without regard to whether
they were young or old, teacher or student.

The first lot fell to Joseph of the Asaph clan and twelve of his sons and
relatives.

The second lot fell to Gedaliah and twelve of his sons and relatives.

The third lot fell to Zaccur and twelve of his sons and relatives.

The fourth lot fell to Zeri and twelve of his sons and relatives.

The fifth lot fell to Nethaniah and twelve of his sons and relatives.

The sixth lot fell to Bukkiah and twelve of his sons and relatives.

The seventh lot fell to Asarelah and twelve of his sons and relatives.

The eighth lot fell to Jeshaiah and twelve of his sons and relatives.

The ninth lot fell to Mattaniah and twelve of his sons and relatives.

The tenth lot fell to Shimei and twelve of his sons and relatives.

The eleventh lot fell to Uzziel and twelve of his sons and relatives.

The twelfth lot fell to Hashabiah and twelve of his sons and relatives.

The thirteenth lot fell to Shubael and twelve of his sons and relatives.

The fourteenth lot fell to Mattithiah and twelve of his sons and relatives.

The fifteenth lot fell to Jerimoth and twelve of his sons and relatives.

The sixteenth lot fell to Hananiah and twelve of his sons and relatives.

The seventeenth lot fell to Joshbekashah and twelve of his sons and relatives.

The eighteenth lot fell to Hanani and twelve of his sons and relatives.

The nineteenth lot fell to Mallothi and twelve of his sons and relatives.

The twentieth lot fell to Eliathah and twelve of his sons and relatives.

The twenty-first lot fell to Hothir and twelve of his sons and relatives.

The twenty-second lot fell to Giddalti and twelve of his sons and relatives.

The twenty-third lot fell to Mahazioth and twelve of his sons and relatives.

The twenty-fourth lot fell to Romamti-ezer and twelve of his sons and relatives.

These are the divisions of the gatekeepers:

From the Korahites, there was Meshelemiah son of Kore, of the family of Abiasaph. The sons of Meshelemiah were Zechariah (the oldest), Jediael (the second), Zebadiah (the third), Jathniel (the fourth), Elam (the fifth), Jehohanan (the sixth), and Eliehoenai (the seventh).

The sons of Obed-edom, also gatekeepers, were Shemaiah (the oldest), Jehozabad (the second), Joah (the third), Sacar (the fourth), Nethanel (the fifth), Ammiel (the sixth), Issachar (the seventh), and Peullethai (the eighth). God had richly blessed Obed-edom.

Obed-edom's son Shemaiah had sons with great ability who earned positions of great authority in the clan. Their names were Othni, Rephael, Obed, and Elzabad. Their relatives, Elihu and Semakiah, were also very capable men.

All of these descendants of Obed-edom, including their sons and grandsons—sixty-two of them in all—were very capable men, well qualified for their work.

Meshelemiah's eighteen sons and relatives were also very capable men.

Hosah, of the Merari clan, appointed Shimri as the leader among his sons, though he was not the oldest. His other sons included Hilkiah (the second), Tebaliah (the third), and Zechariah (the fourth). Hosah's sons and relatives, who served as gatekeepers, numbered thirteen in all.

These divisions of the gatekeepers were named for their family leaders, and like the other Levites, they served at the house of the LORD. They were assigned by families for guard duty at the various gates, without regard to age or training, for it was all decided by means of sacred lots.

The responsibility for the east gate went to Meshelemiah and his group. The north gate was assigned to his son Zechariah, a man of unusual wisdom. The south gate went to Obed-edom, and his sons were put in charge of the storehouse. Shuppim and Hosah were assigned the west gate and the gateway leading up to the Temple. Guard duties were divided evenly. Six Levites were assigned each day to the east gate, four to the north gate, four to the south gate, and two pairs at the storehouse. Six were assigned each day to the west gate, four to the gateway leading up to the Temple, and two to the courtyard.

These were the divisions of the gatekeepers from the clans of Korah and Merari.

Other Levites, led by Ahijah, were in charge of the treasuries of the house of God and the treasuries of the gifts dedicated to the LORD. From the family of Libni in the clan of Gershon, Jehiel was the leader. The sons of Jehiel, Zetham and his brother Joel, were in charge of the treasuries of the house of the LORD.

These are the leaders that descended from Amram, Izhar, Hebron, and Uzziel:

From the clan of Amram, Shebuel was a descendant of Gershom son of Moses. He was the chief officer of the treasuries. His relatives through Eliezer were Rehabiah, Jeshaiah, Joram, Zicri, and Shelomoth.

Shelomoth and his relatives were in charge of the treasuries containing the gifts that King David, the family leaders, and the generals and captains and other officers of the army had dedicated to the LORD. These men dedicated some of the plunder they had gained in battle to maintain the house of the LORD. Shelomoth and his relatives also cared for the gifts dedicated to the LORD by Samuel the seer, Saul son of Kish, Abner son of Ner, and Joab son of Zeruiah. All the other dedicated gifts were in their care, too.

From the clan of Izhar came Kenaniah. He and his sons were given administrative responsibilities over Israel as officials and judges.

From the clan of Hebron came Hashabiah. He and his relatives—1,700 capable men—were put in charge of the Israelite lands west of the Jordan River. They were responsible for all matters related to the things of the LORD and the service of the king in that area.

Also from the clan of Hebron came Jeriah, who was the leader of the Hebronites according to the genealogical records. (In the fortieth year of David's reign, a search was made in the records, and capable men from the clan of Hebron were found at Jazer in the land of Gilead.) There were 2,700 capable men among the relatives of Jeriah. King David sent them to the east side of the Jordan River and put them in charge of the tribes of Reuben and Gad and the half-tribe of Manasseh. They were responsible for all matters related to God and to the king.

This is the list of Israelite generals and captains, and their officers, who served the king by supervising the army divisions that were on duty each month of the year. Each division served for one month and had 24,000 troops.

Jashobeam son of Zabdiel was commander of the first division of 24,000 troops, which was on duty during the first month. He was a descendant of Perez and was in charge of all the army officers for the first month.

Dodai, a descendant of Ahoah, was commander of the second division of 24,000 troops, which was on duty during the second month. Mikloth was his chief officer.

Benaiah son of Jehoiada the priest was commander of the third division of 24,000 troops, which was on duty during the third month. This was the Benaiah who commanded David's elite military group known as the Thirty. His son Ammizabad was his chief officer.

Asahel, the brother of Joab, was commander of the fourth division of 24,000 troops, which was on duty during the fourth month. Asahel was succeeded by his son Zebadiah.

Shammah the Izrahite was commander of the fifth division of 24,000 troops, which was on duty during the fifth month.

Ira son of Ikkesh from Tekoa was commander of the sixth division of 24,000 troops, which was on duty during the sixth month.

Helez, a descendant of Ephraim from Pelon, was commander of the seventh division of 24,000 troops, which was on duty during the seventh month.

Sibbecai, a descendant of Zerah from Hushah, was commander of the eighth division of 24,000 troops, which was on duty during the eighth month.

Abiezer from Anathoth in the territory of Benjamin was commander of the ninth division of 24,000 troops, which was on duty during the ninth month.

Maharai, a descendant of Zerah from Netophah, was commander of the tenth division of 24,000 troops, which was on duty during the tenth month.

Benaiah from Pirathon in Ephraim was commander of the eleventh division of 24,000 troops, which was on duty during the eleventh month.

Heled, a descendant of Othniel from Netophah, was commander of the twelfth division of 24,000 troops, which was on duty during the twelfth month.

The following were the tribes of Israel and their leaders:

Tribe	Leader
Reuben	Eliezer son of Zicri
Simeon	Shephatiah son of Maacah
Levi	Hashabiah son of Kemuel
Aaron (the priests)	Zadok
Judah	Elihu (a brother of David)
Issachar	Omri son of Michael
Zebulun	Ishmaiah son of Obadiah
Naphtali	Jeremoth son of Azriel
Ephraim	Hoshea son of Azaziah
Manasseh (west)	Joel son of Pedaiah
Manasseh in Gilead (east)	Iddo son of Zechariah
Benjamin	Jaasiel son of Abner
Dan	Azarel son of Jeroham

These were the leaders of the tribes of Israel.

When David took his census, he did not count those who were younger than twenty years of age, because the LORD had promised to make the Israelites as numerous as the stars in heaven. Joab son of Zeruiah began the census but never finished it because the anger of God fell on Israel. The total number was never recorded in King David's official records.

Azmaveth son of Adiel was in charge of the palace treasuries.

Jonathan son of Uzziah was in charge of the regional treasuries throughout the towns, villages, and fortresses of Israel.

Ezri son of Kelub was in charge of the field workers who farmed the king's lands.

Shimei from Ramah was in charge of the king's vineyards.

Zabdi from Shepham was responsible for the grapes and the supplies of wine.

Baal-hanan from Geder was in charge of the king's olive groves and sycamore-fig trees in the foothills of Judah.

Joash was responsible for the supplies of olive oil.

Shitrai from Sharon was in charge of the cattle on the Sharon Plain.

Shaphat son of Adlai was responsible for the cattle in the valleys.

Obil the Ishmaelite was in charge of the camels.

Jehdeiah from Meronoth was in charge of the donkeys.

Jaziz the Hagrite was in charge of the king's flocks of sheep and goats.

All these officials were overseers of King David's property.

Jonathan, David's uncle, was a wise counselor to the king, a man of great insight, and a scribe. Jehiel the Hacmonite was responsible for teaching the king's sons. Ahithophel was the royal adviser. Hushai the Arkite was the king's friend. Ahithophel was succeeded by Jehoiada son of Benaiah and by Abiathar. Joab was commander of the king's army.

+

David summoned all the officials of Israel to Jerusalem—the leaders of the tribes, the commanders of the army divisions, the other generals and captains, the overseers of the royal property and livestock, the palace officials, the mighty men, and all the other brave warriors in the kingdom. David rose to his feet and said: "My brothers and my people! It was my desire to build a Temple where the Ark of the LORD's Covenant, God's footstool, could rest permanently. I made the necessary preparations for building it, but God said to me, 'You must not build a Temple to honor my name, for you are a warrior and have shed much blood.'

"Yet the LORD, the God of Israel, has chosen me from among all my father's family to be king over Israel forever. For he has chosen the tribe of Judah to rule, and from among the families of Judah he chose my father's family. And from among my father's sons the LORD was pleased to make me king over all Israel. And from among my sons—for the LORD has given me many—he chose Solomon to succeed me on the throne of Israel and to rule over the LORD's kingdom. He said to me, 'Your son Solomon will build my Temple and its courtyards, for I have chosen him as my son, and I will be his father. And if he continues to obey my commands and regulations as he does now, I will make his kingdom last forever.'

"So now, with God as our witness, and in the sight of all Israel—the LORD's assembly—I give you this charge. Be careful to obey all the commands of the LORD your God, so that you may continue to possess this good land and leave it to your children as a permanent inheritance.

"And Solomon, my son, learn to know the God of your ancestors intimately. Worship and serve him with your whole heart and a willing mind. For the LORD sees every heart and knows every plan and thought. If you seek him, you will find him. But if you forsake him, he will reject you forever. So take this seriously. The LORD has chosen you to build a Temple as his sanctuary. Be strong, and do the work."

Then David gave Solomon the plans for the Temple and its surroundings, including the entry room, the storerooms, the upstairs rooms, the inner rooms, and the inner sanctuary—which was the place of atonement. David also gave Solomon all the plans he had in mind for the courtyards of the LORD's Temple, the outside rooms, the treasuries, and the rooms for the gifts dedicated to the LORD. The king also gave Solomon the instructions concerning the work of the various divisions of priests and Levites in the Temple of the LORD. And he gave specifications for the items in the Temple that were to be used for worship.

David gave instructions regarding how much gold and silver should be used to make the items needed for service. He told Solomon the amount of gold needed for the gold lampstands and lamps, and the amount of silver for the silver lampstands and lamps, depending on how each would be used. He designated the amount of gold for the table on which the Bread of the Presence would be placed and the amount of silver for other tables.

David also designated the amount of gold for the solid gold meat hooks used to handle the sacrificial meat and for the basins, pitchers, and dishes, as well as the amount of silver for every dish. He designated the amount of refined gold for the altar of incense. Finally, he gave him a plan for the LORD's "chariot"—the gold cherubim whose wings were stretched out over the Ark of the LORD's Covenant. "Every part of this plan," David told Solomon, "was given to me in writing from the hand of the LORD."

Then David continued, "Be strong and courageous, and do the work. Don't be afraid or discouraged, for the LORD God, my God, is with you. He will not fail you or forsake you. He will see to it that all the work related to the Temple of the LORD is finished correctly. The various divisions of priests and Levites will serve in the Temple of God. Others with skills of every kind will volunteer, and the officials and the entire nation are at your command."

Then King David turned to the entire assembly and said, "My son Solomon, whom God has clearly chosen as the next king of Israel, is still young and inexperienced. The work ahead of him is enormous, for the Temple he will build is not for mere mortals—it is for the LORD God himself! Using every resource at my command, I have gathered as much as I could for building the Temple of my God. Now there is enough gold, silver, bronze, iron, and wood, as well as great quantities of onyx, other precious stones, costly jewels, and all kinds of fine stone and marble.

"And now, because of my devotion to the Temple of my God, I am giving all of my own private treasures of gold and silver to help in the construction. This is in addition to the building materials I have already collected for his holy Temple. I am donating more than 112 tons of gold from Ophir and 262 tons of refined silver to be used for overlaying the walls of the buildings and for the other gold and silver work to be done by the craftsmen. Now then, who will follow my example and give offerings to the LORD today?"

Then the family leaders, the leaders of the tribes of Israel, the generals and captains of the army, and the king's administrative officers all gave willingly. For the construction of the Temple of God, they gave about 188 tons of gold, 10,000 gold coins, 375 tons of silver, 675 tons of bronze, and 3,750 tons of iron. They also contributed numerous precious stones, which were deposited in the treasury of the house of the LORD under the care of Jehiel, a descendant of Gershon. The people rejoiced over the offerings, for they had given freely and wholeheartedly to the LORD, and King David was filled with joy.

Then David praised the LORD in the presence of the whole assembly:

"O LORD, the God of our ancestor Israel, may you be praised forever and ever! Yours, O LORD, is the greatness, the power, the glory, the victory, and the majesty. Everything in the heavens and on earth is yours, O LORD, and this is your kingdom. We adore you as the one who is over all things. Wealth and honor come from you alone, for you rule over everything. Power and might are in your hand, and at your discretion people are made great and given strength.

"O our God, we thank you and praise your glorious name! But who am I, and who are my people, that we could give anything to you? Everything we have has come from you, and we give you only what you first gave us! We are here for only a moment, visitors and strangers in the land as our ancestors were before us. Our days on earth are like a passing shadow, gone so soon without a trace.

"O LORD our God, even this material we have gathered to build a

Temple to honor your holy name comes from you! It all belongs to
you! I know, my God, that you examine our hearts and rejoice when
you find integrity there. You know I have done all this with good
motives, and I have watched your people offer their gifts willingly and
joyously.

"O LORD, the God of our ancestors Abraham, Isaac, and Israel,
make your people always want to obey you. See to it that their love for
you never changes. Give my son Solomon the wholehearted desire
to obey all your commands, laws, and decrees, and to do everything
necessary to build this Temple, for which I have made these
preparations."

Then David said to the whole assembly, "Give praise to the LORD your
God!" And the entire assembly praised the LORD, the God of their ancestors, and they bowed low and knelt before the LORD and the king.

The next day they brought 1,000 bulls, 1,000 rams, and 1,000 male lambs
as burnt offerings to the LORD. They also brought liquid offerings and
many other sacrifices on behalf of all Israel. They feasted and drank in the
LORD's presence with great joy that day.

And again they crowned David's son Solomon as their new king. They
anointed him before the LORD as their leader, and they anointed Zadok
as priest. So Solomon took the throne of the LORD in place of his father,
David, and he succeeded in everything, and all Israel obeyed him. All the
officials, the warriors, and the sons of King David pledged their loyalty to
King Solomon. And the LORD exalted Solomon in the sight of all Israel, and
he gave Solomon greater royal splendor than any king in Israel before him.

So David son of Jesse reigned over all Israel. He reigned over Israel for
forty years, seven of them in Hebron and thirty-three in Jerusalem. He
died at a ripe old age, having enjoyed long life, wealth, and honor. Then
his son Solomon ruled in his place.

All the events of King David's reign, from beginning to end, are written
in *The Record of Samuel the Seer, The Record of Nathan the Prophet,* and
The Record of Gad the Seer. These accounts include the mighty deeds of
his reign and everything that happened to him and to Israel and to all the
surrounding kingdoms.

+ + +

Solomon son of David took firm control of his kingdom, for the LORD his
God was with him and made him very powerful.

Solomon called together all the leaders of Israel—the generals and captains of the army, the judges, and all the political and clan leaders. Then he led the entire assembly to the place of worship in Gibeon, for God's Tabernacle was located there. (This was the Tabernacle that Moses, the LORD's servant, had made in the wilderness.)

David had already moved the Ark of God from Kiriath-jearim to the tent he had prepared for it in Jerusalem. But the bronze altar made by Bezalel son of Uri and grandson of Hur was there at Gibeon in front of the Tabernacle of the LORD. So Solomon and the people gathered in front of it to consult the LORD. There in front of the Tabernacle, Solomon went up to the bronze altar in the LORD's presence and sacrificed 1,000 burnt offerings on it.

That night God appeared to Solomon and said, "What do you want? Ask, and I will give it to you!"

Solomon replied to God, "You showed great and faithful love to David, my father, and now you have made me king in his place. O LORD God, please continue to keep your promise to David my father, for you have made me king over a people as numerous as the dust of the earth! Give me the wisdom and knowledge to lead them properly, for who could possibly govern this great people of yours?"

God said to Solomon, "Because your greatest desire is to help your people, and you did not ask for wealth, riches, fame, or even the death of your enemies or a long life, but rather you asked for wisdom and knowledge to properly govern my people—I will certainly give you the wisdom and knowledge you requested. But I will also give you wealth, riches, and fame such as no other king has had before you or will ever have in the future!"

Then Solomon returned to Jerusalem from the Tabernacle at the place of worship in Gibeon, and he reigned over Israel.

Solomon built up a huge force of chariots and horses. He had 1,400 chariots and 12,000 horses. He stationed some of them in the chariot cities and some near him in Jerusalem. The king made silver and gold as plentiful in Jerusalem as stone. And valuable cedar timber was as common as the sycamore-fig trees that grow in the foothills of Judah. Solomon's horses were imported from Egypt and from Cilicia; the king's traders acquired them from Cilicia at the standard price. At that time chariots from Egypt could be purchased for 600 pieces of silver, and horses for 150 pieces of silver. They were then exported to the kings of the Hittites and the kings of Aram.

+

Solomon decided to build a Temple to honor the name of the LORD, and also a royal palace for himself. He enlisted a force of 70,000 laborers, 80,000 men to quarry stone in the hill country, and 3,600 foremen.

Solomon also sent this message to King Hiram at Tyre:

"Send me cedar logs as you did for my father, David, when he was building his palace. I am about to build a Temple to honor the name of the LORD my God. It will be a place set apart to burn fragrant incense before him, to display the special sacrificial bread, and to sacrifice burnt offerings each morning and evening, on the Sabbaths, at new moon celebrations, and at the other appointed festivals of the LORD our God. He has commanded Israel to do these things forever.

"This must be a magnificent Temple because our God is greater than all other gods. But who can really build him a worthy home? Not even the highest heavens can contain him! So who am I to consider building a Temple for him, except as a place to burn sacrifices to him?

"So send me a master craftsman who can work with gold, silver, bronze, and iron, as well as with purple, scarlet, and blue cloth. He must be a skilled engraver who can work with the craftsmen of Judah and Jerusalem who were selected by my father, David.

"Also send me cedar, cypress, and red sandalwood logs from Lebanon, for I know that your men are without equal at cutting timber in Lebanon. I will send my men to help them. An immense amount of timber will be needed, for the Temple I am going to build will be very large and magnificent. In payment for your woodcutters, I will send 100,000 bushels of crushed wheat, 100,000 bushels of barley, 110,000 gallons of wine, and 110,000 gallons of olive oil."

King Hiram sent this letter of reply to Solomon:

"It is because the LORD loves his people that he has made you their king! Praise the LORD, the God of Israel, who made the heavens and the earth! He has given King David a wise son, gifted with skill and understanding, who will build a Temple for the LORD and a royal palace for himself.

"I am sending you a master craftsman named Huram-abi, who is extremely talented. His mother is from the tribe of Dan in Israel, and his father is from Tyre. He is skillful at making things from gold, silver, bronze, and iron, and he also works with stone and wood. He can work with purple, blue, and scarlet cloth and fine linen. He is also an engraver and can follow any design given to him. He will work with your craftsmen and those appointed by my lord David, your father.

"Send along the wheat, barley, olive oil, and wine that my lord has mentioned. We will cut whatever timber you need from the Lebanon mountains and will float the logs in rafts down the coast of the Mediterranean Sea to Joppa. From there you can transport the logs up to Jerusalem."

Solomon took a census of all foreigners in the land of Israel, like the census his father had taken, and he counted 153,600. He assigned 70,000 of them as common laborers, 80,000 as quarry workers in the hill country, and 3,600 as foremen.

So Solomon began to build the Temple of the LORD in Jerusalem on Mount Moriah, where the LORD had appeared to David, his father. The Temple was built on the threshing floor of Araunah the Jebusite, the site that David had selected. The construction began in midspring, during the fourth year of Solomon's reign.

These are the dimensions Solomon used for the foundation of the Temple of God (using the old standard of measurement). It was 90 feet long and 30 feet wide. The entry room at the front of the Temple was 30 feet wide, running across the entire width of the Temple, and 30 feet high. He overlaid the inside with pure gold.

He paneled the main room of the Temple with cypress wood, overlaid it with fine gold, and decorated it with carvings of palm trees and chains. He decorated the walls of the Temple with beautiful jewels and with gold from the land of Parvaim. He overlaid the beams, thresholds, walls, and doors throughout the Temple with gold, and he carved figures of cherubim on the walls.

He made the Most Holy Place 30 feet wide, corresponding to the width of the Temple, and 30 feet deep. He overlaid its interior with 23 tons of fine gold. The gold nails that were used weighed 20 ounces each. He also overlaid the walls of the upper rooms with gold.

He made two figures shaped like cherubim, overlaid them with gold, and placed them in the Most Holy Place. The total wingspan of the two cherubim standing side by side was 30 feet. One wing of the first figure was 7½ feet long, and it touched the Temple wall. The other wing, also 7½ feet long, touched one of the wings of the second figure. In the same way, the second figure had one wing 7½ feet long that touched the opposite wall. The other wing, also 7½ feet long, touched the wing of the first figure. So the wingspan of the two cherubim side by side was 30 feet. They stood on their feet and faced out toward the main room of the Temple.

Across the entrance of the Most Holy Place he hung a curtain made of fine linen, decorated with blue, purple, and scarlet thread and embroidered with figures of cherubim.

For the front of the Temple, he made two pillars that were 27 feet tall, each topped by a capital extending upward another 7½ feet. He made a network of interwoven chains and used them to decorate the tops of the pillars. He also made 100 decorative pomegranates and attached them to the chains. Then he set up the two pillars at the entrance of the Temple, one to the south of the entrance and the other to the north. He named the one on the south Jakin, and the one on the north Boaz.

Solomon also made a bronze altar 30 feet long, 30 feet wide, and 15 feet high. Then he cast a great round basin, 15 feet across from rim to rim, called the Sea. It was 7½ feet deep and about 45 feet in circumference. It was encircled just below its rim by two rows of figures that resembled oxen. There were about six oxen per foot all the way around, and they were cast as part of the basin.

The Sea was placed on a base of twelve bronze oxen, all facing outward. Three faced north, three faced west, three faced south, and three faced east, and the Sea rested on them. The walls of the Sea were about three inches thick, and its rim flared out like a cup and resembled a water lily blossom. It could hold about 16,500 gallons of water.

He also made ten smaller basins for washing the utensils for the burnt offerings. He set five on the south side and five on the north. But the priests washed themselves in the Sea.

He then cast ten gold lampstands according to the specifications that had been given, and he put them in the Temple. Five were placed against the south wall, and five were placed against the north wall.

He also built ten tables and placed them in the Temple, five along the south wall and five along the north wall. Then he molded 100 gold basins.

He then built a courtyard for the priests, and also the large outer courtyard. He made doors for the courtyard entrances and overlaid them with bronze. The great bronze basin called the Sea was placed near the southeast corner of the Temple.

Huram-abi also made the necessary washbasins, shovels, and bowls.

So at last Huram-abi completed everything King Solomon had assigned him to make for the Temple of God:

> the two pillars;
> the two bowl-shaped capitals on top of the pillars;
> the two networks of interwoven chains that decorated the capitals;
> the 400 pomegranates that hung from the chains on the capitals (two rows of pomegranates for each of the chain networks that decorated the capitals on top of the pillars);
> the water carts holding the basins;
> the Sea and the twelve oxen under it;
> the ash buckets, the shovels, the meat hooks, and all the related articles.

Huram-abi made all these things of burnished bronze for the Temple of the LORD, just as King Solomon had directed. The king had them cast in clay molds in the Jordan Valley between Succoth and Zarethan. Solomon used such great quantities of bronze that its weight could not be determined.

Solomon also made all the furnishings for the Temple of God:

the gold altar;
the tables for the Bread of the Presence;
the lampstands and their lamps of solid gold, to burn in front of the Most Holy Place as prescribed;
the flower decorations, lamps, and tongs—all of the purest gold;
the lamp snuffers, bowls, ladles, and incense burners—all of solid gold;
the doors for the entrances to the Most Holy Place and the main room of the Temple, overlaid with gold.

So Solomon finished all his work on the Temple of the LORD. Then he brought all the gifts his father, David, had dedicated—the silver, the gold, and the various articles—and he stored them in the treasuries of the Temple of God.

Solomon then summoned to Jerusalem the elders of Israel and all the heads of tribes—the leaders of the ancestral families of Israel. They were to bring the Ark of the LORD's Covenant to the Temple from its location in the City of David, also known as Zion. So all the men of Israel assembled before the king at the annual Festival of Shelters, which is held in early autumn.

When all the elders of Israel arrived, the Levites picked up the Ark. The priests and Levites brought up the Ark along with the special tent and all the sacred items that had been in it. There, before the Ark, King Solomon and the entire community of Israel sacrificed so many sheep, goats, and cattle that no one could keep count!

Then the priests carried the Ark of the LORD's Covenant into the inner sanctuary of the Temple—the Most Holy Place—and placed it beneath the wings of the cherubim. The cherubim spread their wings over the Ark, forming a canopy over the Ark and its carrying poles. These poles were so long that their ends could be seen from the Holy Place, which is in front of the Most Holy Place, but not from the outside. They are still there to this day. Nothing was in the Ark except the two stone tablets that Moses had placed in it at Mount Sinai, where the LORD made a covenant with the people of Israel when they left Egypt.

Then the priests left the Holy Place. All the priests who were present had purified themselves, whether or not they were on duty that day. And the Levites who were musicians—Asaph, Heman, Jeduthun, and all their sons and brothers—were dressed in fine linen robes and stood at the east side of the altar playing cymbals, lyres, and harps. They were joined by 120 priests who were playing trumpets. The trumpeters and singers performed together in unison to praise and give thanks to the LORD. Accompanied by trumpets, cymbals, and other instruments, they raised their voices and praised the LORD with these words:

"He is good!
His faithful love endures forever!"

At that moment a thick cloud filled the Temple of the LORD. The priests could not continue their service because of the cloud, for the glorious presence of the LORD filled the Temple of God.

Then Solomon prayed, "O LORD, you have said that you would live in a thick cloud of darkness. Now I have built a glorious Temple for you, a place where you can live forever!"

Then the king turned around to the entire community of Israel standing before him and gave this blessing: "Praise the LORD, the God of Israel, who has kept the promise he made to my father, David. For he told my father, 'From the day I brought my people out of the land of Egypt, I have never chosen a city among any of the tribes of Israel as the place where a Temple should be built to honor my name. Nor have I chosen a king to lead my people Israel. But now I have chosen Jerusalem as the place for my name to be honored, and I have chosen David to be king over my people Israel.'"

Then Solomon said, "My father, David, wanted to build this Temple to honor the name of the LORD, the God of Israel. But the LORD told him, 'You wanted to build the Temple to honor my name. Your intention is good, but you are not the one to do it. One of your own sons will build the Temple to honor me.'

"And now the LORD has fulfilled the promise he made, for I have become king in my father's place, and now I sit on the throne of Israel, just as the LORD promised. I have built this Temple to honor the name of the LORD, the God of Israel. There I have placed the Ark, which contains the covenant that the LORD made with the people of Israel."

Then Solomon stood before the altar of the LORD in front of the entire community of Israel, and he lifted his hands in prayer. Now Solomon had made a bronze platform 7½ feet long, 7½ feet wide, and 4½ feet high and had placed it at the center of the Temple's outer courtyard. He stood on the platform, and then he knelt in front of the entire community of Israel and lifted his hands toward heaven. He prayed,

"O LORD, God of Israel, there is no God like you in all of heaven and earth. You keep your covenant and show unfailing love to all who walk before you in wholehearted devotion. You have kept your promise to your servant David, my father. You made that promise with your own mouth, and with your own hands you have fulfilled it today.

"And now, O LORD, God of Israel, carry out the additional promise you made to your servant David, my father. For you said to him, 'If your descendants guard their behavior and faithfully follow my Law as you have done, one of them will always sit on the throne of Israel.' Now, O LORD, God of Israel, fulfill this promise to your servant David.

"But will God really live on earth among people? Why, even the highest heavens cannot contain you. How much less this Temple I have built! Nevertheless, listen to my prayer and my plea, O LORD my God. Hear the cry and the prayer that your servant is making to you. May you watch over this Temple day and night, this place where you have said you would put your name. May you always hear the prayers I make toward this place. May you hear the humble and earnest requests from me and your people Israel when we pray toward this place. Yes, hear us from heaven where you live, and when you hear, forgive.

"If someone wrongs another person and is required to take an oath of innocence in front of your altar at this Temple, then hear from heaven and judge between your servants—the accuser and the accused. Pay back the guilty as they deserve. Acquit the innocent because of their innocence.

"If your people Israel are defeated by their enemies because they have sinned against you, and if they turn back and acknowledge your name and pray to you here in this Temple, then hear from heaven and forgive the sin of your people Israel and return them to this land you gave to them and to their ancestors.

"If the skies are shut up and there is no rain because your people have sinned against you, and if they pray toward this Temple and acknowledge your name and turn from their sins because you have punished them, then hear from heaven and forgive the sins of your servants, your people Israel. Teach them to follow the right path, and send rain on your land that you have given to your people as their special possession.

"If there is a famine in the land or a plague or crop disease or attacks of locusts or caterpillars, or if your people's enemies are in the land besieging their towns—whatever disaster or disease there is—and if your people Israel pray about their troubles or sorrow, raising their hands toward this Temple, then hear from heaven where you live, and forgive. Give your people what their actions deserve, for you alone know each human heart. Then they will fear you and walk in your ways as long as they live in the land you gave to our ancestors.

"In the future, foreigners who do not belong to your people Israel
will hear of you. They will come from distant lands when they hear
of your great name and your strong hand and your powerful arm. And
when they pray toward this Temple, then hear from heaven where you
live, and grant what they ask of you. In this way, all the people of the
earth will come to know and fear you, just as your own people Israel do.
They, too, will know that this Temple I have built honors your name.

"If your people go out where you send them to fight their enemies,
and if they pray to you by turning toward this city you have chosen
and toward this Temple I have built to honor your name, then hear
their prayers from heaven and uphold their cause.

"If they sin against you—and who has never sinned?—you might
become angry with them and let their enemies conquer them and
take them captive to a foreign land far away or near. But in that land of
exile, they might turn to you in repentance and pray, 'We have sinned,
done evil, and acted wickedly.' If they turn to you with their whole
heart and soul in the land of their captivity and pray toward the land
you gave to their ancestors—toward this city you have chosen, and
toward this Temple I have built to honor your name—then hear their
prayers and their petitions from heaven where you live, and uphold
their cause. Forgive your people who have sinned against you.

"O my God, may your eyes be open and your ears attentive to all the
prayers made to you in this place.

"And now arise, O Lord God, and enter your resting place,
    along with the Ark, the symbol of your power.
May your priests, O Lord God, be clothed with salvation;
    may your loyal servants rejoice in your goodness.
O Lord God, do not reject the king you have anointed.
    Remember your unfailing love for your servant David."

When Solomon finished praying, fire flashed down from heaven and
burned up the burnt offerings and sacrifices, and the glorious presence
of the Lord filled the Temple. The priests could not enter the Temple of
the Lord because the glorious presence of the Lord filled it. When all
the people of Israel saw the fire coming down and the glorious presence
of the Lord filling the Temple, they fell face down on the ground and
worshiped and praised the Lord, saying,

"He is good!
    His faithful love endures forever!"

Then the king and all the people offered sacrifices to the Lord. King
Solomon offered a sacrifice of 22,000 cattle and 120,000 sheep and goats.

And so the king and all the people dedicated the Temple of God. The priests took their assigned positions, and so did the Levites who were singing, "His faithful love endures forever!" They accompanied the singing with music from the instruments King David had made for praising the LORD. Across from the Levites, the priests blew the trumpets, while all Israel stood.

Solomon then consecrated the central area of the courtyard in front of the LORD's Temple. He offered burnt offerings and the fat of peace offerings there, because the bronze altar he had built could not hold all the burnt offerings, grain offerings, and sacrificial fat.

For the next seven days Solomon and all Israel celebrated the Festival of Shelters. A large congregation had gathered from as far away as Lebo-hamath in the north and the Brook of Egypt in the south. On the eighth day they had a closing ceremony, for they had celebrated the dedication of the altar for seven days and the Festival of Shelters for seven days. Then at the end of the celebration, Solomon sent the people home. They were all joyful and glad because the LORD had been so good to David and to Solomon and to his people Israel.

So Solomon finished the Temple of the LORD, as well as the royal palace. He completed everything he had planned to do in the construction of the Temple and the palace. Then one night the LORD appeared to Solomon and said,

"I have heard your prayer and have chosen this Temple as the place for making sacrifices. At times I might shut up the heavens so that no rain falls, or command grasshoppers to devour your crops, or send plagues among you. Then if my people who are called by my name will humble themselves and pray and seek my face and turn from their wicked ways, I will hear from heaven and will forgive their sins and restore their land. My eyes will be open and my ears attentive to every prayer made in this place. For I have chosen this Temple and set it apart to be holy—a place where my name will be honored forever. I will always watch over it, for it is dear to my heart.

"As for you, if you faithfully follow me as David your father did, obeying all my commands, decrees, and regulations, then I will establish the throne of your dynasty. For I made this covenant with your father, David, when I said, 'One of your descendants will always rule over Israel.'

"But if you or your descendants abandon me and disobey the decrees and commands I have given you, and if you serve and worship other gods, then I will uproot the people from this land that I have given them. I will reject this Temple that I have made holy to honor my name. I will make it an object of mockery and ridicule among the nations. And though this Temple is impressive now, all who pass by will be appalled. They will ask, 'Why did the Lord do such terrible things to this land and to this Temple?'

"And the answer will be, 'Because his people abandoned the Lord, the God of their ancestors, who brought them out of Egypt, and they worshiped other gods instead and bowed down to them. That is why he has brought all these disasters on them.'"

+

It took Solomon twenty years to build the Lord's Temple and his own royal palace. At the end of that time, Solomon turned his attention to rebuilding the towns that King Hiram had given him, and he settled Israelites in them.

Solomon also fought against the town of Hamath-zobah and conquered it. He rebuilt Tadmor in the wilderness and built towns in the region of Hamath as supply centers. He fortified the towns of Upper Beth-horon and Lower Beth-horon, rebuilding their walls and installing barred gates. He also rebuilt Baalath and other supply centers and constructed towns where his chariots and horses could be stationed. He built everything he desired in Jerusalem and Lebanon and throughout his entire realm.

There were still some people living in the land who were not Israelites, including the Hittites, Amorites, Perizzites, Hivites, and Jebusites. These were descendants of the nations whom the people of Israel had not destroyed. So Solomon conscripted them for his labor force, and they serve as forced laborers to this day. But Solomon did not conscript any of the Israelites for his labor force. Instead, he assigned them to serve as fighting men, officers in his army, commanders of his chariots, and charioteers. King Solomon appointed 250 of them to supervise the people.

Solomon moved his wife, Pharaoh's daughter, from the City of David to the new palace he had built for her. He said, "My wife must not live in King David's palace, for the Ark of the Lord has been there, and it is holy ground."

Then Solomon presented burnt offerings to the Lord on the altar he had built for him in front of the entry room of the Temple. He offered the sacrifices for the Sabbaths, the new moon festivals, and the three annual festivals—the Passover celebration, the Festival of Harvest, and the Festival of Shelters—as Moses had commanded.

In assigning the priests to their duties, Solomon followed the regulations of his father, David. He also assigned the Levites to lead the people in praise and to assist the priests in their daily duties. And he assigned the gatekeepers to their gates by their divisions, following the commands of David, the man of God. Solomon did not deviate in any way from David's commands concerning the priests and Levites and the treasuries.

So Solomon made sure that all the work related to building the Temple of the LORD was carried out, from the day its foundation was laid to the day of its completion.

Later Solomon went to Ezion-geber and Elath, ports along the shore of the Red Sea in the land of Edom. Hiram sent him ships commanded by his own officers and manned by experienced crews of sailors. These ships sailed to Ophir with Solomon's men and brought back to Solomon almost seventeen tons of gold.

When the queen of Sheba heard of Solomon's fame, she came to Jerusalem to test him with hard questions. She arrived with a large group of attendants and a great caravan of camels loaded with spices, large quantities of gold, and precious jewels. When she met with Solomon, she talked with him about everything she had on her mind. Solomon had answers for all her questions; nothing was too hard for him to explain to her. When the queen of Sheba realized how wise Solomon was, and when she saw the palace he had built, she was overwhelmed. She was also amazed at the food on his tables, the organization of his officials and their splendid clothing, the cup-bearers and their robes, and the burnt offerings Solomon made at the Temple of the LORD.

She exclaimed to the king, "Everything I heard in my country about your achievements and wisdom is true! I didn't believe what was said until I arrived here and saw it with my own eyes. In fact, I had not heard the half of your great wisdom! It is far beyond what I was told. How happy your people must be! What a privilege for your officials to stand here day after day, listening to your wisdom! Praise the LORD your God, who delights in you and has placed you on the throne as king to rule for him. Because God loves Israel and desires this kingdom to last forever, he has made you king over them so you can rule with justice and righteousness."

Then she gave the king a gift of 9,000 pounds of gold, great quantities of spices, and precious jewels. Never before had there been spices as fine as those the queen of Sheba gave to King Solomon.

(In addition, the crews of Hiram and Solomon brought gold from Ophir, and they also brought red sandalwood and precious jewels. The king used the sandalwood to make steps for the Temple of the LORD and the royal palace, and to construct lyres and harps for the musicians. Never before had such beautiful things been seen in Judah.)

King Solomon gave the queen of Sheba whatever she asked for—gifts of greater value than the gifts she had given him. Then she and all her attendants returned to their own land.

Each year Solomon received about 25 tons of gold. This did not include the additional revenue he received from merchants and traders. All the kings of Arabia and the governors of the provinces also brought gold and silver to Solomon.

King Solomon made 200 large shields of hammered gold, each weighing more than 15 pounds. He also made 300 smaller shields of hammered gold, each weighing more than 7½ pounds. The king placed these shields in the Palace of the Forest of Lebanon.

Then the king made a huge throne, decorated with ivory and overlaid with pure gold. The throne had six steps, with a footstool of gold. There were armrests on both sides of the seat, and the figure of a lion stood on each side of the throne. There were also twelve other lions, one standing on each end of the six steps. No other throne in all the world could be compared with it!

All of King Solomon's drinking cups were solid gold, as were all the utensils in the Palace of the Forest of Lebanon. They were not made of silver, for silver was considered worthless in Solomon's day!

The king had a fleet of trading ships of Tarshish manned by the sailors sent by Hiram. Once every three years the ships returned, loaded with gold, silver, ivory, apes, and peacocks.

So King Solomon became richer and wiser than any other king on earth. Kings from every nation came to consult him and to hear the wisdom God had given him. Year after year everyone who visited brought him gifts of silver and gold, clothing, weapons, spices, horses, and mules.

Solomon had 4,000 stalls for his horses and chariots, and he had 12,000 horses. He stationed some of them in the chariot cities, and some near him in Jerusalem. He ruled over all the kings from the Euphrates River in the north to the land of the Philistines and the border of Egypt in the south. The king made silver as plentiful in Jerusalem as stone. And valuable cedar timber was as common as the sycamore-fig trees that grow in the foothills of Judah. Solomon's horses were imported from Egypt and many other countries.

The rest of the events of Solomon's reign, from beginning to end, are recorded in *The Record of Nathan the Prophet,* and *The Prophecy of Ahijah from Shiloh,* and also in *The Visions of Iddo the Seer,* concerning Jeroboam son of Nebat. Solomon ruled in Jerusalem over all Israel for forty years. When he died, he was buried in the City of David, named for his father. Then his son Rehoboam became the next king.

+ + +

Rehoboam went to Shechem, where all Israel had gathered to make him king. When Jeroboam son of Nebat heard of this, he returned from Egypt, for he had fled to Egypt to escape from King Solomon. The leaders of Israel summoned him, and Jeroboam and all Israel went to speak with Rehoboam. "Your father was a hard master," they said. "Lighten the harsh labor demands and heavy taxes that your father imposed on us. Then we will be your loyal subjects."

Rehoboam replied, "Come back in three days for my answer." So the people went away.

Then King Rehoboam discussed the matter with the older men who had counseled his father, Solomon. "What is your advice?" he asked. "How should I answer these people?"

The older counselors replied, "If you are good to these people and do your best to please them and give them a favorable answer, they will always be your loyal subjects."

But Rehoboam rejected the advice of the older men and instead asked the opinion of the young men who had grown up with him and were now his advisers. "What is your advice?" he asked them. "How should I answer these people who want me to lighten the burdens imposed by my father?"

The young men replied, "This is what you should tell those complainers who want a lighter burden: 'My little finger is thicker than my father's waist! Yes, my father laid heavy burdens on you, but I'm going to make them even heavier! My father beat you with whips, but I will beat you with scorpions!'"

Three days later Jeroboam and all the people returned to hear Rehoboam's decision, just as the king had ordered. But Rehoboam spoke harshly to them, for he rejected the advice of the older counselors and followed the counsel of his younger advisers. He told the people, "My father laid heavy burdens on you, but I'm going to make them even heavier! My father beat you with whips, but I will beat you with scorpions!"

So the king paid no attention to the people. This turn of events was the will of God, for it fulfilled the LORD's message to Jeroboam son of Nebat through the prophet Ahijah from Shiloh.

When all Israel realized that the king had refused to listen to them, they responded,

"Down with the dynasty of David!
    We have no interest in the son of Jesse.
Back to your homes, O Israel!
    Look out for your own house, O David!"

So all the people of Israel returned home. But Rehoboam continued to rule over the Israelites who lived in the towns of Judah.

King Rehoboam sent Adoniram, who was in charge of forced labor, to restore order, but the people of Israel stoned him to death. When this news reached King Rehoboam, he quickly jumped into his chariot and fled to Jerusalem. And to this day the northern tribes of Israel have refused to be ruled by a descendant of David.

When Rehoboam arrived at Jerusalem, he mobilized the men of Judah and Benjamin—180,000 select troops—to fight against Israel and to restore the kingdom to himself.

But the LORD said to Shemaiah, the man of God, "Say to Rehoboam son of Solomon, king of Judah, and to all the Israelites in Judah and Benjamin: 'This is what the LORD says: Do not fight against your relatives. Go back home, for what has happened is my doing!'" So they obeyed the message of the LORD and did not fight against Jeroboam.

Rehoboam remained in Jerusalem and fortified various towns for the defense of Judah. He built up Bethlehem, Etam, Tekoa, Beth-zur, Soco, Adullam, Gath, Mareshah, Ziph, Adoraim, Lachish, Azekah, Zorah, Aijalon, and Hebron. These became the fortified towns of Judah and Benjamin. Rehoboam strengthened their defenses and stationed commanders in them, and he stored supplies of food, olive oil, and wine. He also put shields and spears in these towns as a further safety measure. So only Judah and Benjamin remained under his control.

But all the priests and Levites living among the northern tribes of Israel sided with Rehoboam. The Levites even abandoned their pasturelands and property and moved to Judah and Jerusalem, because Jeroboam and his sons would not allow them to serve the LORD as priests. Jeroboam appointed his own priests to serve at the pagan shrines, where they worshiped the goat and calf idols he had made. From all the tribes of Israel, those who sincerely wanted to worship the LORD, the God of Israel, followed the Levites to Jerusalem, where they could offer sacrifices to the LORD, the God of their ancestors. This strengthened the kingdom of Judah, and for three years they supported Rehoboam son of Solomon, for during those years they faithfully followed in the footsteps of David and Solomon.

Rehoboam married his cousin Mahalath, the daughter of David's son Jerimoth and of Abihail, the daughter of Eliab son of Jesse. Mahalath had three sons—Jeush, Shemariah, and Zaham.

Later Rehoboam married another cousin, Maacah, the granddaughter of Absalom. Maacah gave birth to Abijah, Attai, Ziza, and Shelomith.

Rehoboam loved Maacah more than any of his other wives and concubines. In all, he had eighteen wives and sixty concubines, and they gave birth to twenty-eight sons and sixty daughters.

Rehoboam appointed Maacah's son Abijah as leader among the princes, making it clear that he would be the next king. Rehoboam also wisely gave responsibilities to his other sons and stationed some of them in the fortified towns throughout the land of Judah and Benjamin. He provided them with generous provisions, and he found many wives for them.

But when Rehoboam was firmly established and strong, he abandoned the Law of the LORD, and all Israel followed him in this sin. Because they were unfaithful to the LORD, King Shishak of Egypt came up and attacked Jerusalem in the fifth year of King Rehoboam's reign. He came with 1,200 chariots, 60,000 horses, and a countless army of foot soldiers, including Libyans, Sukkites, and Ethiopians. Shishak conquered Judah's fortified towns and then advanced to attack Jerusalem.

The prophet Shemaiah then met with Rehoboam and Judah's leaders, who had all fled to Jerusalem because of Shishak. Shemaiah told them, "This is what the LORD says: You have abandoned me, so I am abandoning you to Shishak."

Then the leaders of Israel and the king humbled themselves and said, "The LORD is right in doing this to us!"

When the LORD saw their change of heart, he gave this message to Shemaiah: "Since the people have humbled themselves, I will not completely destroy them and will soon give them some relief. I will not use Shishak to pour out my anger on Jerusalem. But they will become his subjects, so they will know the difference between serving me and serving earthly rulers."

So King Shishak of Egypt came up and attacked Jerusalem. He ransacked the treasuries of the LORD's Temple and the royal palace; he stole everything, including all the gold shields Solomon had made. King Rehoboam later replaced them with bronze shields as substitutes, and he entrusted them to the care of the commanders of the guard who protected the entrance to the royal palace. Whenever the king went to the Temple of the LORD, the guards would also take the shields and then return them to the guardroom. Because Rehoboam humbled himself, the LORD's anger was turned away, and he did not destroy him completely. There were still some good things in the land of Judah.

King Rehoboam firmly established himself in Jerusalem and continued to rule. He was forty-one years old when he became king, and he reigned seventeen years in Jerusalem, the city the LORD had chosen from among all the tribes of Israel as the place to honor his name. Rehoboam's mother was Naamah, a woman from Ammon. But he was an evil king, for he did not seek the LORD with all his heart.

The rest of the events of Rehoboam's reign, from beginning to end, are recorded in *The Record of Shemaiah the Prophet* and *The Record of Iddo the Seer,* which are part of the genealogical record. Rehoboam and Jeroboam were continually at war with each other. When Rehoboam died, he was buried in the City of David. Then his son Abijah became the next king.

+ + +

Abijah began to rule over Judah in the eighteenth year of Jeroboam's reign in Israel. He reigned in Jerusalem three years. His mother was Maacah, the daughter of Uriel from Gibeah.

Then war broke out between Abijah and Jeroboam. Judah, led by King Abijah, fielded 400,000 select warriors, while Jeroboam mustered 800,000 select troops from Israel.

When the army of Judah arrived in the hill country of Ephraim, Abijah stood on Mount Zemaraim and shouted to Jeroboam and all Israel: "Listen to me! Don't you realize that the LORD, the God of Israel, made a lasting covenant with David, giving him and his descendants the throne of Israel forever? Yet Jeroboam son of Nebat, a mere servant of David's son Solomon, rebelled against his master. Then a whole gang of scoundrels joined him, defying Solomon's son Rehoboam when he was young and inexperienced and could not stand up to them.

"Do you really think you can stand against the kingdom of the LORD that is led by the descendants of David? You may have a vast army, and you have those gold calves that Jeroboam made as your gods. But you have chased away the priests of the LORD (the descendants of Aaron) and the Levites, and you have appointed your own priests, just like the pagan nations. You let anyone become a priest these days! Whoever comes to be dedicated with a young bull and seven rams can become a priest of these so-called gods of yours!

"But as for us, the LORD is our God, and we have not abandoned him. Only the descendants of Aaron serve the LORD as priests, and the Levites alone may help them in their work. They present burnt offerings and fragrant incense to the LORD every morning and evening. They place the Bread of the Presence on the holy table, and they light the gold lampstand every evening. We are following the instructions of the LORD our God, but you have abandoned him. So you see, God is with us. He is our leader. His priests blow their trumpets and lead us into battle against you. O people of Israel, do not fight against the LORD, the God of your ancestors, for you will not succeed!"

Meanwhile, Jeroboam had secretly sent part of his army around behind the men of Judah to ambush them. When Judah realized that they were being attacked from the front and the rear, they cried out to the LORD for help. Then the priests blew the trumpets, and the men of Judah began to shout. At the sound of their battle cry, God defeated Jeroboam and all Israel and routed them before Abijah and the army of Judah.

The Israelite army fled from Judah, and God handed them over to Judah in defeat. Abijah and his army inflicted heavy losses on them; 500,000 of Israel's select troops were killed that day. So Judah defeated Israel on that occasion because they trusted in the LORD, the God of their ancestors. Abijah and his army pursued Jeroboam's troops and captured some of his towns, including Bethel, Jeshanah, and Ephron, along with their surrounding villages.

So Jeroboam of Israel never regained his power during Abijah's lifetime, and finally the LORD struck him down and he died. Meanwhile, Abijah of Judah grew more and more powerful. He married fourteen wives and had twenty-two sons and sixteen daughters.

The rest of the events of Abijah's reign, including his words and deeds, are recorded in *The Commentary of Iddo the Prophet*.

+ + +

When Abijah died, he was buried in the City of David. Then his son Asa became the next king. There was peace in the land for ten years.

Asa did what was pleasing and good in the sight of the LORD his God. He removed the foreign altars and the pagan shrines. He smashed the sacred pillars and cut down the Asherah poles. He commanded the people of Judah to seek the LORD, the God of their ancestors, and to obey his law and his commands. Asa also removed the pagan shrines, as well as the incense altars from every one of Judah's towns. So Asa's kingdom enjoyed a period of peace. During those peaceful years, he was able to build up the fortified towns throughout Judah. No one tried to make war against him at this time, for the LORD was giving him rest from his enemies.

Asa told the people of Judah, "Let us build towns and fortify them with walls, towers, gates, and bars. The land is still ours because we sought the LORD our God, and he has given us peace on every side." So they went ahead with these projects and brought them to completion.

King Asa had an army of 300,000 warriors from the tribe of Judah, armed with large shields and spears. He also had an army of 280,000 warriors from the tribe of Benjamin, armed with small shields and bows. Both armies were composed of well-trained fighting men.

Once an Ethiopian named Zerah attacked Judah with an army of 1,000,000 men and 300 chariots. They advanced to the town of Mareshah, so Asa deployed his armies for battle in the valley north of Mareshah. Then Asa cried out to the LORD his God, "O LORD, no one but you can help the powerless against the mighty! Help us, O LORD our God, for we trust in you alone. It is in your name that we have come against this vast horde. O LORD, you are our God; do not let mere men prevail against you!"

So the LORD defeated the Ethiopians in the presence of Asa and the army of Judah, and the enemy fled. Asa and his army pursued them as far as Gerar, and so many Ethiopians fell that they were unable to rally. They were destroyed by the LORD and his army, and the army of Judah carried off a vast amount of plunder.

While they were at Gerar, they attacked all the towns in that area, and terror from the LORD came upon the people there. As a result, a vast amount of plunder was taken from these towns, too. They also attacked the camps of herdsmen and captured many sheep, goats, and camels before finally returning to Jerusalem.

Then the Spirit of God came upon Azariah son of Oded, and he went out to meet King Asa as he was returning from the battle. "Listen to me, Asa!" he shouted. "Listen, all you people of Judah and Benjamin! The LORD will stay with you as long as you stay with him! Whenever you seek him, you will find him. But if you abandon him, he will abandon you. For a long time Israel was without the true God, without a priest to teach them, and without the Law to instruct them. But whenever they were in trouble and turned to the LORD, the God of Israel, and sought him out, they found him.

"During those dark times, it was not safe to travel. Problems troubled the people of every land. Nation fought against nation, and city against city, for God was troubling them with every kind of problem. But as for you, be strong and courageous, for your work will be rewarded."

When Asa heard this message from Azariah the prophet, he took courage and removed all the detestable idols from the land of Judah and Benjamin and in the towns he had captured in the hill country of Ephraim. And he repaired the altar of the LORD, which stood in front of the entry room of the LORD's Temple.

Then Asa called together all the people of Judah and Benjamin, along with the people of Ephraim, Manasseh, and Simeon who had settled among them. For many from Israel had moved to Judah during Asa's reign when they saw that the LORD his God was with him. The people gathered at Jerusalem in late spring, during the fifteenth year of Asa's reign.

On that day they sacrificed to the LORD 700 cattle and 7,000 sheep and goats from the plunder they had taken in the battle. Then they entered into a covenant to seek the LORD, the God of their ancestors, with all their heart and soul. They agreed that anyone who refused to seek the LORD, the God of Israel, would be put to death—whether young or old, man or woman. They shouted out their oath of loyalty to the LORD with trumpets blaring and rams' horns sounding. All in Judah were happy about this covenant, for they had entered into it with all their heart. They earnestly sought after God, and they found him. And the LORD gave them rest from their enemies on every side.

King Asa even deposed his grandmother Maacah from her position as queen mother because she had made an obscene Asherah pole. He cut down her obscene pole, broke it up, and burned it in the Kidron Valley. Although the pagan shrines were not removed from Israel, Asa's heart remained completely faithful throughout his life. He brought into the Temple of God the silver and gold and the various items that he and his father had dedicated.

So there was no more war until the thirty-fifth year of Asa's reign.

In the thirty-sixth year of Asa's reign, King Baasha of Israel invaded Judah and fortified Ramah in order to prevent anyone from entering or leaving King Asa's territory in Judah.

Asa responded by removing the silver and gold from the treasuries of the Temple of the LORD and the royal palace. He sent it to King Ben-hadad of Aram, who was ruling in Damascus, along with this message:

"Let there be a treaty between you and me like the one between your father and my father. See, I am sending you silver and gold. Break your treaty with King Baasha of Israel so that he will leave me alone."

Ben-hadad agreed to King Asa's request and sent the commanders of his army to attack the towns of Israel. They conquered the towns of Ijon, Dan, Abel-beth-maacah, and all the store cities in Naphtali. As soon as Baasha of Israel heard what was happening, he abandoned his project of fortifying Ramah and stopped all work on it. Then King Asa called out all the men of Judah to carry away the building stones and timbers that Baasha had been using to fortify Ramah. Asa used these materials to fortify the towns of Geba and Mizpah.

At that time Hanani the seer came to King Asa and told him, "Because you have put your trust in the king of Aram instead of in the LORD your

God, you missed your chance to destroy the army of the king of Aram. Don't you remember what happened to the Ethiopians and Libyans and their vast army, with all of their chariots and charioteers? At that time you relied on the LORD, and he handed them over to you. The eyes of the LORD search the whole earth in order to strengthen those whose hearts are fully committed to him. What a fool you have been! From now on you will be at war."

Asa became so angry with Hanani for saying this that he threw him into prison and put him in stocks. At that time Asa also began to oppress some of his people.

The rest of the events of Asa's reign, from beginning to end, are recorded in *The Book of the Kings of Judah and Israel.* In the thirty-ninth year of his reign, Asa developed a serious foot disease. Yet even with the severity of his disease, he did not seek the LORD's help but turned only to his physicians. So he died in the forty-first year of his reign. He was buried in the tomb he had carved out for himself in the City of David. He was laid on a bed perfumed with sweet spices and fragrant ointments, and the people built a huge funeral fire in his honor.

+ + +

Then Jehoshaphat, Asa's son, became the next king. He strengthened Judah to stand against any attack from Israel. He stationed troops in all the fortified towns of Judah, and he assigned additional garrisons to the land of Judah and to the towns of Ephraim that his father, Asa, had captured.

The LORD was with Jehoshaphat because he followed the example of his father's early years and did not worship the images of Baal. He sought his father's God and obeyed his commands instead of following the evil practices of the kingdom of Israel. So the LORD established Jehoshaphat's control over the kingdom of Judah. All the people of Judah brought gifts to Jehoshaphat, so he became very wealthy and highly esteemed. He was deeply committed to the ways of the LORD. He removed the pagan shrines and Asherah poles from Judah.

In the third year of his reign Jehoshaphat sent his officials to teach in all the towns of Judah. These officials included Ben-hail, Obadiah, Zechariah, Nethanel, and Micaiah. He sent Levites along with them, including Shemaiah, Nethaniah, Zebadiah, Asahel, Shemiramoth, Jehonathan, Adonijah, Tobijah, and Tob-adonijah. He also sent out the priests Elishama and Jehoram. They took copies of the Book of the Law of the LORD and traveled around through all the towns of Judah, teaching the people.

Then the fear of the LORD fell over all the surrounding kingdoms so that none of them wanted to declare war on Jehoshaphat. Some of the Philistines brought him gifts and silver as tribute, and the Arabs brought 7,700 rams and 7,700 male goats.

So Jehoshaphat became more and more powerful and built fortresses and storage cities throughout Judah. He stored numerous supplies in Judah's towns and stationed an army of seasoned troops at Jerusalem. His army was enrolled according to ancestral clans.

From Judah there were 300,000 troops organized in units of 1,000, under the command of Adnah. Next in command was Jehohanan, who commanded 280,000 troops. Next was Amasiah son of Zicri, who volunteered for the LORD's service, with 200,000 troops under his command.
From Benjamin there were 200,000 troops equipped with bows and shields. They were under the command of Eliada, a veteran soldier. Next in command was Jehozabad, who commanded 180,000 armed men.

These were the troops stationed in Jerusalem to serve the king, besides those Jehoshaphat stationed in the fortified towns throughout Judah.

Jehoshaphat enjoyed great riches and high esteem, and he made an alliance with Ahab of Israel by having his son marry Ahab's daughter. A few years later he went to Samaria to visit Ahab, who prepared a great banquet for him and his officials. They butchered great numbers of sheep, goats, and cattle for the feast. Then Ahab enticed Jehoshaphat to join forces with him to recover Ramoth-gilead.

"Will you go with me to Ramoth-gilead?" King Ahab of Israel asked King Jehoshaphat of Judah.

Jehoshaphat replied, "Why, of course! You and I are as one, and my troops are your troops. We will certainly join you in battle." Then Jehoshaphat added, "But first let's find out what the LORD says."

So the king of Israel summoned the prophets, 400 of them, and asked them, "Should we go to war against Ramoth-gilead, or should I hold back?"

They all replied, "Yes, go right ahead! God will give the king victory."

But Jehoshaphat asked, "Is there not also a prophet of the LORD here? We should ask him the same question."

The king of Israel replied to Jehoshaphat, "There is one more man who could consult the LORD for us, but I hate him. He never prophesies anything but trouble for me! His name is Micaiah son of Imlah."

Jehoshaphat replied, "That's not the way a king should talk! Let's hear what he has to say."

So the king of Israel called one of his officials and said, "Quick! Bring Micaiah son of Imlah."

King Ahab of Israel and King Jehoshaphat of Judah, dressed in their royal robes, were sitting on thrones at the threshing floor near the gate of Samaria. All of Ahab's prophets were prophesying there in front of them. One of them, Zedekiah son of Kenaanah, made some iron horns and proclaimed, "This is what the LORD says: With these horns you will gore the Arameans to death!"

All the other prophets agreed. "Yes," they said, "go up to Ramoth-gilead and be victorious, for the LORD will give the king victory!"

Meanwhile, the messenger who went to get Micaiah said to him, "Look, all the prophets are promising victory for the king. Be sure that you agree with them and promise success."

But Micaiah replied, "As surely as the LORD lives, I will say only what my God says."

When Micaiah arrived before the king, Ahab asked him, "Micaiah, should we go to war against Ramoth-gilead, or should I hold back?"

Micaiah replied sarcastically, "Yes, go up and be victorious, for you will have victory over them!"

But the king replied sharply, "How many times must I demand that you speak only the truth to me when you speak for the LORD?"

Then Micaiah told him, "In a vision I saw all Israel scattered on the mountains, like sheep without a shepherd. And the LORD said, 'Their master has been killed. Send them home in peace.'"

"Didn't I tell you?" the king of Israel exclaimed to Jehoshaphat. "He never prophesies anything but trouble for me."

Then Micaiah continued, "Listen to what the LORD says! I saw the LORD sitting on his throne with all the armies of heaven around him, on his right and on his left. And the LORD said, 'Who can entice King Ahab of Israel to go into battle against Ramoth-gilead so he can be killed?'

"There were many suggestions, and finally a spirit approached the LORD and said, 'I can do it!'

"'How will you do this?' the LORD asked.

"And the spirit replied, 'I will go out and inspire all of Ahab's prophets to speak lies.'

"'You will succeed,' said the LORD. 'Go ahead and do it.'

"So you see, the LORD has put a lying spirit in the mouths of your prophets. For the LORD has pronounced your doom."

Then Zedekiah son of Kenaanah walked up to Micaiah and slapped him across the face. "Since when did the Spirit of the LORD leave me to speak to you?" he demanded.

And Micaiah replied, "You will find out soon enough when you are try-ing to hide in some secret room!"

"Arrest him!" the king of Israel ordered. "Take him back to Amon, the governor of the city, and to my son Joash. Give them this order from the king: 'Put this man in prison, and feed him nothing but bread and water until I return safely from the battle!'"

But Micaiah replied, "If you return safely, it will mean that the LORD has not spoken through me!" Then he added to those standing around, "Everyone mark my words!"

So King Ahab of Israel and King Jehoshaphat of Judah led their armies against Ramoth-gilead. The king of Israel said to Jehoshaphat, "As we go into battle, I will disguise myself so no one will recognize me, but you wear your royal robes." So the king of Israel disguised himself, and they went into battle.

Meanwhile, the king of Aram had issued these orders to his chariot com-manders: "Attack only the king of Israel! Don't bother with anyone else." So when the Aramean chariot commanders saw Jehoshaphat in his royal robes, they went after him. "There is the king of Israel!" they shouted. But Jehoshaphat called out, and the LORD saved him. God helped him by turning the attackers away from him. As soon as the chariot commanders realized he was not the king of Israel, they stopped chasing him.

An Aramean soldier, however, randomly shot an arrow at the Israelite troops and hit the king of Israel between the joints of his armor. "Turn the horses and get me out of here!" Ahab groaned to the driver of the chariot. "I'm badly wounded!"

The battle raged all that day, and the king of Israel propped himself up in his chariot facing the Arameans. In the evening, just as the sun was set-ting, he died.

When King Jehoshaphat of Judah arrived safely home in Jerusalem, Jehu son of Hanani the seer went out to meet him. "Why should you help the wicked and love those who hate the LORD?" he asked the king. "Because of what you have done, the LORD is very angry with you. Even so, there is some good in you, for you have removed the Asherah poles throughout the land, and you have committed yourself to seeking God."

Jehoshaphat lived in Jerusalem, but he went out among the people, traveling from Beersheba to the hill country of Ephraim, encouraging the people to return to the LORD, the God of their ancestors. He appointed judges throughout the nation in all the fortified towns, and he said to them, "Always think carefully before pronouncing judgment. Remember that you do not judge to please people but to please the LORD. He will be with you when you render the verdict in each case. Fear the LORD and judge with integrity, for the LORD our God does not tolerate perverted justice, partiality, or the taking of bribes."

In Jerusalem, Jehoshaphat appointed some of the Levites and priests and clan leaders in Israel to serve as judges for cases involving the LORD's regulations and for civil disputes. These were his instructions to them: "You must always act in the fear of the LORD, with faithfulness and an undivided heart. Whenever a case comes to you from fellow citizens in an outlying town, whether a murder case or some other violation of God's laws, commands, decrees, or regulations, you must warn them not to sin against the LORD, so that he will not be angry with you and them. Do this and you will not be guilty.

"Amariah the high priest will have final say in all cases involving the LORD. Zebadiah son of Ishmael, a leader from the tribe of Judah, will have final say in all civil cases. The Levites will assist you in making sure that justice is served. Take courage as you fulfill your duties, and may the LORD be with those who do what is right."

After this, the armies of the Moabites, Ammonites, and some of the Meunites declared war on Jehoshaphat. Messengers came and told Jehoshaphat, "A vast army from Edom is marching against you from beyond the Dead Sea. They are already at Hazazon-tamar." (This was another name for En-gedi.)

Jehoshaphat was terrified by this news and begged the LORD for guidance. He also ordered everyone in Judah to begin fasting. So people from all the towns of Judah came to Jerusalem to seek the LORD's help.

Jehoshaphat stood before the community of Judah and Jerusalem in front of the new courtyard at the Temple of the LORD. He prayed, "O LORD, God of our ancestors, you alone are the God who is in heaven. You are ruler of all the kingdoms of the earth. You are powerful and mighty; no one can stand against you! O our God, did you not drive out those who lived in this land when your people Israel arrived? And did you not give this land forever to the descendants of your friend Abraham? Your people settled here and built this Temple to honor your name. They said, 'Whenever we are faced with any calamity such as war, plague, or famine, we can come to stand in your presence before this Temple where your name is honored. We can cry out to you to save us, and you will hear us and rescue us.'

"And now see what the armies of Ammon, Moab, and Mount Seir are doing. You would not let our ancestors invade those nations when Israel left Egypt, so they went around them and did not destroy them. Now see how they reward us! For they have come to throw us out of your land, which you gave us as an inheritance. O our God, won't you stop them? We are powerless against this mighty army that is about to attack us. We do not know what to do, but we are looking to you for help."

As all the men of Judah stood before the LORD with their little ones, wives, and children, the Spirit of the LORD came upon one of the men standing there. His name was Jahaziel son of Zechariah, son of Benaiah, son of Jeiel, son of Mattaniah, a Levite who was a descendant of Asaph.

He said, "Listen, all you people of Judah and Jerusalem! Listen, King Jehoshaphat! This is what the LORD says: Do not be afraid! Don't be discouraged by this mighty army, for the battle is not yours, but God's. Tomorrow, march out against them. You will find them coming up through the ascent of Ziz at the end of the valley that opens into the wilderness of Jeruel. But you will not even need to fight. Take your positions; then stand still and watch the LORD's victory. He is with you, O people of Judah and Jerusalem. Do not be afraid or discouraged. Go out against them tomorrow, for the LORD is with you!"

Then King Jehoshaphat bowed low with his face to the ground. And all the people of Judah and Jerusalem did the same, worshiping the LORD. Then the Levites from the clans of Kohath and Korah stood to praise the LORD, the God of Israel, with a very loud shout.

Early the next morning the army of Judah went out into the wilderness of Tekoa. On the way Jehoshaphat stopped and said, "Listen to me, all you people of Judah and Jerusalem! Believe in the LORD your God, and you will be able to stand firm. Believe in his prophets, and you will succeed."

After consulting the people, the king appointed singers to walk ahead of the army, singing to the LORD and praising him for his holy splendor. This is what they sang:

"Give thanks to the LORD;
    his faithful love endures forever!"

At the very moment they began to sing and give praise, the LORD caused the armies of Ammon, Moab, and Mount Seir to start fighting among themselves. The armies of Moab and Ammon turned against their allies from Mount Seir and killed every one of them. After they had destroyed the army of Seir, they began attacking each other. So when the army of Judah arrived at the lookout point in the wilderness, all they saw were dead bodies lying on the ground as far as they could see. Not a single one of the enemy had escaped.

King Jehoshaphat and his men went out to gather the plunder. They found vast amounts of equipment, clothing, and other valuables—more than they could carry. There was so much plunder that it took them three days just to collect it all! On the fourth day they gathered in the Valley of Blessing, which got its name that day because the people praised and thanked the LORD there. It is still called the Valley of Blessing today.

Then all the men returned to Jerusalem, with Jehoshaphat leading them, overjoyed that the LORD had given them victory over their enemies. They marched into Jerusalem to the music of harps, lyres, and trumpets, and they proceeded to the Temple of the LORD.

When all the surrounding kingdoms heard that the LORD himself had fought against the enemies of Israel, the fear of God came over them. So Jehoshaphat's kingdom was at peace, for his God had given him rest on every side.

So Jehoshaphat ruled over the land of Judah. He was thirty-five years old when he became king, and he reigned in Jerusalem twenty-five years. His mother was Azubah, the daughter of Shilhi.

Jehoshaphat was a good king, following the ways of his father, Asa. He did what was pleasing in the LORD's sight. During his reign, however, he failed to remove all the pagan shrines, and the people never fully committed themselves to follow the God of their ancestors.

The rest of the events of Jehoshaphat's reign, from beginning to end, are recorded in *The Record of Jehu Son of Hanani,* which is included in *The Book of the Kings of Israel.*

Some time later King Jehoshaphat of Judah made an alliance with King Ahaziah of Israel, who was very wicked. Together they built a fleet of trading ships at the port of Ezion-geber. Then Eliezer son of Dodavahu from Mareshah prophesied against Jehoshaphat. He said, "Because you have allied yourself with King Ahaziah, the LORD will destroy your work." So the ships met with disaster and never put out to sea.

+ + +

When Jehoshaphat died, he was buried with his ancestors in the City of David. Then his son Jehoram became the next king.

Jehoram's brothers—the other sons of Jehoshaphat—were Azariah, Jehiel, Zechariah, Azariahu, Michael, and Shephatiah; all these were the sons of Jehoshaphat king of Judah. Their father had given each of them valuable gifts of silver, gold, and costly items, and also some of Judah's fortified towns. However, he designated Jehoram as the next king because he was the oldest. But when Jehoram had become solidly established as king, he killed all his brothers and some of the other leaders of Judah.

Jehoram was thirty-two years old when he became king, and he reigned in Jerusalem eight years. But Jehoram followed the example of the kings of Israel and was as wicked as King Ahab, for he had married one of Ahab's daughters. So Jehoram did what was evil in the LORD's sight. But the LORD did not want to destroy David's dynasty, for he had made a covenant with David and promised that his descendants would continue to rule, shining like a lamp forever.

During Jehoram's reign, the Edomites revolted against Judah and crowned their own king. So Jehoram went out with his full army and all his chariots. The Edomites surrounded him and his chariot commanders, but he went out at night and attacked them under cover of darkness. Even so, Edom has been independent from Judah to this day. The town of Libnah also revolted about that same time. All this happened because Jehoram had abandoned the LORD, the God of his ancestors. He had built pagan shrines in the hill country of Judah and had led the people of Jerusalem and Judah to give themselves to pagan gods and to go astray.

Then Elijah the prophet wrote Jehoram this letter:

"This is what the LORD, the God of your ancestor David, says: You have not followed the good example of your father, Jehoshaphat, or your grandfather King Asa of Judah. Instead, you have been as evil as the kings of Israel. You have led the people of Jerusalem and Judah to worship idols, just as King Ahab did in Israel. And you have even killed your own brothers, men who were better than you. So now the LORD is about to strike you, your people, your children, your wives, and all that is yours with a heavy blow. You yourself will suffer with a severe intestinal disease that will get worse each day until your bowels come out."

Then the LORD stirred up the Philistines and the Arabs, who lived near the Ethiopians, to attack Jehoram. They marched against Judah, broke down its defenses, and carried away everything of value in the royal palace, including the king's sons and his wives. Only his youngest son, Ahaziah, was spared.

After all this, the LORD struck Jehoram with an incurable intestinal disease. The disease grew worse and worse, and at the end of two years it caused his bowels to come out, and he died in agony. His people did not build a great funeral fire to honor him as they had done for his ancestors.

Jehoram was thirty-two years old when he became king, and he reigned in Jerusalem eight years. No one was sorry when he died. They buried him in the City of David, but not in the royal cemetery.

+ + +

Then the people of Jerusalem made Ahaziah, Jehoram's youngest son, their next king, since the marauding bands who came with the Arabs had killed all the older sons. So Ahaziah son of Jehoram reigned as king of Judah.

Ahaziah was twenty-two years old when he became king, and he reigned in Jerusalem one year. His mother was Athaliah, a granddaughter of King Omri. Ahaziah also followed the evil example of King Ahab's family, for his mother encouraged him in doing wrong. He did what was evil in the LORD's sight, just as Ahab's family had done. They even became his advisers after the death of his father, and they led him to ruin.

Following their evil advice, Ahaziah joined Joram, the son of King Ahab of Israel, in his war against King Hazael of Aram at Ramoth-gilead. When the Arameans wounded Joram in the battle, he returned to Jezreel to recover from the wounds he had received at Ramoth. Because Joram was wounded, King Ahaziah of Judah went to Jezreel to visit him.

But God had decided that this visit would be Ahaziah's downfall. While he was there, Ahaziah went out with Joram to meet Jehu grandson of Nimshi, whom the LORD had appointed to destroy the dynasty of Ahab.

While Jehu was executing judgment against the family of Ahab, he happened to meet some of Judah's officials and Ahaziah's relatives who were traveling with Ahaziah. So Jehu killed them all. Then Jehu's men searched for Ahaziah, and they found him hiding in the city of Samaria. They brought him to Jehu, who killed him. Ahaziah was given a decent burial because the people said, "He was the grandson of Jehoshaphat—a man who sought the LORD with all his heart." But none of the surviving members of Ahaziah's family was capable of ruling the kingdom.

When Athaliah, the mother of King Ahaziah of Judah, learned that her son was dead, she began to destroy the rest of Judah's royal family. But Ahaziah's sister Jehosheba, the daughter of King Jehoram, took Ahaziah's infant son, Joash, and stole him away from among the rest of the king's children, who were about to be killed. She put Joash and his nurse in a bedroom. In this way, Jehosheba, wife of Jehoiada the priest and sister of Ahaziah, hid the child so that Athaliah could not murder him. Joash remained hidden in the Temple of God for six years while Athaliah ruled over the land.

In the seventh year of Athaliah's reign, Jehoiada the priest decided to act. He summoned his courage and made a pact with five army commanders: Azariah son of Jeroham, Ishmael son of Jehohanan, Azariah son of Obed, Maaseiah son of Adaiah, and Elishaphat son of Zicri. These men traveled secretly throughout Judah and summoned the Levites and clan leaders in all the towns to come to Jerusalem. They all gathered at the Temple of God, where they made a solemn pact with Joash, the young king.

Jehoiada said to them, "Here is the king's son! The time has come for him to reign! The LORD has promised that a descendant of David will be our king. This is what you must do. When you priests and Levites come on duty on the Sabbath, a third of you will serve as gatekeepers. Another third will go over to the royal palace, and the final third will be at the Foundation Gate. Everyone else should stay in the courtyards of the LORD's Temple. Remember, only the priests and Levites on duty may enter the Temple of the LORD, for they are set apart as holy. The rest of the people must obey the LORD's instructions and stay outside. You Levites, form a bodyguard around the king and keep your weapons in hand. Kill anyone who tries to enter the Temple. Stay with the king wherever he goes."

So the Levites and all the people of Judah did everything as Jehoiada the priest ordered. The commanders took charge of the men reporting for duty that Sabbath, as well as those who were going off duty. Jehoiada the priest did not let anyone go home after their shift ended. Then Jehoiada supplied the commanders with the spears and the large and small shields that had once belonged to King David and were stored in the Temple of God. He stationed all the people around the king, with their weapons ready. They formed a line from the south side of the Temple around to the north side and all around the altar.

Then Jehoiada and his sons brought out Joash, the king's son, placed the crown on his head, and presented him with a copy of God's laws. They anointed him and proclaimed him king, and everyone shouted, "Long live the king!"

When Athaliah heard the noise of the people running and the shouts of praise to the king, she hurried to the LORD's Temple to see what was happening. When she arrived, she saw the newly crowned king standing in his place of authority by the pillar at the Temple entrance. The commanders and trumpeters were surrounding him, and people from all over the land were rejoicing and blowing trumpets. Singers with musical instruments were leading the people in a great celebration. When Athaliah saw all this, she tore her clothes in despair and shouted, "Treason! Treason!"

Then Jehoiada the priest ordered the commanders who were in charge of the troops, "Take her to the soldiers in front of the Temple, and kill anyone who tries to rescue her." For the priest had said, "She must not be killed in the Temple of the LORD." So they seized her and led her out to the entrance of the Horse Gate on the palace grounds, and they killed her there.

Then Jehoiada made a covenant between himself and the king and the people that they would be the LORD's people. And all the people went over to the temple of Baal and tore it down. They demolished the altars and smashed the idols, and they killed Mattan the priest of Baal in front of the altars.

Jehoiada now put the priests and Levites in charge of the Temple of the LORD, following all the directions given by David. He also commanded them to present burnt offerings to the LORD, as prescribed by the Law of Moses, and to sing and rejoice as David had instructed. He also stationed gatekeepers at the gates of the LORD's Temple to keep out those who for any reason were ceremonially unclean.

Then the commanders, nobles, rulers, and all the people of the land escorted the king from the Temple of the LORD. They went through the upper gate and into the palace, and they seated the king on the royal throne. So all the people of the land rejoiced, and the city was peaceful because Athaliah had been killed.

+ + +

Joash was seven years old when he became king, and he reigned in Jerusalem forty years. His mother was Zibiah from Beersheba. Joash did what was pleasing in the LORD's sight throughout the lifetime of Jehoiada the priest. Jehoiada chose two wives for Joash, and he had sons and daughters.

At one point Joash decided to repair and restore the Temple of the LORD. He summoned the priests and Levites and gave them these instructions: "Go to all the towns of Judah and collect the required annual offerings, so that we can repair the Temple of your God. Do not delay!" But the Levites did not act immediately.

So the king called for Jehoiada the high priest and asked him, "Why haven't you demanded that the Levites go out and collect the Temple taxes from the towns of Judah and from Jerusalem? Moses, the servant of the LORD, levied this tax on the community of Israel in order to maintain the Tabernacle of the Covenant."

Over the years the followers of wicked Athaliah had broken into the Temple of God, and they had used all the dedicated things from the Temple of the LORD to worship the images of Baal.

So now the king ordered a chest to be made and set outside the gate leading to the Temple of the LORD. Then a proclamation was sent throughout Judah and Jerusalem, telling the people to bring to the LORD the tax that Moses, the servant of God, had required of the Israelites in the wilderness. This pleased all the leaders and the people, and they gladly brought their money and filled the chest with it.

Whenever the chest became full, the Levites would carry it to the king's officials. Then the court secretary and an officer of the high priest would come and empty the chest and take it back to the Temple again. This went on day after day, and a large amount of money was collected. The king and Jehoiada gave the money to the construction supervisors, who hired masons and carpenters to restore the Temple of the LORD. They also hired metalworkers, who made articles of iron and bronze for the LORD's Temple.

The men in charge of the renovation worked hard and made steady progress. They restored the Temple of God according to its original design and strengthened it. When all the repairs were finished, they brought the remaining money to the king and Jehoiada. It was used to make various articles for the Temple of the LORD—articles for worship services and for burnt offerings, including ladles and other articles made of gold and silver. And the burnt offerings were sacrificed continually in the Temple of the LORD during the lifetime of Jehoiada the priest.

Jehoiada lived to a very old age, finally dying at 130. He was buried among the kings in the City of David, because he had done so much good in Israel for God and his Temple.

But after Jehoiada's death, the leaders of Judah came and bowed before King Joash and persuaded him to listen to their advice. They decided to abandon the Temple of the LORD, the God of their ancestors, and they worshiped Asherah poles and idols instead! Because of this sin, divine anger fell on Judah and Jerusalem. Yet the LORD sent prophets to bring them back to him. The prophets warned them, but still the people would not listen.

Then the Spirit of God came upon Zechariah son of Jehoiada the priest. He stood before the people and said, "This is what God says: Why do you disobey the LORD's commands and keep yourselves from prospering? You have abandoned the LORD, and now he has abandoned you!"

Then the leaders plotted to kill Zechariah, and King Joash ordered that they stone him to death in the courtyard of the LORD's Temple. That was how King Joash repaid Jehoiada for his loyalty—by killing his son. Zechariah's last words as he died were, "May the LORD see what they are doing and avenge my death!"

In the spring of the year the Aramean army marched against Joash. They invaded Judah and Jerusalem and killed all the leaders of the nation. Then they sent all the plunder back to their king in Damascus. Although the Arameans attacked with only a small army, the LORD helped them conquer the much larger army of Judah. The people of Judah had abandoned the LORD, the God of their ancestors, so judgment was carried out against Joash.

The Arameans withdrew, leaving Joash severely wounded. But his own officials plotted to kill him for murdering the son of Jehoiada the priest. They assassinated him as he lay in bed. Then he was buried in the City of David, but not in the royal cemetery. The assassins were Jozacar, the son of an Ammonite woman named Shimeath, and Jehozabad, the son of a Moabite woman named Shomer.

The account of the sons of Joash, the prophecies about him, and the record of his restoration of the Temple of God are written in *The Commentary on the Book of the Kings*. His son Amaziah became the next king.

+ + +

Amaziah was twenty-five years old when he became king, and he reigned in Jerusalem twenty-nine years. His mother was Jehoaddin from Jerusalem. Amaziah did what was pleasing in the LORD's sight, but not wholeheartedly.

When Amaziah was well established as king, he executed the officials who had assassinated his father. However, he did not kill the children of the assassins, for he obeyed the command of the LORD as written by Moses in the Book of the Law: "Parents must not be put to death for the sins of their children, nor children for the sins of their parents. Those deserving to die must be put to death for their own crimes."

Then Amaziah organized the army, assigning generals and captains for all Judah and Benjamin. He took a census and found that he had an army of 300,000 select troops, twenty years old and older, all trained in the use of spear and shield. He also paid about 7,500 pounds of silver to hire 100,000 experienced fighting men from Israel.

But a man of God came to him and said, "Your Majesty, do not hire troops from Israel, for the LORD is not with Israel. He will not help those people of Ephraim! If you let them go with your troops into battle, you will be defeated by the enemy no matter how well you fight. God will overthrow you, for he has the power to help you or to trip you up."

Amaziah asked the man of God, "But what about all that silver I paid to hire the army of Israel?"

The man of God replied, "The LORD is able to give you much more than this!" So Amaziah discharged the hired troops and sent them back to Ephraim. This made them very angry with Judah, and they returned home in a great rage.

Then Amaziah summoned his courage and led his army to the Valley of Salt, where they killed 10,000 Edomite troops from Seir. They captured another 10,000 and took them to the top of a cliff and threw them off, dashing them to pieces on the rocks below.

Meanwhile, the hired troops that Amaziah had sent home raided several of the towns of Judah between Samaria and Beth-horon. They killed 3,000 people and carried off great quantities of plunder.

When King Amaziah returned from slaughtering the Edomites, he brought with him idols taken from the people of Seir. He set them up as his own gods, bowed down in front of them, and offered sacrifices to them! This made the LORD very angry, and he sent a prophet to ask, "Why do you turn to gods who could not even save their own people from you?"

But the king interrupted him and said, "Since when have I made you the king's counselor? Be quiet now before I have you killed!"

So the prophet stopped with this warning: "I know that God has determined to destroy you because you have done this and have refused to accept my counsel."

After consulting with his advisers, King Amaziah of Judah sent this challenge to Israel's king Jehoash, the son of Jehoahaz and grandson of Jehu: "Come and meet me in battle!"

But King Jehoash of Israel replied to King Amaziah of Judah with this story: "Out in the Lebanon mountains, a thistle sent a message to a mighty cedar tree: 'Give your daughter in marriage to my son.' But just then a wild animal of Lebanon came by and stepped on the thistle, crushing it!

"You are saying, 'I have defeated Edom,' and you are very proud of it. But my advice is to stay at home. Why stir up trouble that will only bring disaster on you and the people of Judah?"

But Amaziah refused to listen, for God was determined to destroy him for turning to the gods of Edom. So King Jehoash of Israel mobilized his army against King Amaziah of Judah. The two armies drew up their battle lines at Beth-shemesh in Judah. Judah was routed by the army of Israel, and its army scattered and fled for home. King Jehoash of Israel captured Judah's king, Amaziah son of Joash and grandson of Ahaziah, at Beth-shemesh. Then he brought him to Jerusalem, where he demolished 600 feet of Jerusalem's wall, from the Ephraim Gate to the Corner Gate. He carried off all the gold and silver and all the articles from the Temple of God that had been in the care of Obed-edom. He also seized the treasures of the royal palace, along with hostages, and then returned to Samaria.

King Amaziah of Judah lived for fifteen years after the death of King Jehoash of Israel. The rest of the events in Amaziah's reign, from beginning to end, are recorded in *The Book of the Kings of Judah and Israel*.

After Amaziah turned away from the LORD, there was a conspiracy against his life in Jerusalem, and he fled to Lachish. But his enemies sent assassins after him, and they killed him there. They brought his body back on a horse, and he was buried with his ancestors in the City of David.

+ + +

All the people of Judah had crowned Amaziah's sixteen-year-old son, Uzziah, as king in place of his father. After his father's death, Uzziah rebuilt the town of Elath and restored it to Judah.

Uzziah was sixteen years old when he became king, and he reigned in Jerusalem fifty-two years. His mother was Jecoliah from Jerusalem. He did what was pleasing in the LORD's sight, just as his father, Amaziah, had done. Uzziah sought God during the days of Zechariah, who taught him to fear God. And as long as the king sought guidance from the LORD, God gave him success.

Uzziah declared war on the Philistines and broke down the walls of Gath, Jabneh, and Ashdod. Then he built new towns in the Ashdod area and in other parts of Philistia. God helped him in his wars against the Philistines, his battles with the Arabs of Gur, and his wars with the Meunites. The Meunites paid annual tribute to him, and his fame spread even to Egypt, for he had become very powerful.

Uzziah built fortified towers in Jerusalem at the Corner Gate, at the Valley Gate, and at the angle in the wall. He also constructed forts in the wilderness and dug many water cisterns, because he kept great herds of livestock in the foothills of Judah and on the plains. He was also a man who loved the soil. He had many workers who cared for his farms and vineyards, both on the hillsides and in the fertile valleys.

Uzziah had an army of well-trained warriors, ready to march into battle, unit by unit. This army had been mustered and organized by Jeiel, the secretary of the army, and his assistant, Maaseiah. They were under the direction of Hananiah, one of the king's officials. These regiments of mighty warriors were commanded by 2,600 clan leaders. The army consisted of 307,500 men, all elite troops. They were prepared to assist the king against any enemy.

Uzziah provided the entire army with shields, spears, helmets, coats of mail, bows, and sling stones. And he built structures on the walls of Jerusalem, designed by experts to protect those who shot arrows and hurled large stones from the towers and the corners of the wall. His fame spread far and wide, for the LORD gave him marvelous help, and he became very powerful.

But when he had become powerful, he also became proud, which led to his downfall. He sinned against the LORD his God by entering the sanctuary of the LORD's Temple and personally burning incense on the incense altar. Azariah the high priest went in after him with eighty other priests of the LORD, all brave men. They confronted King Uzziah and said, "It is not for you, Uzziah, to burn incense to the LORD. That is the work of the priests alone, the descendants of Aaron who are set apart for this work. Get out of the sanctuary, for you have sinned. The LORD God will not honor you for this!"

Uzziah, who was holding an incense burner, became furious. But as he was standing there raging at the priests before the incense altar in the LORD's Temple, leprosy suddenly broke out on his forehead. When Azariah the high priest and all the other priests saw the leprosy, they rushed him out. And the king himself was eager to get out because the LORD had struck him. So King Uzziah had leprosy until the day he died. He lived in isolation in a separate house, for he was excluded from the Temple of the LORD. His son Jotham was put in charge of the royal palace, and he governed the people of the land.

The rest of the events of Uzziah's reign, from beginning to end, are recorded by the prophet Isaiah son of Amoz. When Uzziah died, he was buried with his ancestors; his grave was in a nearby burial field belonging to the kings, for the people said, "He had leprosy." And his son Jotham became the next king.

+ + +

Jotham was twenty-five years old when he became king, and he reigned in Jerusalem sixteen years. His mother was Jerusha, the daughter of Zadok.

Jotham did what was pleasing in the LORD's sight. He did everything his father, Uzziah, had done, except that Jotham did not sin by entering the Temple of the LORD. But the people continued in their corrupt ways.

Jotham rebuilt the upper gate of the Temple of the LORD. He also did extensive rebuilding on the wall at the hill of Ophel. He built towns in the hill country of Judah and constructed fortresses and towers in the wooded areas. Jotham went to war against the Ammonites and conquered them. Over the next three years he received from them an annual tribute of 7,500 pounds of silver, 50,000 bushels of wheat, and 50,000 bushels of barley.

King Jotham became powerful because he was careful to live in obedience to the LORD his God.

The rest of the events of Jotham's reign, including all his wars and other activities, are recorded in *The Book of the Kings of Israel and Judah*. He was twenty-five years old when he became king, and he reigned in Jerusalem sixteen years. When Jotham died, he was buried in the City of David. And his son Ahaz became the next king.

+ + +

Ahaz was twenty years old when he became king, and he reigned in Jerusalem sixteen years. He did not do what was pleasing in the sight of the LORD, as his ancestor David had done. Instead, he followed the example of the kings of Israel. He cast metal images for the worship of Baal. He offered sacrifices in the valley of Ben-Hinnom, even sacrificing his own sons in the fire. In this way, he followed the detestable practices of the pagan nations the LORD had driven from the land ahead of the Israelites. He offered sacrifices and burned incense at the pagan shrines and on the hills and under every green tree.

Because of all this, the LORD his God allowed the king of Aram to defeat Ahaz and to exile large numbers of his people to Damascus. The armies of the king of Israel also defeated Ahaz and inflicted many casualties on his army. In a single day Pekah son of Remaliah, Israel's king, killed 120,000 of Judah's troops, all of them experienced warriors, because they had abandoned the LORD, the God of their ancestors. Then Zicri, a warrior from Ephraim, killed Maaseiah, the king's son; Azrikam, the king's palace commander; and Elkanah, the king's second-in-command. The armies of Israel captured 200,000 women and children from Judah and seized tremendous amounts of plunder, which they took back to Samaria.

But a prophet of the LORD named Oded was there in Samaria when the army of Israel returned home. He went out to meet them and said, "The LORD, the God of your ancestors, was angry with Judah and let you defeat them. But you have gone too far, killing them without mercy, and all heaven is disturbed. And now you are planning to make slaves of these people from Judah and Jerusalem. What about your own sins against the LORD your God? Listen to me and return these prisoners you have taken, for they are your own relatives. Watch out, because now the LORD's fierce anger has been turned against you!"

Then some of the leaders of Israel—Azariah son of Jehohanan, Berekiah son of Meshillemoth, Jehizkiah son of Shallum, and Amasa son of Hadlai—agreed with this and confronted the men returning from battle. "You must not bring the prisoners here!" they declared. "We cannot afford to add to our sins and guilt. Our guilt is already great, and the LORD's fierce anger is already turned against Israel."

So the warriors released the prisoners and handed over the plunder in the sight of the leaders and all the people. Then the four men just mentioned by name came forward and distributed clothes from the plunder to the prisoners who were naked. They provided clothing and sandals to wear, gave them enough food and drink, and dressed their wounds with olive oil. They put those who were weak on donkeys and took all the prisoners back to their own people in Jericho, the city of palms. Then they returned to Samaria.

At that time King Ahaz of Judah asked the king of Assyria for help. The armies of Edom had again invaded Judah and taken captives. And the Philistines had raided towns located in the foothills of Judah and in the Negev of Judah. They had already captured and occupied Beth-shemesh, Aijalon, Gederoth, Soco with its villages, Timnah with its villages, and Gimzo with its villages. The LORD was humbling Judah because of King Ahaz of Judah, for he had encouraged his people to sin and had been utterly unfaithful to the LORD.

So when King Tiglath-pileser of Assyria arrived, he attacked Ahaz instead of helping him. Ahaz took valuable items from the LORD's Temple, the royal palace, and from the homes of his officials and gave them to the king of Assyria as tribute. But this did not help him.

Even during this time of trouble, King Ahaz continued to reject the LORD. He offered sacrifices to the gods of Damascus who had defeated him, for he said, "Since these gods helped the kings of Aram, they will help me, too, if I sacrifice to them." But instead, they led to his ruin and the ruin of all Judah.

The king took the various articles from the Temple of God and broke them into pieces. He shut the doors of the LORD's Temple so that no one could worship there, and he set up altars to pagan gods in every corner of Jerusalem. He made pagan shrines in all the towns of Judah for offering sacrifices to other gods. In this way, he aroused the anger of the LORD, the God of his ancestors.

The rest of the events of Ahaz's reign and everything he did, from beginning to end, are recorded in *The Book of the Kings of Judah and Israel.* When Ahaz died, he was buried in Jerusalem but not in the royal cemetery of the kings of Judah. Then his son Hezekiah became the next king.

+ + +

Hezekiah was twenty-five years old when he became the king of Judah, and he reigned in Jerusalem twenty-nine years. His mother was Abijah, the daughter of Zechariah. He did what was pleasing in the LORD's sight, just as his ancestor David had done.

In the very first month of the first year of his reign, Hezekiah reopened the doors of the Temple of the LORD and repaired them. He summoned the priests and Levites to meet him at the courtyard east of the Temple. He said to them, "Listen to me, you Levites! Purify yourselves, and purify the Temple of the LORD, the God of your ancestors. Remove all the defiled things from the sanctuary. Our ancestors were unfaithful and did what was evil in the sight of the LORD our God. They abandoned the LORD and his dwelling place; they turned their backs on him. They also shut the doors to the Temple's entry room, and they snuffed out the lamps. They stopped burning incense and presenting burnt offerings at the sanctuary of the God of Israel.

"That is why the LORD's anger has fallen upon Judah and Jerusalem. He has made them an object of dread, horror, and ridicule, as you can see with your own eyes. Because of this, our fathers have been killed in battle, and our sons and daughters and wives have been captured. But now I will make a covenant with the LORD, the God of Israel, so that his fierce anger will turn away from us. My sons, do not neglect your duties any longer! The LORD has chosen you to stand in his presence, to minister to him, and to lead the people in worship and present offerings to him."

Then these Levites got right to work:

From the clan of Kohath: Mahath son of Amasai and Joel son of Azariah.
From the clan of Merari: Kish son of Abdi and Azariah son of Jehallelel.
From the clan of Gershon: Joah son of Zimmah and Eden son of Joah.
From the family of Elizaphan: Shimri and Jeiel.
From the family of Asaph: Zechariah and Mattaniah.
From the family of Heman: Jehiel and Shimei.
From the family of Jeduthun: Shemaiah and Uzziel.

These men called together their fellow Levites, and they all purified themselves. Then they began to cleanse the Temple of the LORD, just as the king had commanded. They were careful to follow all the LORD's instructions in their work. The priests went into the sanctuary of the Temple of the LORD to cleanse it, and they took out to the Temple courtyard all the defiled things they found. From there the Levites carted it all out to the Kidron Valley.

They began the work in early spring, on the first day of the new year, and in eight days they had reached the entry room of the LORD's Temple. Then they purified the Temple of the LORD itself, which took another eight days. So the entire task was completed in sixteen days.

Then the Levites went to King Hezekiah and gave him this report: "We have cleansed the entire Temple of the Lord, the altar of burnt offering with all its utensils, and the table of the Bread of the Presence with all its utensils. We have also recovered all the items discarded by King Ahaz when he was unfaithful and closed the Temple. They are now in front of the altar of the Lord, purified and ready for use."

Early the next morning King Hezekiah gathered the city officials and went to the Temple of the Lord. They brought seven bulls, seven rams, and seven male lambs as a burnt offering, together with seven male goats as a sin offering for the kingdom, for the Temple, and for Judah. The king commanded the priests, who were descendants of Aaron, to sacrifice the animals on the altar of the Lord.

So they killed the bulls, and the priests took the blood and sprinkled it on the altar. Next they killed the rams and sprinkled their blood on the altar. And finally, they did the same with the male lambs. The male goats for the sin offering were then brought before the king and the assembly of people, who laid their hands on them. The priests then killed the goats as a sin offering and sprinkled their blood on the altar to make atonement for the sins of all Israel. The king had specifically commanded that this burnt offering and sin offering should be made for all Israel.

King Hezekiah then stationed the Levites at the Temple of the Lord with cymbals, lyres, and harps. He obeyed all the commands that the Lord had given to King David through Gad, the king's seer, and the prophet Nathan. The Levites then took their positions around the Temple with the instruments of David, and the priests took their positions with the trumpets.

Then Hezekiah ordered that the burnt offering be placed on the altar. As the burnt offering was presented, songs of praise to the Lord were begun, accompanied by the trumpets and other instruments of David, the former king of Israel. The entire assembly worshiped the Lord as the singers sang and the trumpets blew, until all the burnt offerings were finished. Then the king and everyone with him bowed down in worship. King Hezekiah and the officials ordered the Levites to praise the Lord with the psalms written by David and by Asaph the seer. So they offered joyous praise and bowed down in worship.

Then Hezekiah declared, "Now that you have consecrated yourselves to the Lord, bring your sacrifices and thanksgiving offerings to the Temple of the Lord." So the people brought their sacrifices and thanksgiving offerings, and all whose hearts were willing brought burnt offerings, too. The people brought to the Lord 70 bulls, 100 rams, and 200 male lambs for burnt offerings. They also brought 600 cattle and 3,000 sheep and goats as sacred offerings.

But there were too few priests to prepare all the burnt offerings. So their relatives the Levites helped them until the work was finished and more priests had been purified, for the Levites had been more conscientious about purifying themselves than the priests had been. There was an abundance of burnt offerings, along with the usual liquid offerings, and a great deal of fat from the many peace offerings.

So the Temple of the LORD was restored to service. And Hezekiah and all the people rejoiced because of what God had done for the people, for everything had been accomplished so quickly.

King Hezekiah now sent word to all Israel and Judah, and he wrote letters of invitation to the people of Ephraim and Manasseh. He asked everyone to come to the Temple of the LORD at Jerusalem to celebrate the Passover of the LORD, the God of Israel. The king, his officials, and all the community of Jerusalem decided to celebrate Passover a month later than usual. They were unable to celebrate it at the prescribed time because not enough priests could be purified by then, and the people had not yet assembled at Jerusalem.

This plan for keeping the Passover seemed right to the king and all the people. So they sent a proclamation throughout all Israel, from Beersheba in the south to Dan in the north, inviting everyone to come to Jerusalem to celebrate the Passover of the LORD, the God of Israel. The people had not been celebrating it in great numbers as required in the Law.

At the king's command, runners were sent throughout Israel and Judah. They carried letters that said:

"O people of Israel, return to the LORD, the God of Abraham, Isaac, and Israel, so that he will return to the few of us who have survived the conquest of the Assyrian kings. Do not be like your ancestors and relatives who abandoned the LORD, the God of their ancestors, and became an object of derision, as you yourselves can see. Do not be stubborn, as they were, but submit yourselves to the LORD. Come to his Temple, which he has set apart as holy forever. Worship the LORD your God so that his fierce anger will turn away from you.

"For if you return to the LORD, your relatives and your children will be treated mercifully by their captors, and they will be able to return to this land. For the LORD your God is gracious and merciful. If you return to him, he will not continue to turn his face from you."

The runners went from town to town throughout Ephraim and Manasseh and as far as the territory of Zebulun. But most of the people just laughed at the runners and made fun of them. However, some people from Asher, Manasseh, and Zebulun humbled themselves and went to Jerusalem.

At the same time, God's hand was on the people in the land of Judah, giving them all one heart to obey the orders of the king and his officials, who were following the word of the LORD. So a huge crowd assembled at Jerusalem in midspring to celebrate the Festival of Unleavened Bread. They set to work and removed the pagan altars from Jerusalem. They took away all the incense altars and threw them into the Kidron Valley.

On the fourteenth day of the second month, one month later than usual, the people slaughtered the Passover lamb. This shamed the priests and Levites, so they purified themselves and brought burnt offerings to the Temple of the LORD. Then they took their places at the Temple as prescribed in the Law of Moses, the man of God. The Levites brought the sacrificial blood to the priests, who then sprinkled it on the altar.

Since many of the people had not purified themselves, the Levites had to slaughter their Passover lamb for them, to set them apart for the LORD. Most of those who came from Ephraim, Manasseh, Issachar, and Zebulun had not purified themselves. But King Hezekiah prayed for them, and they were allowed to eat the Passover meal anyway, even though this was contrary to the requirements of the Law. For Hezekiah said, "May the LORD, who is good, pardon those who decide to follow the LORD, the God of their ancestors, even though they are not properly cleansed for the ceremony." And the LORD listened to Hezekiah's prayer and healed the people.

So the people of Israel who were present in Jerusalem joyously celebrated the Festival of Unleavened Bread for seven days. Each day the Levites and priests sang to the LORD, accompanied by loud instruments. Hezekiah encouraged all the Levites regarding the skill they displayed as they served the LORD. The celebration continued for seven days. Peace offerings were sacrificed, and the people gave thanks to the LORD, the God of their ancestors.

The entire assembly then decided to continue the festival another seven days, so they celebrated joyfully for another week. King Hezekiah gave the people 1,000 bulls and 7,000 sheep and goats for offerings, and the officials donated 1,000 bulls and 10,000 sheep and goats. Meanwhile, many more priests purified themselves.

The entire assembly of Judah rejoiced, including the priests, the Levites, all who came from the land of Israel, the foreigners who came to the festival, and all those who lived in Judah. There was great joy in the city, for Jerusalem had not seen a celebration like this one since the days of Solomon, King David's son. Then the priests and Levites stood and blessed the people, and God heard their prayer from his holy dwelling in heaven.

When the festival ended, the Israelites who attended went to all the towns of Judah, Benjamin, Ephraim, and Manasseh, and they smashed all the sacred pillars, cut down the Asherah poles, and removed the pagan shrines and altars. After this, the Israelites returned to their own towns and homes.

Hezekiah then organized the priests and Levites into divisions to offer the burnt offerings and peace offerings, and to worship and give thanks and praise to the LORD at the gates of the Temple. The king also made a personal contribution of animals for the daily morning and evening burnt offerings, the weekly Sabbath festivals, the monthly new moon festivals, and the annual festivals as prescribed in the Law of the LORD. In addition, he required the people in Jerusalem to bring a portion of their goods to the priests and Levites, so they could devote themselves fully to the Law of the LORD.

When the people of Israel heard these requirements, they responded generously by bringing the first share of their grain, new wine, olive oil, honey, and all the produce of their fields. They brought a large quantity— a tithe of all they produced. The people who had moved to Judah from Israel, and the people of Judah themselves, brought in the tithes of their cattle, sheep, and goats and a tithe of the things that had been dedicated to the LORD their God, and they piled them up in great heaps. They began piling them up in late spring, and the heaps continued to grow until early autumn. When Hezekiah and his officials came and saw these huge piles, they thanked the LORD and his people Israel!

"Where did all this come from?" Hezekiah asked the priests and Levites.

And Azariah the high priest, from the family of Zadok, replied, "Since the people began bringing their gifts to the LORD's Temple, we have had enough to eat and plenty to spare. The LORD has blessed his people, and all this is left over."

Hezekiah ordered that storerooms be prepared in the Temple of the LORD. When this was done, the people faithfully brought all the gifts, tithes, and other items dedicated for use in the Temple. Conaniah the Levite was put in charge, assisted by his brother Shimei. The supervisors under them were Jehiel, Azaziah, Nahath, Asahel, Jerimoth, Jozabad, Eliel, Ismakiah, Mahath, and Benaiah. These appointments were made by King Hezekiah and Azariah, the chief official in the Temple of God.

Kore son of Imnah the Levite, who was the gatekeeper at the East Gate, was put in charge of distributing the voluntary offerings given to God, the gifts, and the things that had been dedicated to the LORD. His faithful assistants were Eden, Miniamin, Jeshua, Shemaiah, Amariah, and Shecaniah. They distributed the gifts among the families of priests in their towns by their divisions, dividing the gifts fairly among old and young alike. They distributed the gifts to all males three years old or older, regardless of their place in the genealogical records. The distribution went to all who would come to the LORD's Temple to perform their daily duties according to their divisions. They distributed gifts to the priests who were listed by their families in the genealogical records, and to the Levites twenty years old or older who were listed according to their jobs and their divisions. Food allotments were also given to the families of all those listed in the genealogical records, including their little babies, wives, sons, and daughters. For they had all been faithful in purifying themselves.

As for the priests, the descendants of Aaron, who were living in the open villages around the towns, men were appointed by name to distribute portions to every male among the priests and to all the Levites listed in the genealogical records.

In this way, King Hezekiah handled the distribution throughout all Judah, doing what was pleasing and good in the sight of the LORD his God. In all that he did in the service of the Temple of God and in his efforts to follow God's laws and commands, Hezekiah sought his God wholeheartedly. As a result, he was very successful.

After Hezekiah had faithfully carried out this work, King Sennacherib of Assyria invaded Judah. He laid siege to the fortified towns, giving orders for his army to break through their walls. When Hezekiah realized that Sennacherib also intended to attack Jerusalem, he consulted with his officials and military advisers, and they decided to stop the flow of the springs outside the city. They organized a huge work crew to stop the flow of the springs, cutting off the brook that ran through the fields. For they said, "Why should the kings of Assyria come here and find plenty of water?"

Then Hezekiah worked hard at repairing all the broken sections of the wall, erecting towers, and constructing a second wall outside the first. He also reinforced the supporting terraces in the City of David and manufactured large numbers of weapons and shields. He appointed military officers over the people and assembled them before him in the square at the city gate. Then Hezekiah encouraged them by saying: "Be strong and courageous! Don't be afraid or discouraged because of the king of Assyria or his mighty army, for there is a power far greater on our side! He may have a great army, but they are merely men. We have the LORD our God to help us and to fight our battles for us!" Hezekiah's words greatly encouraged the people.

While King Sennacherib of Assyria was still besieging the town of Lachish, he sent his officers to Jerusalem with this message for Hezekiah and all the people in the city:

"This is what King Sennacherib of Assyria says: What are you trusting in that makes you think you can survive my siege of Jerusalem? Hezekiah has said, 'The LORD our God will rescue us from the king of Assyria.' Surely Hezekiah is misleading you, sentencing you to death by famine and thirst! Don't you realize that Hezekiah is the very person who destroyed all the LORD's shrines and altars? He commanded Judah and Jerusalem to worship only at the altar at the Temple and to offer sacrifices on it alone.

"Surely you must realize what I and the other kings of Assyria before me have done to all the people of the earth! Were any of the gods of those nations able to rescue their people from my power? Which of their gods was able to rescue its people from the destructive power of my predecessors? What makes you think your God can rescue you from me? Don't let Hezekiah deceive you! Don't let him fool you like this! I say it again—no god of any nation or kingdom has ever yet been able to rescue his people from me or my ancestors. How much less will your God rescue you from my power!"

And Sennacherib's officers further mocked the LORD God and his servant Hezekiah, heaping insult upon insult. The king also sent letters scorning the LORD, the God of Israel. He wrote, "Just as the gods of all the other nations failed to rescue their people from my power, so the God of Hezekiah will also fail." The Assyrian officials who brought the letters shouted this in Hebrew to the people gathered on the walls of the city, trying to terrify them so it would be easier to capture the city. These officers talked about the God of Jerusalem as though he were one of the pagan gods, made by human hands.

Then King Hezekiah and the prophet Isaiah son of Amoz cried out in prayer to God in heaven. And the LORD sent an angel who destroyed the Assyrian army with all its commanders and officers. So Sennacherib was forced to return home in disgrace to his own land. And when he entered the temple of his god, some of his own sons killed him there with a sword.

That is how the LORD rescued Hezekiah and the people of Jerusalem from King Sennacherib of Assyria and from all the others who threatened them. So there was peace throughout the land. From then on King Hezekiah became highly respected among all the surrounding nations, and many gifts for the LORD arrived at Jerusalem, with valuable presents for King Hezekiah, too.

About that time Hezekiah became deathly ill. He prayed to the LORD, who healed him and gave him a miraculous sign. But Hezekiah did not respond appropriately to the kindness shown him, and he became proud. So the LORD's anger came against him and against Judah and Jerusalem. Then Hezekiah humbled himself and repented of his pride, as did the people of Jerusalem. So the LORD's anger did not fall on them during Hezekiah's lifetime.

Hezekiah was very wealthy and highly honored. He built special treasury buildings for his silver, gold, precious stones, and spices, and for his shields and other valuable items. He also constructed many storehouses for his grain, new wine, and olive oil; and he made many stalls for his cattle and pens for his flocks of sheep and goats. He built many towns and acquired vast flocks and herds, for God had given him great wealth. He blocked up the upper spring of Gihon and brought the water down through a tunnel to the west side of the City of David. And so he succeeded in everything he did.

However, when ambassadors arrived from Babylon to ask about the remarkable events that had taken place in the land, God withdrew from Hezekiah in order to test him and to see what was really in his heart.

The rest of the events in Hezekiah's reign and his acts of devotion are recorded in *The Vision of the Prophet Isaiah Son of Amoz,* which is included in *The Book of the Kings of Judah and Israel.* When Hezekiah died, he was buried in the upper area of the royal cemetery, and all Judah and Jerusalem honored him at his death. And his son Manasseh became the next king.

+ + +

Manasseh was twelve years old when he became king, and he reigned in Jerusalem fifty-five years. He did what was evil in the LORD's sight, following the detestable practices of the pagan nations that the LORD had driven from the land ahead of the Israelites.

He rebuilt the pagan shrines his father, Hezekiah, had broken down. He constructed altars for the images of Baal and set up Asherah poles. He also bowed before all the powers of the heavens and worshiped them.

He built pagan altars in the Temple of the LORD, the place where the LORD had said, "My name will remain in Jerusalem forever." He built these altars for all the powers of the heavens in both courtyards of the LORD's Temple. Manasseh also sacrificed his own sons in the fire in the valley of Ben-Hinnom. He practiced sorcery, divination, and witchcraft, and he consulted with mediums and psychics. He did much that was evil in the LORD's sight, arousing his anger.

Manasseh even took a carved idol he had made and set it up in God's Temple, the very place where God had told David and his son Solomon: "My name will be honored forever in this Temple and in Jerusalem—the city I have chosen from among all the tribes of Israel. If the Israelites will be careful to obey my commands—all the laws, decrees, and regulations given through Moses—I will not send them into exile from this land that

I set aside for your ancestors." But Manasseh led the people of Judah and Jerusalem to do even more evil than the pagan nations that the LORD had destroyed when the people of Israel entered the land.

The LORD spoke to Manasseh and his people, but they ignored all his warnings. So the LORD sent the commanders of the Assyrian armies, and they took Manasseh prisoner. They put a ring through his nose, bound him in bronze chains, and led him away to Babylon. But while in deep distress, Manasseh sought the LORD his God and sincerely humbled himself before the God of his ancestors. And when he prayed, the LORD listened to him and was moved by his request. So the LORD brought Manasseh back to Jerusalem and to his kingdom. Then Manasseh finally realized that the LORD alone is God!

After this Manasseh rebuilt the outer wall of the City of David, from west of the Gihon Spring in the Kidron Valley to the Fish Gate, and continuing around the hill of Ophel. He built the wall very high. And he stationed his military officers in all of the fortified towns of Judah. Manasseh also removed the foreign gods and the idol from the LORD's Temple. He tore down all the altars he had built on the hill where the Temple stood and all the altars that were in Jerusalem, and he dumped them outside the city. Then he restored the altar of the LORD and sacrificed peace offerings and thanksgiving offerings on it. He also encouraged the people of Judah to worship the LORD, the God of Israel. However, the people still sacrificed at the pagan shrines, though only to the LORD their God.

The rest of the events of Manasseh's reign, his prayer to God, and the words the seers spoke to him in the name of the LORD, the God of Israel, are recorded in *The Book of the Kings of Israel*. Manasseh's prayer, the account of the way God answered him, and an account of all his sins and unfaithfulness are recorded in *The Record of the Seers*. It includes a list of the locations where he built pagan shrines and set up Asherah poles and idols before he humbled himself and repented. When Manasseh died, he was buried in his palace. Then his son Amon became the next king.

+ + +

Amon was twenty-two years old when he became king, and he reigned in Jerusalem two years. He did what was evil in the LORD's sight, just as his father, Manasseh, had done. He worshiped and sacrificed to all the idols his father had made. But unlike his father, he did not humble himself before the LORD. Instead, Amon sinned even more.

Then Amon's own officials conspired against him and assassinated him in his palace. But the people of the land killed all those who had conspired against King Amon, and they made his son Josiah the next king.

+ + +

Josiah was eight years old when he became king, and he reigned in Jerusalem thirty-one years. He did what was pleasing in the LORD's sight and followed the example of his ancestor David. He did not turn away from doing what was right.

During the eighth year of his reign, while he was still young, Josiah began to seek the God of his ancestor David. Then in the twelfth year he began to purify Judah and Jerusalem, destroying all the pagan shrines, the Asherah poles, and the carved idols and cast images. He ordered that the altars of Baal be demolished and that the incense altars which stood above them be broken down. He also made sure that the Asherah poles, the carved idols, and the cast images were smashed and scattered over the graves of those who had sacrificed to them. He burned the bones of the pagan priests on their own altars, and so he purified Judah and Jerusalem.

He did the same thing in the towns of Manasseh, Ephraim, and Simeon, even as far as Naphtali, and in the regions all around them. He destroyed the pagan altars and the Asherah poles, and he crushed the idols into dust. He cut down all the incense altars throughout the land of Israel. Finally, he returned to Jerusalem.

In the eighteenth year of his reign, after he had purified the land and the Temple, Josiah appointed Shaphan son of Azaliah, Maaseiah the governor of Jerusalem, and Joah son of Joahaz, the royal historian, to repair the Temple of the LORD his God. They gave Hilkiah the high priest the money that had been collected by the Levites who served as gatekeepers at the Temple of God. The gifts were brought by people from Manasseh, Ephraim, and from all the remnant of Israel, as well as from all Judah, Benjamin, and the people of Jerusalem.

He entrusted the money to the men assigned to supervise the restoration of the LORD's Temple. Then they paid the workers who did the repairs and renovation of the Temple. They hired carpenters and builders, who purchased finished stone for the walls and timber for the rafters and beams. They restored what earlier kings of Judah had allowed to fall into ruin.

The workers served faithfully under the leadership of Jahath and Obadiah, Levites of the Merarite clan, and Zechariah and Meshullam, Levites of the Kohathite clan. Other Levites, all of whom were skilled musicians, were put in charge of the laborers of the various trades. Still others assisted as secretaries, officials, and gatekeepers.

While they were bringing out the money collected at the LORD's Temple, Hilkiah the priest found the Book of the Law of the LORD that was written by Moses. Hilkiah said to Shaphan the court secretary, "I have found the Book of the Law in the LORD's Temple!" Then Hilkiah gave the scroll to Shaphan.

Shaphan took the scroll to the king and reported, "Your officials are doing everything they were assigned to do. The money that was collected at the Temple of the LORD has been turned over to the supervisors and workmen." Shaphan also told the king, "Hilkiah the priest has given me a scroll." So Shaphan read it to the king.

When the king heard what was written in the Law, he tore his clothes in despair. Then he gave these orders to Hilkiah, Ahikam son of Shaphan, Acbor son of Micaiah, Shaphan the court secretary, and Asaiah the king's personal adviser: "Go to the Temple and speak to the LORD for me and for all the remnant of Israel and Judah. Inquire about the words written in the scroll that has been found. For the LORD's great anger has been poured out on us because our ancestors have not obeyed the word of the LORD. We have not been doing everything this scroll says we must do."

So Hilkiah and the other men went to the New Quarter of Jerusalem to consult with the prophet Huldah. She was the wife of Shallum son of Tikvah, son of Harhas, the keeper of the Temple wardrobe.

She said to them, "The LORD, the God of Israel, has spoken! Go back and tell the man who sent you, 'This is what the LORD says: I am going to bring disaster on this city and its people. All the curses written in the scroll that was read to the king of Judah will come true. For my people have abandoned me and offered sacrifices to pagan gods, and I am very angry with them for everything they have done. My anger will be poured out on this place, and it will not be quenched.'

"But go to the king of Judah who sent you to seek the LORD and tell him: 'This is what the LORD, the God of Israel, says concerning the message you have just heard: You were sorry and humbled yourself before God when you heard his words against this city and its people. You humbled yourself and tore your clothing in despair and wept before me in repentance. And I have indeed heard you, says the LORD. So I will not send the promised disaster until after you have died and been buried in peace. You yourself will not see the disaster I am going to bring on this city and its people.'"

So they took her message back to the king.

Then the king summoned all the elders of Judah and Jerusalem. And the king went up to the Temple of the LORD with all the people of Judah and Jerusalem, along with the priests and the Levites—all the people from the greatest to the least. There the king read to them the entire Book of the Covenant that had been found in the LORD's Temple. The king took his place of authority beside the pillar and renewed the covenant in the LORD's presence. He pledged to obey the LORD by keeping all his commands, laws, and decrees with all his heart and soul. He promised to obey all the terms of the covenant that were written in the scroll. And he required everyone in Jerusalem and the people of Benjamin to make a similar pledge. The people of Jerusalem did so, renewing their covenant with God, the God of their ancestors.

So Josiah removed all detestable idols from the entire land of Israel and required everyone to worship the LORD their God. And throughout the rest of his lifetime, they did not turn away from the LORD, the God of their ancestors.

Then Josiah announced that the Passover of the LORD would be celebrated in Jerusalem, and so the Passover lamb was slaughtered on the fourteenth day of the first month. Josiah also assigned the priests to their duties and encouraged them in their work at the Temple of the LORD. He issued this order to the Levites, who were to teach all Israel and who had been set apart to serve the LORD: "Put the holy Ark in the Temple that was built by Solomon son of David, the king of Israel. You no longer need to carry it back and forth on your shoulders. Now spend your time serving the LORD your God and his people Israel. Report for duty according to the family divisions of your ancestors, following the directions of King David of Israel and the directions of his son Solomon.

"Then stand in the sanctuary at the place appointed for your family division and help the families assigned to you as they bring their offerings to the Temple. Slaughter the Passover lambs, purify yourselves, and prepare to help those who come. Follow all the directions that the LORD gave through Moses."

Then Josiah provided 30,000 lambs and young goats for the people's Passover offerings, along with 3,000 cattle, all from the king's own flocks and herds. The king's officials also made willing contributions to the people, priests, and Levites. Hilkiah, Zechariah, and Jehiel, the administrators of God's Temple, gave the priests 2,600 lambs and young goats and 300 cattle as Passover offerings. The Levite leaders—Conaniah and his brothers Shemaiah and Nethanel, as well as Hashabiah, Jeiel, and Jozabad—gave 5,000 lambs and young goats and 500 cattle to the Levites for their Passover offerings.

When everything was ready for the Passover celebration, the priests and the Levites took their places, organized by their divisions, as the king had commanded. The Levites then slaughtered the Passover lambs and presented the blood to the priests, who sprinkled the blood on the altar while the Levites prepared the animals. They divided the burnt offerings among the people by their family groups, so they could offer them to the LORD as prescribed in the Book of Moses. They did the same with the cattle. Then they roasted the Passover lambs as prescribed; and they boiled the holy offerings in pots, kettles, and pans, and brought them out quickly so the people could eat them.

Afterward the Levites prepared Passover offerings for themselves and for the priests—the descendants of Aaron—because the priests had been busy from morning till night offering the burnt offerings and the fat portions. The Levites took responsibility for all these preparations.

The musicians, descendants of Asaph, were in their assigned places, following the commands that had been given by David, Asaph, Heman, and Jeduthun, the king's seer. The gatekeepers guarded the gates and did not need to leave their posts of duty, for their Passover offerings were prepared for them by their fellow Levites.

The entire ceremony for the LORD's Passover was completed that day. All the burnt offerings were sacrificed on the altar of the LORD, as King Josiah had commanded. All the Israelites present in Jerusalem celebrated Passover and the Festival of Unleavened Bread for seven days. Never since the time of the prophet Samuel had there been such a Passover. None of the kings of Israel had ever kept a Passover as Josiah did, involving all the priests and Levites, all the people of Jerusalem, and people from all over Judah and Israel. This Passover was celebrated in the eighteenth year of Josiah's reign.

After Josiah had finished restoring the Temple, King Neco of Egypt led his army up from Egypt to do battle at Carchemish on the Euphrates River, and Josiah and his army marched out to fight him. But King Neco sent messengers to Josiah with this message:

> "What do you want with me, king of Judah? I have no quarrel with you today! I am on my way to fight another nation, and God has told me to hurry! Do not interfere with God, who is with me, or he will destroy you."

But Josiah refused to listen to Neco, to whom God had indeed spoken, and he would not turn back. Instead, he disguised himself and led his army into battle on the plain of Megiddo. But the enemy archers hit King Josiah with their arrows and wounded him. He cried out to his men, "Take me from the battle, for I am badly wounded!"

So they lifted Josiah out of his chariot and placed him in another chariot.

Then they brought him back to Jerusalem, where he died. He was buried there in the royal cemetery. And all Judah and Jerusalem mourned for him. The prophet Jeremiah composed funeral songs for Josiah, and to this day choirs still sing these sad songs about his death. These songs of sorrow have become a tradition and are recorded in *The Book of Laments.*

The rest of the events of Josiah's reign and his acts of devotion (carried out according to what was written in the Law of the LORD), from beginning to end—all are recorded in *The Book of the Kings of Israel and Judah.*

+ + +

Then the people of the land took Josiah's son Jehoahaz and made him the next king in Jerusalem.

Jehoahaz was twenty-three years old when he became king, and he reigned in Jerusalem three months.

Then he was deposed by the king of Egypt, who demanded that Judah pay 7,500 pounds of silver and 75 pounds of gold as tribute.

+ + +

The king of Egypt then installed Eliakim, the brother of Jehoahaz, as the next king of Judah and Jerusalem, and he changed Eliakim's name to Jehoiakim. Then Neco took Jehoahaz to Egypt as a prisoner.

Jehoiakim was twenty-five years old when he became king, and he reigned in Jerusalem eleven years. He did what was evil in the sight of the LORD his God.

Then King Nebuchadnezzar of Babylon came to Jerusalem and captured it, and he bound Jehoiakim in bronze chains and led him away to Babylon. Nebuchadnezzar also took some of the treasures from the Temple of the LORD, and he placed them in his palace in Babylon.

The rest of the events in Jehoiakim's reign, including all the evil things he did and everything found against him, are recorded in *The Book of the Kings of Israel and Judah.* Then his son Jehoiachin became the next king.

+ + +

Jehoiachin was eighteen years old when he became king, and he reigned in Jerusalem three months and ten days. Jehoiachin did what was evil in the LORD's sight.

In the spring of the year King Nebuchadnezzar took Jehoiachin to Babylon. Many treasures from the Temple of the LORD were also taken to

Babylon at that time. And Nebuchadnezzar installed Jehoiachin's uncle, Zedekiah, as the next king in Judah and Jerusalem.

+ + +

Zedekiah was twenty-one years old when he became king, and he reigned in Jerusalem eleven years. But Zedekiah did what was evil in the sight of the Lord his God, and he refused to humble himself when the prophet Jeremiah spoke to him directly from the Lord. He also rebelled against King Nebuchadnezzar, even though he had taken an oath of loyalty in God's name. Zedekiah was a hard and stubborn man, refusing to turn to the Lord, the God of Israel.

Likewise, all the leaders of the priests and the people became more and more unfaithful. They followed all the pagan practices of the surrounding nations, desecrating the Temple of the Lord that had been consecrated in Jerusalem.

The Lord, the God of their ancestors, repeatedly sent his prophets to warn them, for he had compassion on his people and his Temple. But the people mocked these messengers of God and despised their words. They scoffed at the prophets until the Lord's anger could no longer be restrained and nothing could be done.

So the Lord brought the king of Babylon against them. The Babylonians killed Judah's young men, even chasing after them into the Temple. They had no pity on the people, killing both young men and young women, the old and the infirm. God handed all of them over to Nebuchadnezzar. The king took home to Babylon all the articles, large and small, used in the Temple of God, and the treasures from both the Lord's Temple and from the palace of the king and his officials. Then his army burned the Temple of God, tore down the walls of Jerusalem, burned all the palaces, and completely destroyed everything of value. The few who survived were taken as exiles to Babylon, and they became servants to the king and his sons until the kingdom of Persia came to power.

So the message of the Lord spoken through Jeremiah was fulfilled. The land finally enjoyed its Sabbath rest, lying desolate until the seventy years were fulfilled, just as the prophet had said.

IN THE FIRST YEAR of King Cyrus of Persia, the LORD fulfilled the prophecy he had given through Jeremiah. He stirred the heart of Cyrus to put this proclamation in writing and to send it throughout his kingdom:

"This is what King Cyrus of Persia says:

"The LORD, the God of heaven, has given me all the kingdoms of the earth. He has appointed me to build him a Temple at Jerusalem, which is in Judah. Any of you who are his people may go to Jerusalem in Judah to rebuild this Temple of the LORD, the God of Israel, who lives in Jerusalem. And may your God be with you! Wherever this Jewish remnant is found, let their neighbors contribute toward their expenses by giving them silver and gold, supplies for the journey, and livestock, as well as a voluntary offering for the Temple of God in Jerusalem."

Then God stirred the hearts of the priests and Levites and the leaders of the tribes of Judah and Benjamin to go to Jerusalem to rebuild the Temple of the LORD. And all their neighbors assisted by giving them articles of silver and gold, supplies for the journey, and livestock. They gave them many valuable gifts in addition to all the voluntary offerings.

King Cyrus himself brought out the articles that King Nebuchadnezzar had taken from the LORD's Temple in Jerusalem and had placed in the temple of his own gods. Cyrus directed Mithredath, the treasurer of Persia, to count these items and present them to Sheshbazzar, the leader of the exiles returning to Judah. This is a list of the items that were returned:

gold basins 30
silver basins 1,000
silver incense burners 29
gold bowls 30
silver bowls 410
other items 1,000

In all, there were 5,400 articles of gold and silver. Sheshbazzar brought all of these along when the exiles went from Babylon to Jerusalem.

Here is the list of the Jewish exiles of the provinces who returned from their captivity. King Nebuchadnezzar had deported them to Babylon, but now they returned to Jerusalem and the other towns in Judah where they originally lived. Their leaders were Zerubbabel, Jeshua, Nehemiah, Seraiah, Reelaiah, Mordecai, Bilshan, Mispar, Bigvai, Rehum, and Baanah.

This is the number of the men of Israel who returned from exile:
The family of Parosh 2,172
The family of Shephatiah 372

The family of Arah..775
The family of Pahath-moab (descendants of Jeshua and Joab)... 2,812
The family of Elam...1,254
The family of Zattu..945
The family of Zaccai...760
The family of Bani...642
The family of Bebai..623
The family of Azgad.......................................1,222
The family of Adonikam.......................................666
The family of Bigvai......................................2,056
The family of Adin...454
The family of Ater (descendants of Hezekiah)..................98
The family of Bezai..323
The family of Jorah..112
The family of Hashum...223
The family of Gibbar..95
The people of Bethlehem......................................123
The people of Netophah..56
The people of Anathoth.......................................128
The people of Beth-azmaveth...................................42
The people of Kiriath-jearim, Kephirah, and Beeroth..........743
The people of Ramah and Geba.................................621
The people of Micmash..122
The people of Bethel and Ai..................................223
The citizens of Nebo..52
The citizens of Magbish......................................156
The citizens of West Elam..................................1,254
The citizens of Harim..320
The citizens of Lod, Hadid, and Ono..........................725
The citizens of Jericho......................................345
The citizens of Senaah.....................................3,630

These are the priests who returned from exile:
The family of Jedaiah (through the line of Jeshua)............973
The family of Immer..1,052
The family of Pashhur......................................1,247
The family of Harim..1,017

These are the Levites who returned from exile:
The families of Jeshua and Kadmiel (descendants of
    Hodaviah)...74
The singers of the family of Asaph...........................128

The gatekeepers of the families of Shallum, Ater, Talmon, Akkub, Hatita, and Shobai. 139

The descendants of the following Temple servants returned from exile:
Ziha, Hasupha, Tabbaoth,
Keros, Siaha, Padon,
Lebanah, Hagabah, Akkub,
Hagab, Shalmai, Hanan,
Giddel, Gahar, Reaiah,
Rezin, Nekoda, Gazzam,
Uzza, Paseah, Besai,
Asnah, Meunim, Nephusim,
Bakbuk, Hakupha, Harhur,
Bazluth, Mehida, Harsha,
Barkos, Sisera, Temah,
Neziah, and Hatipha.

The descendants of these servants of King Solomon returned from exile:
Sotai, Hassophereth, Peruda,
Jaalah, Darkon, Giddel,
Shephatiah, Hattil, Pokereth-hazzebaim, and Ami.

In all, the Temple servants and the descendants of Solomon's servants numbered 392.

Another group returned at this time from the towns of Tel-melah, Tel-harsha, Kerub, Addan, and Immer. However, they could not prove that they or their families were descendants of Israel. This group included the families of Delaiah, Tobiah, and Nekoda—a total of 652 people.

Three families of priests—Hobaiah, Hakkoz, and Barzillai—also returned. (This Barzillai had married a woman who was a descendant of Barzillai of Gilead, and he had taken her family name.) They searched for their names in the genealogical records, but they were not found, so they were disqualified from serving as priests. The governor told them not to eat the priests' share of food from the sacrifices until a priest could consult the LORD about the matter by using the Urim and Thummim—the sacred lots.

So a total of 42,360 people returned to Judah, in addition to 7,337 servants and 200 singers, both men and women. They took with them 736 horses, 245 mules, 435 camels, and 6,720 donkeys.

When they arrived at the Temple of the LORD in Jerusalem, some of the family leaders made voluntary offerings toward the rebuilding of God's Temple on its original site, and each leader gave as much as he could. The total of their gifts came to 61,000 gold coins, 6,250 pounds of silver, and 100 robes for the priests.

So the priests, the Levites, the singers, the gatekeepers, the Temple servants, and some of the common people settled in villages near Jerusalem. The rest of the people returned to their own towns throughout Israel.

In early autumn, when the Israelites had settled in their towns, all the people assembled in Jerusalem with a unified purpose. Then Jeshua son of Jehozadak joined his fellow priests and Zerubbabel son of Shealtiel with his family in rebuilding the altar of the God of Israel. They wanted to sacrifice burnt offerings on it, as instructed in the Law of Moses, the man of God. Even though the people were afraid of the local residents, they rebuilt the altar at its old site. Then they began to sacrifice burnt offerings on the altar to the LORD each morning and evening.

They celebrated the Festival of Shelters as prescribed in the Law, sacrificing the number of burnt offerings specified for each day of the festival. They also offered the regular burnt offerings and the offerings required for the new moon celebrations and the annual festivals as prescribed by the LORD. The people also gave voluntary offerings to the LORD. Fifteen days before the Festival of Shelters began, the priests had begun to sacrifice burnt offerings to the LORD. This was even before they had started to lay the foundation of the LORD's Temple.

Then the people hired masons and carpenters and bought cedar logs from the people of Tyre and Sidon, paying them with food, wine, and olive oil. The logs were brought down from the Lebanon mountains and floated along the coast of the Mediterranean Sea to Joppa, for King Cyrus had given permission for this.

The construction of the Temple of God began in midspring, during the second year after they arrived in Jerusalem. The work force was made up of everyone who had returned from exile, including Zerubbabel son of Shealtiel, Jeshua son of Jehozadak and his fellow priests, and all the Levites. The Levites who were twenty years old or older were put in charge of rebuilding the LORD's Temple. The workers at the Temple of God were supervised by Jeshua with his sons and relatives, and Kadmiel and his sons, all descendants of Hodaviah. They were helped in this task by the Levites of the family of Henadad.

When the builders completed the foundation of the LORD's Temple, the priests put on their robes and took their places to blow their trumpets. And the Levites, descendants of Asaph, clashed their cymbals to praise the LORD, just as King David had prescribed. With praise and thanks, they sang this song to the LORD:

"He is so good!
His faithful love for Israel endures forever!"

Then all the people gave a great shout, praising the LORD because the foundation of the LORD's Temple had been laid.

But many of the older priests, Levites, and other leaders who had seen the first Temple wept aloud when they saw the new Temple's foundation. The others, however, were shouting for joy. The joyful shouting and weeping mingled together in a loud noise that could be heard far in the distance.

+

The enemies of Judah and Benjamin heard that the exiles were rebuilding a Temple to the LORD, the God of Israel. So they approached Zerubbabel and the other leaders and said, "Let us build with you, for we worship your God just as you do. We have sacrificed to him ever since King Esarhaddon of Assyria brought us here."

But Zerubbabel, Jeshua, and the other leaders of Israel replied, "You may have no part in this work. We alone will build the Temple for the LORD, the God of Israel, just as King Cyrus of Persia commanded us."

Then the local residents tried to discourage and frighten the people of Judah to keep them from their work. They bribed agents to work against them and to frustrate their plans. This went on during the entire reign of King Cyrus of Persia and lasted until King Darius of Persia took the throne.

Years later when Xerxes began his reign, the enemies of Judah wrote a letter of accusation against the people of Judah and Jerusalem.

Even later, during the reign of King Artaxerxes of Persia, the enemies of Judah, led by Bishlam, Mithredath, and Tabeel, sent a letter to Artaxerxes in the Aramaic language, and it was translated for the king.

Rehum the governor and Shimshai the court secretary wrote the letter, telling King Artaxerxes about the situation in Jerusalem. They greeted the king for all their colleagues—the judges and local leaders, the people of Tarpel, the Persians, the Babylonians, and the people of Erech and Susa (that is, Elam). They also sent greetings from the rest of the people whom the great and noble Ashurbanipal had deported and relocated in Samaria and throughout the neighboring lands of the province west of the Euphrates River. This is a copy of their letter:

"To King Artaxerxes, from your loyal subjects in the province west of the Euphrates River.

"The king should know that the Jews who came here to Jerusalem from Babylon are rebuilding this rebellious and evil city. They have already laid the foundation and will soon finish its walls. And the king should know that if this city is rebuilt and its walls are completed, it will be much to your disadvantage, for the Jews will then refuse to pay their tribute, customs, and tolls to you.

"Since we are your loyal subjects and do not want to see the king dishonored in this way, we have sent the king this information. We suggest that a search be made in your ancestors' records, where you will discover what a rebellious city this has been in the past. In fact, it was destroyed because of its long and troublesome history of revolt against the kings and countries who controlled it. We declare to the king that if this city is rebuilt and its walls are completed, the province west of the Euphrates River will be lost to you."

Then King Artaxerxes sent this reply:

"To Rehum the governor, Shimshai the court secretary, and their colleagues living in Samaria and throughout the province west of the Euphrates River. Greetings.

"The letter you sent has been translated and read to me. I ordered a search of the records and have found that Jerusalem has indeed been a hotbed of insurrection against many kings. In fact, rebellion and revolt are normal there! Powerful kings have ruled over Jerusalem and the entire province west of the Euphrates River, receiving tribute, customs, and tolls. Therefore, issue orders to have these men stop their work. That city must not be rebuilt except at my express command. Be diligent, and don't neglect this matter, for we must not permit the situation to harm the king's interests."

When this letter from King Artaxerxes was read to Rehum, Shimshai, and their colleagues, they hurried to Jerusalem. Then, with a show of strength, they forced the Jews to stop building.

+

So the work on the Temple of God in Jerusalem had stopped, and it remained at a standstill until the second year of the reign of King Darius of Persia.

At that time the prophets Haggai and Zechariah son of Iddo prophesied to the Jews in Judah and Jerusalem. They prophesied in the name of the God of Israel who was over them. Zerubbabel son of Shealtiel and Jeshua son of Jehozadak responded by starting again to rebuild the Temple of God in Jerusalem. And the prophets of God were with them and helped them. But Tattenai, governor of the province west of the Euphrates River, and Shethar-bozenai and their colleagues soon arrived in Jerusalem and asked, "Who gave you permission to rebuild this Temple and restore this structure?" They also asked for the names of all the men working on the Temple. But because their God was watching over them, the leaders of the Jews were not prevented from building until a report was sent to Darius and he returned his decision.

This is a copy of the letter that Tattenai the governor, Shethar-bozenai, and the other officials of the province west of the Euphrates River sent to King Darius:

"To King Darius. Greetings.

"The king should know that we went to the construction site of the Temple of the great God in the province of Judah. It is being rebuilt with specially prepared stones, and timber is being laid in its walls. The work is going forward with great energy and success.

"We asked the leaders, 'Who gave you permission to rebuild this Temple and restore this structure?' And we demanded their names so that we could tell you who the leaders were.

"This was their answer: 'We are the servants of the God of heaven and earth, and we are rebuilding the Temple that was built here many years ago by a great king of Israel. But because our ancestors angered the God of heaven, he abandoned them to King Nebuchadnezzar of Babylon, who destroyed this Temple and exiled the people to Babylonia. However, King Cyrus of Babylon, during the first year of his reign, issued a decree that the Temple of God should be rebuilt. King Cyrus returned the gold and silver cups that Nebuchadnezzar had taken from the Temple of God in Jerusalem and had placed in the temple of Babylon. These cups were taken from that temple and presented to a man named Sheshbazzar, whom King Cyrus appointed as governor of Judah. The king instructed him to return the cups to their place in Jerusalem and to rebuild the Temple of God there on its original site. So this Sheshbazzar came and laid the foundations of the Temple of God in Jerusalem. The people have been working on it ever since, though it is not yet completed.'

"Therefore, if it pleases the king, we request that a search be made in the royal archives of Babylon to discover whether King Cyrus ever issued a decree to rebuild God's Temple in Jerusalem. And then let the king send us his decision in this matter."

So King Darius issued orders that a search be made in the Babylonian archives, which were stored in the treasury. But it was at the fortress at Ecbatana in the province of Media that a scroll was found. This is what it said:

"Memorandum:

"In the first year of King Cyrus's reign, a decree was sent out concerning the Temple of God at Jerusalem.

"Let the Temple be rebuilt on the site where Jews used to offer their sacrifices, using the original foundations. Its height will be ninety feet, and its width will be ninety feet. Every three layers of specially prepared stones will be topped by a layer of timber. All expenses will be paid by the royal treasury. Furthermore, the gold and silver cups, which were taken to Babylon by Nebuchadnezzar from the Temple of God in Jerusalem, must be returned to Jerusalem and put back where they belong. Let them be taken back to the Temple of God."

So King Darius sent this message:

"Now therefore, Tattenai, governor of the province west of the Euphrates River, and Shethar-bozenai, and your colleagues and other officials west of the Euphrates River—stay away from there! Do not disturb the construction of the Temple of God. Let it be rebuilt on its original site, and do not hinder the governor of Judah and the elders of the Jews in their work.

"Moreover, I hereby decree that you are to help these elders of the Jews as they rebuild this Temple of God. You must pay the full construction costs, without delay, from my taxes collected in the province west of the Euphrates River so that the work will not be interrupted.

"Give the priests in Jerusalem whatever is needed in the way of young bulls, rams, and male lambs for the burnt offerings presented to the God of heaven. And without fail, provide them with as much wheat, salt, wine, and olive oil as they need each day. Then they will be able to offer acceptable sacrifices to the God of heaven and pray for the welfare of the king and his sons.

"Those who violate this decree in any way will have a beam pulled from their house. Then they will be lifted up and impaled on it, and their house will be reduced to a pile of rubble. May the God who has chosen the city of Jerusalem as the place to honor his name destroy any king or nation that violates this command and destroys this Temple.

"I, Darius, have issued this decree. Let it be obeyed with all diligence."

Tattenai, governor of the province west of the Euphrates River, and Shethar-bozenai and their colleagues complied at once with the command of King Darius. So the Jewish elders continued their work, and they were greatly encouraged by the preaching of the prophets Haggai and Zechariah son of Iddo. The Temple was finally finished, as had been commanded by the God of Israel and decreed by Cyrus, Darius, and Artaxerxes, the kings of Persia. The Temple was completed on March 12, during the sixth year of King Darius's reign.

The Temple of God was then dedicated with great joy by the people of Israel, the priests, the Levites, and the rest of the people who had returned from exile. During the dedication ceremony for the Temple of God, 100 young bulls, 200 rams, and 400 male lambs were sacrificed. And 12 male goats were presented as a sin offering for the twelve tribes of Israel. Then the priests and Levites were divided into their various divisions to serve at the Temple of God in Jerusalem, as prescribed in the Book of Moses.

On April 21 the returned exiles celebrated Passover. The priests and Levites had purified themselves and were ceremonially clean. So they slaughtered the Passover lamb for all the returned exiles, for their fellow priests, and for themselves. The Passover meal was eaten by the people of Israel who had returned from exile and by the others in the land who had turned from their corrupt practices to worship the LORD, the God of Israel. Then they celebrated the Festival of Unleavened Bread for seven days. There was great joy throughout the land because the LORD had caused the king of Assyria to be favorable to them, so that he helped them to rebuild the Temple of God, the God of Israel.

+ + +

Many years later, during the reign of King Artaxerxes of Persia, there was a man named Ezra. He was the son of Seraiah, son of Azariah, son of Hilkiah, son of Shallum, son of Zadok, son of Ahitub, son of Amariah, son of Azariah, son of Meraioth, son of Zerahiah, son of Uzzi, son of Bukki, son of Abishua, son of Phinehas, son of Eleazar, son of Aaron the high priest. This Ezra was a scribe who was well versed in the Law of Moses, which the LORD, the God of Israel, had given to the people of Israel. He came up to Jerusalem from Babylon, and the king gave him everything he asked for, because the gracious hand of the LORD his God was on him. Some of the people of Israel, as well as some of the priests, Levites, singers, gatekeepers, and Temple servants, traveled up to Jerusalem with him in the seventh year of King Artaxerxes' reign.

Ezra arrived in Jerusalem in August of that year. He had arranged to leave Babylon on April 8, the first day of the new year, and he arrived at Jerusalem on August 4, for the gracious hand of his God was on him. This was

because Ezra had determined to study and obey the Law of the LORD and
to teach those decrees and regulations to the people of Israel.

King Artaxerxes had given a copy of the following letter to Ezra, the
priest and scribe who studied and taught the commands and decrees of
the LORD to Israel:

> "From Artaxerxes, the king of kings, to Ezra the priest, the teacher of
> the law of the God of heaven. Greetings.
>
> "I decree that any of the people of Israel in my kingdom, including
> the priests and Levites, may volunteer to return to Jerusalem with you.
> I and my council of seven hereby instruct you to conduct an inquiry
> into the situation in Judah and Jerusalem, based on your God's law,
> which is in your hand. We also commission you to take with you silver
> and gold, which we are freely presenting as an offering to the God of
> Israel who lives in Jerusalem.
>
> "Furthermore, you are to take any silver and gold that you may
> obtain from the province of Babylon, as well as the voluntary offerings
> of the people and the priests that are presented for the Temple of
> their God in Jerusalem. These donations are to be used specifically
> for the purchase of bulls, rams, male lambs, and the appropriate grain
> offerings and liquid offerings, all of which will be offered on the altar
> of the Temple of your God in Jerusalem. Any silver and gold that is left
> over may be used in whatever way you and your colleagues feel is the
> will of your God.
>
> "But as for the cups we are entrusting to you for the service of the
> Temple of your God, deliver them all to the God of Jerusalem. If you
> need anything else for your God's Temple or for any similar needs,
> you may take it from the royal treasury.
>
> "I, Artaxerxes the king, hereby send this decree to all the treasurers
> in the province west of the Euphrates River: 'You are to give Ezra,
> the priest and teacher of the law of the God of heaven, whatever he
> requests of you. You are to give him up to 7,500 pounds of silver,
> 500 bushels of wheat, 550 gallons of wine, 550 gallons of olive oil, and
> an unlimited supply of salt. Be careful to provide whatever the God
> of heaven demands for his Temple, for why should we risk bringing
> God's anger against the realm of the king and his sons? I also decree
> that no priest, Levite, singer, gatekeeper, Temple servant, or other
> worker in this Temple of God will be required to pay tribute, customs,
> or tolls of any kind.'
>
> "And you, Ezra, are to use the wisdom your God has given you to
> appoint magistrates and judges who know your God's laws to govern
> all the people in the province west of the Euphrates River. Teach

the law to anyone who does not know it. Anyone who refuses to obey the law of your God and the law of the king will be punished immediately, either by death, banishment, confiscation of goods, or imprisonment."

Praise the LORD, the God of our ancestors, who made the king want to beautify the Temple of the LORD in Jerusalem! And praise him for demonstrating such unfailing love to me by honoring me before the king, his council, and all his mighty nobles! I felt encouraged because the gracious hand of the LORD my God was on me. And I gathered some of the leaders of Israel to return with me to Jerusalem.

Here is a list of the family leaders and the genealogies of those who came with me from Babylon during the reign of King Artaxerxes:

From the family of Phinehas: Gershom.
From the family of Ithamar: Daniel.
From the family of David: Hattush, a descendant of Shecaniah.
From the family of Parosh: Zechariah and 150 other men were registered.
From the family of Pahath-moab: Eliehoenai son of Zerahiah and 200 other men.
From the family of Zattu: Shecaniah son of Jahaziel and 300 other men.
From the family of Adin: Ebed son of Jonathan and 50 other men.
From the family of Elam: Jeshaiah son of Athaliah and 70 other men.
From the family of Shephatiah: Zebadiah son of Michael and 80 other men.
From the family of Joab: Obadiah son of Jehiel and 218 other men.
From the family of Bani: Shelomith son of Josiphiah and 160 other men.
From the family of Bebai: Zechariah son of Bebai and 28 other men.
From the family of Azgad: Johanan son of Hakkatan and 110 other men.
From the family of Adonikam, who came later: Eliphelet, Jeuel, Shemaiah, and 60 other men.
From the family of Bigvai: Uthai, Zaccur, and 70 other men.

I assembled the exiles at the Ahava Canal, and we camped there for three days while I went over the lists of the people and the priests who had arrived. I found that not one Levite had volunteered to come along. So I sent for Eliezer, Ariel, Shemaiah, Elnathan, Jarib, Elnathan, Nathan, Zechariah, and Meshullam, who were leaders of the people. I also sent for Joiarib and Elnathan, who were men of discernment. I sent them to Iddo, the leader of the Levites at Casiphia, to ask him and his relatives and the Temple servants to send us ministers for the Temple of God at Jerusalem.

Since the gracious hand of our God was on us, they sent us a man named Sherebiah, along with eighteen of his sons and brothers. He was a very astute man and a descendant of Mahli, who was a descendant of Levi son of Israel. They also sent Hashabiah, together with Jeshaiah from the descendants of Merari, and twenty of his sons and brothers, and 220 Temple servants. The Temple servants were assistants to the Levites—a group of Temple workers first instituted by King David and his officials. They were all listed by name.

And there by the Ahava Canal, I gave orders for all of us to fast and humble ourselves before our God. We prayed that he would give us a safe journey and protect us, our children, and our goods as we traveled. For I was ashamed to ask the king for soldiers and horsemen to accompany us and protect us from enemies along the way. After all, we had told the king, "Our God's hand of protection is on all who worship him, but his fierce anger rages against those who abandon him." So we fasted and earnestly prayed that our God would take care of us, and he heard our prayer.

I appointed twelve leaders of the priests—Sherebiah, Hashabiah, and ten other priests—to be in charge of transporting the silver, the gold, the gold bowls, and the other items that the king, his council, his officials, and all the people of Israel had presented for the Temple of God. I weighed the treasure as I gave it to them and found the totals to be as follows:

24 tons of silver,
7,500 pounds of silver articles,
7,500 pounds of gold,
20 gold bowls, equal in value to 1,000 gold coins,
2 fine articles of polished bronze, as precious as gold.

And I said to these priests, "You and these treasures have been set apart as holy to the LORD. This silver and gold is a voluntary offering to the LORD, the God of our ancestors. Guard these treasures well until you present them to the leading priests, the Levites, and the leaders of Israel, who will weigh them at the storerooms of the LORD's Temple in Jerusalem." So the priests and the Levites accepted the task of transporting these treasures of silver and gold to the Temple of our God in Jerusalem.

We broke camp at the Ahava Canal on April 19 and started off to Jerusalem. And the gracious hand of our God protected us and saved us from enemies and bandits along the way. So we arrived safely in Jerusalem, where we rested for three days.

On the fourth day after our arrival, the silver, gold, and other valuables were weighed at the Temple of our God and entrusted to Meremoth son of Uriah the priest and to Eleazar son of Phinehas, along with Jozabad son of Jeshua and Noadiah son of Binnui—both of whom were Levites. Everything was accounted for by number and weight, and the total weight was officially recorded.

Then the exiles who had come out of captivity sacrificed burnt offerings to the God of Israel. They presented twelve bulls for all the people of Israel, as well as ninety-six rams and seventy-seven male lambs. They also offered twelve male goats as a sin offering. All this was given as a burnt offering to the LORD. The king's decrees were delivered to his highest officers and the governors of the province west of the Euphrates River, who then cooperated by supporting the people and the Temple of God.

+

When these things had been done, the Jewish leaders came to me and said, "Many of the people of Israel, and even some of the priests and Levites, have not kept themselves separate from the other peoples living in the land. They have taken up the detestable practices of the Canaanites, Hittites, Perizzites, Jebusites, Ammonites, Moabites, Egyptians, and Amorites. For the men of Israel have married women from these people and have taken them as wives for their sons. So the holy race has become polluted by these mixed marriages. Worse yet, the leaders and officials have led the way in this outrage."

When I heard this, I tore my cloak and my shirt, pulled hair from my head and beard, and sat down utterly shocked. Then all who trembled at the words of the God of Israel came and sat with me because of this outrage committed by the returned exiles. And I sat there utterly appalled until the time of the evening sacrifice.

At the time of the sacrifice, I stood up from where I had sat in mourning with my clothes torn. I fell to my knees and lifted my hands to the LORD my God. I prayed,

"O my God, I am utterly ashamed; I blush to lift up my face to you.
For our sins are piled higher than our heads, and our guilt has reached
to the heavens. From the days of our ancestors until now, we have
been steeped in sin. That is why we and our kings and our priests have
been at the mercy of the pagan kings of the land. We have been killed,
captured, robbed, and disgraced, just as we are today.

"But now we have been given a brief moment of grace, for the LORD
our God has allowed a few of us to survive as a remnant. He has given
us security in this holy place. Our God has brightened our eyes and
granted us some relief from our slavery. For we were slaves, but in his

unfailing love our God did not abandon us in our slavery. Instead, he caused the kings of Persia to treat us favorably. He revived us so we could rebuild the Temple of our God and repair its ruins. He has given us a protective wall in Judah and Jerusalem.

"And now, O our God, what can we say after all of this? For once again we have abandoned your commands! Your servants the prophets warned us when they said, 'The land you are entering to possess is totally defiled by the detestable practices of the people living there. From one end to the other, the land is filled with corruption. Don't let your daughters marry their sons! Don't take their daughters as wives for your sons. Don't ever promote the peace and prosperity of those nations. If you follow these instructions, you will be strong and will enjoy the good things the land produces, and you will leave this prosperity to your children forever.'

"Now we are being punished because of our wickedness and our great guilt. But we have actually been punished far less than we deserve, for you, our God, have allowed some of us to survive as a remnant. But even so, we are again breaking your commands and intermarrying with people who do these detestable things. Won't your anger be enough to destroy us, so that even this little remnant no longer survives? O LORD, God of Israel, you are just. We come before you in our guilt as nothing but an escaped remnant, though in such a condition none of us can stand in your presence."

While Ezra prayed and made this confession, weeping and lying face down on the ground in front of the Temple of God, a very large crowd of people from Israel—men, women, and children—gathered and wept bitterly with him. Then Shecaniah son of Jehiel, a descendant of Elam, said to Ezra, "We have been unfaithful to our God, for we have married these pagan women of the land. But in spite of this there is hope for Israel. Let us now make a covenant with our God to divorce our pagan wives and to send them away with their children. We will follow the advice given by you and by the others who respect the commands of our God. Let it be done according to the Law of God. Get up, for it is your duty to tell us how to proceed in setting things straight. We are behind you, so be strong and take action."

So Ezra stood up and demanded that the leaders of the priests and the Levites and all the people of Israel swear that they would do as Shecaniah had said. And they all swore a solemn oath. Then Ezra left the front of the Temple of God and went to the room of Jehohanan son of Eliashib. He spent the night there without eating or drinking anything. He was still in mourning because of the unfaithfulness of the returned exiles.

Then a proclamation was made throughout Judah and Jerusalem that all the exiles should come to Jerusalem. Those who failed to come within three days would, if the leaders and elders so decided, forfeit all their property and be expelled from the assembly of the exiles.

Within three days, all the people of Judah and Benjamin had gathered in Jerusalem. This took place on December 19, and all the people were sitting in the square before the Temple of God. They were trembling both because of the seriousness of the matter and because it was raining. Then Ezra the priest stood and said to them: "You have committed a terrible sin. By marrying pagan women, you have increased Israel's guilt. So now confess your sin to the LORD, the God of your ancestors, and do what he demands. Separate yourselves from the people of the land and from these pagan women."

Then the whole assembly raised their voices and answered, "Yes, you are right; we must do as you say!" Then they added, "This isn't something that can be done in a day or two, for many of us are involved in this extremely sinful affair. And this is the rainy season, so we cannot stay out here much longer. Let our leaders act on behalf of us all. Let everyone who has a pagan wife come at a scheduled time, accompanied by the leaders and judges of his city, so that the fierce anger of our God concerning this affair may be turned away from us."

Only Jonathan son of Asahel and Jahzeiah son of Tikvah opposed this course of action, and they were supported by Meshullam and Shabbethai the Levite.

So this was the plan they followed. Ezra selected leaders to represent their families, designating each of the representatives by name. On December 29, the leaders sat down to investigate the matter. By March 27, the first day of the new year, they had finished dealing with all the men who had married pagan wives.

These are the priests who had married pagan wives:
From the family of Jeshua son of Jehozadak and his brothers: Maaseiah, Eliezer, Jarib, and Gedaliah. They vowed to divorce their wives, and they each acknowledged their guilt by offering a ram as a guilt offering.
From the family of Immer: Hanani and Zebadiah.
From the family of Harim: Maaseiah, Elijah, Shemaiah, Jehiel, and Uzziah.
From the family of Pashhur: Elioenai, Maaseiah, Ishmael, Nethanel, Jozabad, and Elasah.

These are the Levites who were guilty: Jozabad, Shimei, Kelaiah (also called Kelita), Pethahiah, Judah, and Eliezer.

This is the singer who was guilty: Eliashib.

These are the gatekeepers who were guilty: Shallum, Telem, and Uri.

These are the other people of Israel who were guilty:
From the family of Parosh: Ramiah, Izziah, Malkijah, Mijamin, Eleazar, Hashabiah, and Benaiah.
From the family of Elam: Mattaniah, Zechariah, Jehiel, Abdi, Jeremoth, and Elijah.
From the family of Zattu: Elioenai, Eliashib, Mattaniah, Jeremoth, Zabad, and Aziza.
From the family of Bebai: Jehohanan, Hananiah, Zabbai, and Athlai.
From the family of Bani: Meshullam, Malluch, Adaiah, Jashub, Sheal, and Jeremoth.
From the family of Pahath-moab: Adna, Kelal, Benaiah, Maaseiah, Mattaniah, Bezalel, Binnui, and Manasseh.
From the family of Harim: Eliezer, Ishijah, Malkijah, Shemaiah, Shimeon, Benjamin, Malluch, and Shemariah.
From the family of Hashum: Mattenai, Mattattah, Zabad, Eliphelet, Jeremai, Manasseh, and Shimei.
From the family of Bani: Maadai, Amram, Uel, Benaiah, Bedeiah, Keluhi, Vaniah, Meremoth, Eliashib, Mattaniah, Mattenai, and Jaasu.
From the family of Binnui: Shimei, Shelemiah, Nathan, Adaiah, Macnadebai, Shashai, Sharai, Azarel, Shelemiah, Shemariah, Shallum, Amariah, and Joseph.
From the family of Nebo: Jeiel, Mattithiah, Zabad, Zebina, Jaddai, Joel, and Benaiah.

Each of these men had a pagan wife, and some even had children by these wives.

+ + +

These are the memoirs of Nehemiah son of Hacaliah.

In late autumn, in the month of Kislev, in the twentieth year of King Artaxerxes' reign, I was at the fortress of Susa. Hanani, one of my brothers, came to visit me with some other men who had just arrived from Judah. I asked them about the Jews who had returned there from captivity and about how things were going in Jerusalem.

They said to me, "Things are not going well for those who returned to the province of Judah. They are in great trouble and disgrace. The wall of Jerusalem has been torn down, and the gates have been destroyed by fire."

When I heard this, I sat down and wept. In fact, for days I mourned, fasted, and prayed to the God of heaven. Then I said,

"O Lord, God of heaven, the great and awesome God who keeps his covenant of unfailing love with those who love him and obey his commands, listen to my prayer! Look down and see me praying night and day for your people Israel. I confess that we have sinned against you. Yes, even my own family and I have sinned! We have sinned terribly by not obeying the commands, decrees, and regulations that you gave us through your servant Moses.

"Please remember what you told your servant Moses: 'If you are unfaithful to me, I will scatter you among the nations. But if you return to me and obey my commands and live by them, then even if you are exiled to the ends of the earth, I will bring you back to the place I have chosen for my name to be honored.'

"The people you rescued by your great power and strong hand are your servants. O Lord, please hear my prayer! Listen to the prayers of those of us who delight in honoring you. Please grant me success today by making the king favorable to me. Put it into his heart to be kind to me."

In those days I was the king's cup-bearer.

Early the following spring, in the month of Nisan, during the twentieth year of King Artaxerxes' reign, I was serving the king his wine. I had never before appeared sad in his presence. So the king asked me, "Why are you looking so sad? You don't look sick to me. You must be deeply troubled."

Then I was terrified, but I replied, "Long live the king! How can I not be sad? For the city where my ancestors are buried is in ruins, and the gates have been destroyed by fire."

The king asked, "Well, how can I help you?"

With a prayer to the God of heaven, I replied, "If it please the king, and if you are pleased with me, your servant, send me to Judah to rebuild the city where my ancestors are buried."

The king, with the queen sitting beside him, asked, "How long will you be gone? When will you return?" After I told him how long I would be gone, the king agreed to my request.

I also said to the king, "If it please the king, let me have letters addressed to the governors of the province west of the Euphrates River, instructing them to let me travel safely through their territories on my way to Judah. And please give me a letter addressed to Asaph, the manager of the king's forest, instructing him to give me timber. I will need it to make beams for the gates of the Temple fortress, for the city walls, and for a house for myself." And the king granted these requests, because the gracious hand of God was on me.

When I came to the governors of the province west of the Euphrates River, I delivered the king's letters to them. The king, I should add, had sent along army officers and horsemen to protect me. But when Sanballat the Horonite and Tobiah the Ammonite official heard of my arrival, they were very displeased that someone had come to help the people of Israel.

+

So I arrived in Jerusalem. Three days later, I slipped out during the night, taking only a few others with me. I had not told anyone about the plans God had put in my heart for Jerusalem. We took no pack animals with us except the donkey I was riding. After dark I went out through the Valley Gate, past the Jackal's Well, and over to the Dung Gate to inspect the broken walls and burned gates. Then I went to the Fountain Gate and to the King's Pool, but my donkey couldn't get through the rubble. So, though it was still dark, I went up the Kidron Valley instead, inspecting the wall before I turned back and entered again at the Valley Gate.

The city officials did not know I had been out there or what I was doing, for I had not yet said anything to anyone about my plans. I had not yet spoken to the Jewish leaders—the priests, the nobles, the officials, or anyone else in the administration. But now I said to them, "You know very well what trouble we are in. Jerusalem lies in ruins, and its gates have been destroyed by fire. Let us rebuild the wall of Jerusalem and end this disgrace!" Then I told them about how the gracious hand of God had been on me, and about my conversation with the king.

They replied at once, "Yes, let's rebuild the wall!" So they began the good work.

But when Sanballat, Tobiah, and Geshem the Arab heard of our plan, they scoffed contemptuously. "What are you doing? Are you rebelling against the king?" they asked.

I replied, "The God of heaven will help us succeed. We, his servants, will start rebuilding this wall. But you have no share, legal right, or historic claim in Jerusalem."

Then Eliashib the high priest and the other priests started to rebuild at the Sheep Gate. They dedicated it and set up its doors, building the wall as far as the Tower of the Hundred, which they dedicated, and the Tower of Hananel. People from the town of Jericho worked next to them, and beyond them was Zaccur son of Imri.

The Fish Gate was built by the sons of Hassenaah. They laid the beams, set up its doors, and installed its bolts and bars. Meremoth son of Uriah and grandson of Hakkoz repaired the next section of wall. Beside him were Meshullam son of Berekiah and grandson of Meshezabel, and then Zadok son of Baana. Next were the people from Tekoa, though their leaders refused to work with the construction supervisors.

The Old City Gate was repaired by Joiada son of Paseah and Meshullam son of Besodeiah. They laid the beams, set up its doors, and installed its bolts and bars. Next to them were Melatiah from Gibeon, Jadon from Meronoth, people from Gibeon, and people from Mizpah, the headquarters of the governor of the province west of the Euphrates River. Next was Uzziel son of Harhaiah, a goldsmith by trade, who also worked on the wall. Beyond him was Hananiah, a manufacturer of perfumes. They left out a section of Jerusalem as they built the Broad Wall.

Rephaiah son of Hur, the leader of half the district of Jerusalem, was next to them on the wall. Next Jedaiah son of Harumaph repaired the wall across from his own house, and next to him was Hattush son of Hashabneiah. Then came Malkijah son of Harim and Hasshub son of Pahath-moab, who repaired another section of the wall and the Tower of the Ovens. Shallum son of Hallohesh and his daughters repaired the next section. He was the leader of the other half of the district of Jerusalem.

The Valley Gate was repaired by the people from Zanoah, led by Hanun. They set up its doors and installed its bolts and bars. They also repaired the 1,500 feet of wall to the Dung Gate.

The Dung Gate was repaired by Malkijah son of Recab, the leader of the Beth-hakkerem district. He rebuilt it, set up its doors, and installed its bolts and bars.

The Fountain Gate was repaired by Shallum son of Col-hozeh, the leader of the Mizpah district. He rebuilt it, roofed it, set up its doors, and installed its bolts and bars. Then he repaired the wall of the pool of Siloam near the king's garden, and he rebuilt the wall as far as the stairs that descend from the City of David. Next to him was Nehemiah son of Azbuk, the leader of half the district of Beth-zur. He rebuilt the wall from a place across from the tombs of David's family as far as the water reservoir and the House of the Warriors.

Next to him, repairs were made by a group of Levites working under the supervision of Rehum son of Bani. Then came Hashabiah, the leader of half the district of Keilah, who supervised the building of the wall on behalf of his own district. Next down the line were his countrymen led by Binnui son of Henadad, the leader of the other half of the district of Keilah.

Next to them, Ezer son of Jeshua, the leader of Mizpah, repaired another section of wall across from the ascent to the armory near the angle in the wall. Next to him was Baruch son of Zabbai, who zealously repaired an additional section from the angle to the door of the house of Eliashib the high priest. Meremoth son of Uriah and grandson of Hakkoz rebuilt another section of the wall extending from the door of Eliashib's house to the end of the house.

The next repairs were made by the priests from the surrounding region. After them, Benjamin and Hasshub repaired the section across from their house, and Azariah son of Maaseiah and grandson of Ananiah repaired the section across from his house. Next was Binnui son of Henadad, who rebuilt another section of the wall from Azariah's house to the angle and the corner. Palal son of Uzai carried on the work from a point opposite the angle and the tower that projects up from the king's upper house beside the court of the guard. Next to him were Pedaiah son of Parosh, with the Temple servants living on the hill of Ophel, who repaired the wall as far as a point across from the Water Gate to the east and the projecting tower. Then came the people of Tekoa, who repaired another section across from the great projecting tower and over to the wall of Ophel.

Above the Horse Gate, the priests repaired the wall. Each one repaired the section immediately across from his own house. Next Zadok son of Immer also rebuilt the wall across from his own house, and beyond him was Shemaiah son of Shecaniah, the gatekeeper of the East Gate. Next Hananiah son of Shelemiah and Hanun, the sixth son of Zalaph, repaired another section, while Meshullam son of Berekiah rebuilt the wall across from where he lived. Malkijah, one of the goldsmiths, repaired the wall as far as the housing for the Temple servants and merchants, across from the Inspection Gate. Then he continued as far as the upper room at the corner. The other goldsmiths and merchants repaired the wall from that corner to the Sheep Gate.

Sanballat was very angry when he learned that we were rebuilding the wall. He flew into a rage and mocked the Jews, saying in front of his friends and the Samarian army officers, "What does this bunch of poor, feeble Jews think they're doing? Do they think they can build the wall in a single day by just offering a few sacrifices? Do they actually think they can make something of stones from a rubbish heap—and charred ones at that?"

Tobiah the Ammonite, who was standing beside him, remarked, "That stone wall would collapse if even a fox walked along the top of it!"

Then I prayed, "Hear us, our God, for we are being mocked. May their scoffing fall back on their own heads, and may they themselves become captives in a foreign land! Do not ignore their guilt. Do not blot out their sins, for they have provoked you to anger here in front of the builders."

At last the wall was completed to half its height around the entire city, for the people had worked with enthusiasm.

But when Sanballat and Tobiah and the Arabs, Ammonites, and Ashdodites heard that the work was going ahead and that the gaps in the wall of Jerusalem were being repaired, they were furious. They all made plans to come and fight against Jerusalem and throw us into confusion. But we prayed to our God and guarded the city day and night to protect ourselves.

Then the people of Judah began to complain, "The workers are getting tired, and there is so much rubble to be moved. We will never be able to build the wall by ourselves."

Meanwhile, our enemies were saying, "Before they know what's happening, we will swoop down on them and kill them and end their work."

The Jews who lived near the enemy came and told us again and again, "They will come from all directions and attack us!" So I placed armed guards behind the lowest parts of the wall in the exposed areas. I stationed the people to stand guard by families, armed with swords, spears, and bows.

Then as I looked over the situation, I called together the nobles and the rest of the people and said to them, "Don't be afraid of the enemy! Remember the Lord, who is great and glorious, and fight for your brothers, your sons, your daughters, your wives, and your homes!"

When our enemies heard that we knew of their plans and that God had frustrated them, we all returned to our work on the wall. But from then on, only half my men worked while the other half stood guard with spears, shields, bows, and coats of mail. The leaders stationed themselves behind the people of Judah who were building the wall. The laborers carried on their work with one hand supporting their load and one hand holding a weapon. All the builders had a sword belted to their side. The trumpeter stayed with me to sound the alarm.

Then I explained to the nobles and officials and all the people, "The work is very spread out, and we are widely separated from each other along the wall. When you hear the blast of the trumpet, rush to wherever it is sounding. Then our God will fight for us!"

We worked early and late, from sunrise to sunset. And half the men were always on guard. I also told everyone living outside the walls to stay in Jerusalem. That way they and their servants could help with guard duty at night and work during the day. During this time, none of us—not I, nor my relatives, nor my servants, nor the guards who were with me—ever took off our clothes. We carried our weapons with us at all times, even when we went for water.

About this time some of the men and their wives raised a cry of protest against their fellow Jews. They were saying, "We have such large families. We need more food to survive."

Others said, "We have mortgaged our fields, vineyards, and homes to get food during the famine."

And others said, "We have had to borrow money on our fields and vineyards to pay our taxes. We belong to the same family as those who are wealthy, and our children are just like theirs. Yet we must sell our children into slavery just to get enough money to live. We have already sold some of our daughters, and we are helpless to do anything about it, for our fields and vineyards are already mortgaged to others."

When I heard their complaints, I was very angry. After thinking it over, I spoke out against these nobles and officials. I told them, "You are hurting your own relatives by charging interest when they borrow money!" Then I called a public meeting to deal with the problem.

At the meeting I said to them, "We are doing all we can to redeem our Jewish relatives who have had to sell themselves to pagan foreigners, but you are selling them back into slavery again. How often must we redeem them?" And they had nothing to say in their defense.

Then I pressed further, "What you are doing is not right! Should you not walk in the fear of our God in order to avoid being mocked by enemy nations? I myself, as well as my brothers and my workers, have been lending the people money and grain, but now let us stop this business of charging interest. You must restore their fields, vineyards, olive groves, and homes to them this very day. And repay the interest you charged when you lent them money, grain, new wine, and olive oil."

They replied, "We will give back everything and demand nothing more from the people. We will do as you say." Then I called the priests and made the nobles and officials swear to do what they had promised.

I shook out the folds of my robe and said, "If you fail to keep your promise, may God shake you like this from your homes and from your property!"

The whole assembly responded, "Amen," and they praised the LORD. And the people did as they had promised.

For the entire twelve years that I was governor of Judah—from the twentieth year to the thirty-second year of the reign of King Artaxerxes— neither I nor my officials drew on our official food allowance. The former governors, in contrast, had laid heavy burdens on the people, demanding a daily ration of food and wine, besides forty pieces of silver. Even their assistants took advantage of the people. But because I feared God, I did not act that way.

I also devoted myself to working on the wall and refused to acquire any land. And I required all my servants to spend time working on the wall. I asked for nothing, even though I regularly fed 150 Jewish officials at my table, besides all the visitors from other lands! The provisions I paid for each day included one ox, six choice sheep or goats, and a large number of poultry. And every ten days we needed a large supply of all kinds of wine. Yet I refused to claim the governor's food allowance because the people already carried a heavy burden.

Remember, O my God, all that I have done for these people, and bless me for it.

Sanballat, Tobiah, Geshem the Arab, and the rest of our enemies found out that I had finished rebuilding the wall and that no gaps remained—though we had not yet set up the doors in the gates. So Sanballat and Geshem sent a message asking me to meet them at one of the villages in the plain of Ono.

But I realized they were plotting to harm me, so I replied by sending this message to them: "I am engaged in a great work, so I can't come. Why should I stop working to come and meet with you?"

Four times they sent the same message, and each time I gave the same reply. The fifth time, Sanballat's servant came with an open letter in his hand, and this is what it said:

"There is a rumor among the surrounding nations, and Geshem tells me it is true, that you and the Jews are planning to rebel and that is why you are building the wall. According to his reports, you plan to be their king. He also reports that you have appointed prophets in Jerusalem to proclaim about you, 'Look! There is a king in Judah!'

"You can be very sure that this report will get back to the king, so I suggest that you come and talk it over with me."

I replied, "There is no truth in any part of your story. You are making up the whole thing."

They were just trying to intimidate us, imagining that they could discourage us and stop the work. So I continued the work with even greater determination.

Later I went to visit Shemaiah son of Delaiah and grandson of Mehetabel, who was confined to his home. He said, "Let us meet together inside the Temple of God and bolt the doors shut. Your enemies are coming to kill you tonight."

But I replied, "Should someone in my position run from danger? Should someone in my position enter the Temple to save his life? No, I won't do it!" I realized that God had not spoken to him, but that he had uttered this prophecy against me because Tobiah and Sanballat had hired him. They were hoping to intimidate me and make me sin. Then they would be able to accuse and discredit me.

Remember, O my God, all the evil things that Tobiah and Sanballat have done. And remember Noadiah the prophet and all the prophets like her who have tried to intimidate me.

So on October 2 the wall was finished—just fifty-two days after we had begun. When our enemies and the surrounding nations heard about it, they were frightened and humiliated. They realized this work had been done with the help of our God.

During those fifty-two days, many letters went back and forth between Tobiah and the nobles of Judah. For many in Judah had sworn allegiance to him because his father-in-law was Shecaniah son of Arah, and his son Jehohanan was married to the daughter of Meshullam son of Berekiah. They kept telling me about Tobiah's good deeds, and then they told him everything I said. And Tobiah kept sending threatening letters to intimidate me.

After the wall was finished and I had set up the doors in the gates, the gatekeepers, singers, and Levites were appointed. I gave the responsibility of governing Jerusalem to my brother Hanani, along with Hananiah, the commander of the fortress, for he was a faithful man who feared God more than most. I said to them, "Do not leave the gates open during the hottest part of the day. And even while the gatekeepers are on duty, have them shut and bar the doors. Appoint the residents of Jerusalem to act as guards, everyone on a regular watch. Some will serve at sentry posts and some in front of their own homes."

At that time the city was large and spacious, but the population was small, and none of the houses had been rebuilt. So my God gave me the idea to call together all the nobles and leaders of the city, along with the ordinary citizens, for registration. I had found the genealogical record of those who had first returned to Judah. This is what was written there:

Here is the list of the Jewish exiles of the provinces who returned from their captivity. King Nebuchadnezzar had deported them to Babylon, but now they returned to Jerusalem and the other towns in Judah where they originally lived. Their leaders were Zerubbabel, Jeshua, Nehemiah, Seraiah, Reelaiah, Nahamani, Mordecai, Bilshan, Mispar, Bigvai, Rehum, and Baanah.

This is the number of the men of Israel who returned from exile:
The family of Parosh..2,172

The family of Shephatiah 372
The family of Arah 652
The family of Pahath-moab (descendants of Jeshua
    and Joab) 2,818
The family of Elam 1,254
The family of Zattu...845
The family of Zaccai..760
The family of Bani...648
The family of Bebai...628
The family of Azgad 2,322
The family of Adonikam.....................................667
The family of Bigvai 2,067
The family of Adin 655
The family of Ater (descendants of Hezekiah) 98
The family of Hashum.......................................328
The family of Bezai..324
The family of Jorah 112
The family of Gibbar 95
The people of Bethlehem and Netophah 188
The people of Anathoth 128
The people of Beth-azmaveth 42
The people of Kiriath-jearim, Kephirah, and Beeroth...........743
The people of Ramah and Geba 621
The people of Micmash.....................................122
The people of Bethel and Ai................................123
The people of West Nebo 52
The citizens of West Elam..................................1,254
The citizens of Harim......................................320
The citizens of Jericho 345
The citizens of Lod, Hadid, and Ono 721
The citizens of Senaah 3,930

These are the priests who returned from exile:
The family of Jedaiah (through the line of Jeshua) 973
The family of Immer..1,052
The family of Pashhur 1,247
The family of Harim..1,017

These are the Levites who returned from exile:
The families of Jeshua and Kadmiel (descendants of Hodaviah). . 74
The singers of the family of Asaph 148
The gatekeepers of the families of Shallum, Ater, Talmon, Akkub,
    Hatita, and Shobai.......................................138

The descendants of the following Temple servants returned from exile:
Ziha, Hasupha, Tabbaoth,
Keros, Siaha, Padon,
Lebanah, Hagabah, Shalmai,
Hanan, Giddel, Gahar,
Reaiah, Rezin, Nekoda,
Gazzam, Uzza, Paseah,
Besai, Meunim, Nephusim,
Bakbuk, Hakupha, Harhur,
Bazluth, Mehida, Harsha,
Barkos, Sisera, Temah,
Neziah, and Hatipha.

The descendants of these servants of King Solomon returned from exile:
Sotai, Hassophereth, Peruda,
Jaalah, Darkon, Giddel,
Shephatiah, Hattil, Pokereth-hazzebaim, and Ami.

In all, the Temple servants and the descendants of Solomon's servants numbered 392.

Another group returned at this time from the towns of Tel-melah, Tel-harsha, Kerub, Addan, and Immer. However, they could not prove that they or their families were descendants of Israel. This group included the families of Delaiah, Tobiah, and Nekoda—a total of 642 people.

Three families of priests—Hobaiah, Hakkoz, and Barzillai—also returned. (This Barzillai had married a woman who was a descendant of Barzillai of Gilead, and he had taken her family name.) They searched for their names in the genealogical records, but they were not found, so they were disqualified from serving as priests. The governor told them not to eat the priests' share of food from the sacrifices until a priest could consult the LORD about the matter by using the Urim and Thummim—the sacred lots.

So a total of 42,360 people returned to Judah, in addition to 7,337 servants and 245 singers, both men and women. They took with them 736 horses, 245 mules, 435 camels, and 6,720 donkeys.

Some of the family leaders gave gifts for the work. The governor gave to the treasury 1,000 gold coins, 50 gold basins, and 530 robes for the priests. The other leaders gave to the treasury a total of 20,000 gold coins and some 2,750 pounds of silver for the work. The rest of the people gave 20,000 gold coins, about 2,500 pounds of silver, and 67 robes for the priests.

So the priests, the Levites, the gatekeepers, the singers, the Temple servants, and some of the common people settled near Jerusalem. The rest of the people returned to their own towns throughout Israel.

+ + +

In October, when the Israelites had settled in their towns, all the people assembled with a unified purpose at the square just inside the Water Gate. They asked Ezra the scribe to bring out the Book of the Law of Moses, which the LORD had given for Israel to obey.

So on October 8 Ezra the priest brought the Book of the Law before the assembly, which included the men and women and all the children old enough to understand. He faced the square just inside the Water Gate from early morning until noon and read aloud to everyone who could understand. All the people listened closely to the Book of the Law.

Ezra the scribe stood on a high wooden platform that had been made for the occasion. To his right stood Mattithiah, Shema, Anaiah, Uriah, Hilkiah, and Maaseiah. To his left stood Pedaiah, Mishael, Malkijah, Hashum, Hashbaddanah, Zechariah, and Meshullam. Ezra stood on the platform in full view of all the people. When they saw him open the book, they all rose to their feet.

Then Ezra praised the LORD, the great God, and all the people chanted, "Amen! Amen!" as they lifted their hands. Then they bowed down and worshiped the LORD with their faces to the ground.

The Levites—Jeshua, Bani, Sherebiah, Jamin, Akkub, Shabbethai, Hodiah, Maaseiah, Kelita, Azariah, Jozabad, Hanan, and Pelaiah—then instructed the people in the Law while everyone remained in their places. They read from the Book of the Law of God and clearly explained the meaning of what was being read, helping the people understand each passage.

Then Nehemiah the governor, Ezra the priest and scribe, and the Levites who were interpreting for the people said to them, "Don't mourn or weep on such a day as this! For today is a sacred day before the LORD your God." For the people had all been weeping as they listened to the words of the Law.

And Nehemiah continued, "Go and celebrate with a feast of rich foods and sweet drinks, and share gifts of food with people who have nothing prepared. This is a sacred day before our Lord. Don't be dejected and sad, for the joy of the LORD is your strength!"

And the Levites, too, quieted the people, telling them, "Hush! Don't weep! For this is a sacred day." So the people went away to eat and drink at a festive meal, to share gifts of food, and to celebrate with great joy because they had heard God's words and understood them.

On October 9 the family leaders of all the people, together with the priests and Levites, met with Ezra the scribe to go over the Law in greater detail. As they studied the Law, they discovered that the LORD had commanded through Moses that the Israelites should live in shelters during the festival to be held that month. He had said that a proclamation should be made throughout their towns and in Jerusalem, telling the people to go to the hills to get branches from olive, wild olive, myrtle, palm, and other leafy trees. They were to use these branches to make shelters in which they would live during the festival, as prescribed in the Law.

So the people went out and cut branches and used them to build shelters on the roofs of their houses, in their courtyards, in the courtyards of God's Temple, or in the squares just inside the Water Gate and the Ephraim Gate. So everyone who had returned from captivity lived in these shelters during the festival, and they were all filled with great joy! The Israelites had not celebrated like this since the days of Joshua son of Nun.

Ezra read from the Book of the Law of God on each of the seven days of the festival. Then on the eighth day they held a solemn assembly, as was required by law.

On October 31 the people assembled again, and this time they fasted and dressed in burlap and sprinkled dust on their heads. Those of Israelite descent separated themselves from all foreigners as they confessed their own sins and the sins of their ancestors. They remained standing in place for three hours while the Book of the Law of the LORD their God was read aloud to them. Then for three more hours they confessed their sins and worshiped the LORD their God. The Levites—Jeshua, Bani, Kadmiel, Shebaniah, Bunni, Sherebiah, Bani, and Kenani—stood on the stairway of the Levites and cried out to the LORD their God with loud voices.

Then the leaders of the Levites—Jeshua, Kadmiel, Bani, Hashabneiah, Sherebiah, Hodiah, Shebaniah, and Pethahiah—called out to the people: "Stand up and praise the LORD your God, for he lives from everlasting to everlasting!" Then they prayed:

"May your glorious name be praised! May it be exalted above all blessing and praise!

"You alone are the LORD. You made the skies and the heavens and all the stars. You made the earth and the seas and everything in them. You preserve them all, and the angels of heaven worship you.

"You are the LORD God, who chose Abram and brought him from Ur of the Chaldeans and renamed him Abraham. When he had proved himself faithful, you made a covenant with him to give him and his descendants the land of the Canaanites, Hittites, Amorites, Perizzites,

Jebusites, and Girgashites. And you have done what you promised, for you are always true to your word.

"You saw the misery of our ancestors in Egypt, and you heard their cries from beside the Red Sea. You displayed miraculous signs and wonders against Pharaoh, his officials, and all his people, for you knew how arrogantly they were treating our ancestors. You have a glorious reputation that has never been forgotten. You divided the sea for your people so they could walk through on dry land! And then you hurled their enemies into the depths of the sea. They sank like stones beneath the mighty waters. You led our ancestors by a pillar of cloud during the day and a pillar of fire at night so that they could find their way.

"You came down at Mount Sinai and spoke to them from heaven. You gave them regulations and instructions that were just, and decrees and commands that were good. You instructed them concerning your holy Sabbath. And you commanded them, through Moses your servant, to obey all your commands, decrees, and instructions.

"You gave them bread from heaven when they were hungry and water from the rock when they were thirsty. You commanded them to go and take possession of the land you had sworn to give them.

"But our ancestors were proud and stubborn, and they paid no attention to your commands. They refused to obey and did not remember the miracles you had done for them. Instead, they became stubborn and appointed a leader to take them back to their slavery in Egypt. But you are a God of forgiveness, gracious and merciful, slow to become angry, and rich in unfailing love. You did not abandon them, even when they made an idol shaped like a calf and said, 'This is your god who brought you out of Egypt!' They committed terrible blasphemies.

"But in your great mercy you did not abandon them to die in the wilderness. The pillar of cloud still led them forward by day, and the pillar of fire showed them the way through the night. You sent your good Spirit to instruct them, and you did not stop giving them manna from heaven or water for their thirst. For forty years you sustained them in the wilderness, and they lacked nothing. Their clothes did not wear out, and their feet did not swell!

"Then you helped our ancestors conquer kingdoms and nations, and you placed your people in every corner of the land. They took over the land of King Sihon of Heshbon and the land of King Og of Bashan. You made their descendants as numerous as the stars in the sky and brought them into the land you had promised to their ancestors.

"They went in and took possession of the land. You subdued whole nations before them. Even the Canaanites, who inhabited the land, were powerless! Your people could deal with these nations and their kings as they pleased. Our ancestors captured fortified cities and fertile land. They took over houses full of good things, with cisterns already dug and vineyards and olive groves and fruit trees in abundance. So they ate until they were full and grew fat and enjoyed themselves in all your blessings.

"But despite all this, they were disobedient and rebelled against you. They turned their backs on your Law, they killed your prophets who warned them to return to you, and they committed terrible blasphemies. So you handed them over to their enemies, who made them suffer. But in their time of trouble they cried to you, and you heard them from heaven. In your great mercy, you sent them liberators who rescued them from their enemies.

"But as soon as they were at peace, your people again committed evil in your sight, and once more you let their enemies conquer them. Yet whenever your people turned and cried to you again for help, you listened once more from heaven. In your wonderful mercy, you rescued them many times!

"You warned them to return to your Law, but they became proud and obstinate and disobeyed your commands. They did not follow your regulations, by which people will find life if only they obey. They stubbornly turned their backs on you and refused to listen. In your love, you were patient with them for many years. You sent your Spirit, who warned them through the prophets. But still they wouldn't listen! So once again you allowed the peoples of the land to conquer them. But in your great mercy, you did not destroy them completely or abandon them forever. What a gracious and merciful God you are!

"And now, our God, the great and mighty and awesome God, who keeps his covenant of unfailing love, do not let all the hardships we have suffered seem insignificant to you. Great trouble has come upon us and upon our kings and leaders and priests and prophets and ancestors—all of your people—from the days when the kings of Assyria first triumphed over us until now. Every time you punished us you were being just. We have sinned greatly, and you gave us only what we deserved. Our kings, leaders, priests, and ancestors did not obey your Law or listen to the warnings in your commands and laws. Even while they had their own kingdom, they did not serve you, though you showered your goodness on them. You gave them a large, fertile land, but they refused to turn from their wickedness.

"So now today we are slaves in the land of plenty that you gave our ancestors for their enjoyment! We are slaves here in this good land. The lush produce of this land piles up in the hands of the kings whom you have set over us because of our sins. They have power over us and our livestock. We serve them at their pleasure, and we are in great misery."

The people responded, "In view of all this, we are making a solemn promise and putting it in writing. On this sealed document are the names of our leaders and Levites and priests."

The document was ratified and sealed with the following names:

The governor:
   Nehemiah son of Hacaliah, and also Zedekiah.
The following priests:
   Seraiah, Azariah, Jeremiah, Pashhur, Amariah, Malkijah, Hattush, Shebaniah, Malluch, Harim, Meremoth, Obadiah, Daniel, Ginnethon, Baruch, Meshullam, Abijah, Mijamin, Maaziah, Bilgai, and Shemaiah. These were the priests.
The following Levites:
   Jeshua son of Azaniah, Binnui from the family of Henadad, Kadmiel, and their fellow Levites: Shebaniah, Hodiah, Kelita, Pelaiah, Hanan, Mica, Rehob, Hashabiah, Zaccur, Sherebiah, Shebaniah, Hodiah, Bani, and Beninu.
The following leaders:
   Parosh, Pahath-moab, Elam, Zattu, Bani, Bunni, Azgad, Bebai, Adonijah, Bigvai, Adin, Ater, Hezekiah, Azzur, Hodiah, Hashum, Bezai, Hariph, Anathoth, Nebai, Magpiash, Meshullam, Hezir, Meshezabel, Zadok, Jaddua, Pelatiah, Hanan, Anaiah, Hoshea, Hananiah, Hasshub, Hallohesh, Pilha, Shobek, Rehum, Hashabnah, Maaseiah, Ahiah, Hanan, Anan, Malluch, Harim, and Baanah.

Then the rest of the people—the priests, Levites, gatekeepers, singers, Temple servants, and all who had separated themselves from the pagan people of the land in order to obey the Law of God, together with their wives, sons, daughters, and all who were old enough to understand— joined their leaders and bound themselves with an oath. They swore a curse on themselves if they failed to obey the Law of God as issued by his servant Moses. They solemnly promised to carefully follow all the commands, regulations, and decrees of the LORD our Lord:

"We promise not to let our daughters marry the pagan people of the land, and not to let our sons marry their daughters.
   "We also promise that if the people of the land should bring any merchandise or grain to be sold on the Sabbath or on any other holy

day, we will refuse to buy it. Every seventh year we will let our land rest, and we will cancel all debts owed to us.

"In addition, we promise to obey the command to pay the annual Temple tax of one-eighth of an ounce of silver for the care of the Temple of our God. This will provide for the Bread of the Presence; for the regular grain offerings and burnt offerings; for the offerings on the Sabbaths, the new moon celebrations, and the annual festivals; for the holy offerings; and for the sin offerings to make atonement for Israel. It will provide for everything necessary for the work of the Temple of our God.

"We have cast sacred lots to determine when—at regular times each year—the families of the priests, Levites, and the common people should bring wood to God's Temple to be burned on the altar of the LORD our God, as is written in the Law.

"We promise to bring the first part of every harvest to the LORD's Temple year after year—whether it be a crop from the soil or from our fruit trees. We agree to give God our oldest sons and the firstborn of all our herds and flocks, as prescribed in the Law. We will present them to the priests who minister in the Temple of our God. We will store the produce in the storerooms of the Temple of our God. We will bring the best of our flour and other grain offerings, the best of our fruit, and the best of our new wine and olive oil. And we promise to bring to the Levites a tenth of everything our land produces, for it is the Levites who collect the tithes in all our rural towns.

"A priest—a descendant of Aaron—will be with the Levites as they receive these tithes. And a tenth of all that is collected as tithes will be delivered by the Levites to the Temple of our God and placed in the storerooms. The people and the Levites must bring these offerings of grain, new wine, and olive oil to the storerooms and place them in the sacred containers near the ministering priests, the gatekeepers, and the singers.

"We promise together not to neglect the Temple of our God."

The leaders of the people were living in Jerusalem, the holy city. A tenth of the people from the other towns of Judah and Benjamin were chosen by sacred lots to live there, too, while the rest stayed where they were. And the people commended everyone who volunteered to resettle in Jerusalem.

Here is a list of the names of the provincial officials who came to live in Jerusalem. (Most of the people, priests, Levites, Temple servants, and descendants of Solomon's servants continued to live in their own homes in the various towns of Judah, but some of the people from Judah and Benjamin resettled in Jerusalem.)

From the tribe of Judah:

Athaiah son of Uzziah, son of Zechariah, son of Amariah, son of Shephatiah, son of Mahalalel, of the family of Perez. Also Maaseiah son of Baruch, son of Col-hozeh, son of Hazaiah, son of Adaiah, son of Joiarib, son of Zechariah, of the family of Shelah. There were 468 descendants of Perez who lived in Jerusalem—all outstanding men.

From the tribe of Benjamin:

Sallu son of Meshullam, son of Joed, son of Pedaiah, son of Kolaiah, son of Maaseiah, son of Ithiel, son of Jeshaiah. After him were Gabbai and Sallai and a total of 928 relatives. Their chief officer was Joel son of Zicri, who was assisted by Judah son of Hassenuah, second-in-command over the city.

From the priests:

Jedaiah son of Joiarib; Jakin; and Seraiah son of Hilkiah, son of Meshullam, son of Zadok, son of Meraioth, son of Ahitub, the supervisor of the Temple of God. Also 822 of their associates, who worked at the Temple. Also Adaiah son of Jeroham, son of Pelaliah, son of Amzi, son of Zechariah, son of Pashhur, son of Malkijah, along with 242 of his associates, who were heads of their families. Also Amashsai son of Azarel, son of Ahzai, son of Meshillemoth, son of Immer, and 128 of his outstanding associates. Their chief officer was Zabdiel son of Haggedolim.

From the Levites:

Shemaiah son of Hasshub, son of Azrikam, son of Hashabiah, son of Bunni. Also Shabbethai and Jozabad, who were in charge of the work outside the Temple of God. Also Mattaniah son of Mica, son of Zabdi, a descendant of Asaph, who led in thanksgiving and prayer. Also Bakbukiah, who was Mattaniah's assistant, and Abda son of Shammua, son of Galal, son of Jeduthun. In all, there were 284 Levites in the holy city.

From the gatekeepers:

Akkub, Talmon, and 172 of their associates, who guarded the gates.

The other priests, Levites, and the rest of the Israelites lived wherever their family inheritance was located in any of the towns of Judah. The Temple servants, however, whose leaders were Ziha and Gishpa, all lived on the hill of Ophel.

The chief officer of the Levites in Jerusalem was Uzzi son of Bani, son of Hashabiah, son of Mattaniah, son of Mica, a descendant of Asaph, whose family served as singers at God's Temple. Their daily responsibilities were carried out according to the terms of a royal command.

Pethahiah son of Meshezabel, a descendant of Zerah son of Judah, was the royal adviser in all matters of public administration.

As for the surrounding villages with their open fields, some of the people of Judah lived in Kiriath-arba with its settlements, Dibon with its settlements, and Jekabzeel with its villages. They also lived in Jeshua, Moladah, Beth-pelet, Hazar-shual, Beersheba with its settlements, Ziklag, and Meconah with its settlements. They also lived in En-rimmon, Zorah, Jarmuth, Zanoah, and Adullam with their surrounding villages. They also lived in Lachish with its nearby fields and Azekah with its surrounding villages. So the people of Judah were living all the way from Beersheba in the south to the valley of Hinnom.

Some of the people of Benjamin lived at Geba, Micmash, Aija, and Bethel with its settlements. They also lived in Anathoth, Nob, Ananiah, Hazor, Ramah, Gittaim, Hadid, Zeboim, Neballat, Lod, Ono, and the Valley of Craftsmen. Some of the Levites who lived in Judah were sent to live with the tribe of Benjamin.

Here is the list of the priests and Levites who returned with Zerubbabel son of Shealtiel and Jeshua the high priest:

> Seraiah, Jeremiah, Ezra,
> Amariah, Malluch, Hattush,
> Shecaniah, Harim, Meremoth,
> Iddo, Ginnethon, Abijah,
> Miniamin, Moadiah, Bilgah,
> Shemaiah, Joiarib, Jedaiah,
> Sallu, Amok, Hilkiah, and Jedaiah.

These were the leaders of the priests and their associates in the days of Jeshua.

The Levites who returned with them were Jeshua, Binnui, Kadmiel, Sherebiah, Judah, and Mattaniah, who with his associates was in charge of the songs of thanksgiving. Their associates, Bakbukiah and Unni, stood opposite them during the service.

> Jeshua the high priest was the father of Joiakim.
> Joiakim was the father of Eliashib.
> Eliashib was the father of Joiada.
> Joiada was the father of Johanan.
> Johanan was the father of Jaddua.

Now when Joiakim was high priest, the family leaders of the priests were as follows:

Meraiah was leader of the family of Seraiah.
Hananiah was leader of the family of Jeremiah.
Meshullam was leader of the family of Ezra.
Jehohanan was leader of the family of Amariah.
Jonathan was leader of the family of Malluch.
Joseph was leader of the family of Shecaniah.
Adna was leader of the family of Harim.
Helkai was leader of the family of Meremoth.
Zechariah was leader of the family of Iddo.
Meshullam was leader of the family of Ginnethon.
Zicri was leader of the family of Abijah.
There was also a leader of the family of Miniamin.
Piltai was leader of the family of Moadiah.
Shammua was leader of the family of Bilgah.
Jehonathan was leader of the family of Shemaiah.
Mattenai was leader of the family of Joiarib.
Uzzi was leader of the family of Jedaiah.
Kallai was leader of the family of Sallu.
Eber was leader of the family of Amok.
Hashabiah was leader of the family of Hilkiah.
Nethanel was leader of the family of Jedaiah.

A record of the Levite families was kept during the years when Eliashib, Joiada, Johanan, and Jaddua served as high priest. Another record of the priests was kept during the reign of Darius the Persian. A record of the heads of the Levite families was kept in *The Book of History* down to the days of Johanan, the grandson of Eliashib.

These were the family leaders of the Levites: Hashabiah, Sherebiah, Jeshua, Binnui, Kadmiel, and other associates, who stood opposite them during the ceremonies of praise and thanksgiving, one section responding to the other, as commanded by David, the man of God. This included Mattaniah, Bakbukiah, and Obadiah.

Meshullam, Talmon, and Akkub were the gatekeepers in charge of the storerooms at the gates. These all served in the days of Joiakim son of Jeshua, son of Jehozadak, and in the days of Nehemiah the governor and of Ezra the priest and scribe.

✛ ✛ ✛

For the dedication of the new wall of Jerusalem, the Levites throughout the land were asked to come to Jerusalem to assist in the ceremonies. They were to take part in the joyous occasion with their songs of thanksgiving and with the music of cymbals, harps, and lyres. The singers were

brought together from the region around Jerusalem and from the villages
of the Netophathites. They also came from Beth-gilgal and the rural areas
near Geba and Azmaveth, for the singers had built their own settlements
around Jerusalem. The priests and Levites first purified themselves; then
they purified the people, the gates, and the wall.

I led the leaders of Judah to the top of the wall and organized two large
choirs to give thanks. One of the choirs proceeded southward along the
top of the wall to the Dung Gate. Hoshaiah and half the leaders of Judah
followed them, along with Azariah, Ezra, Meshullam, Judah, Benjamin,
Shemaiah, and Jeremiah. Then came some priests who played trumpets,
including Zechariah son of Jonathan, son of Shemaiah, son of Mattaniah,
son of Micaiah, son of Zaccur, a descendant of Asaph. And Zechariah's
colleagues were Shemaiah, Azarel, Milalai, Gilalai, Maai, Nethanel, Judah,
and Hanani. They used the musical instruments prescribed by David, the
man of God. Ezra the scribe led this procession. At the Fountain Gate they
went straight up the steps on the ascent of the city wall toward the City of
David. They passed the house of David and then proceeded to the Water
Gate on the east.

The second choir giving thanks went northward around the other way
to meet them. I followed them, together with the other half of the people,
along the top of the wall past the Tower of the Ovens to the Broad Wall,
then past the Ephraim Gate to the Old City Gate, past the Fish Gate and
the Tower of Hananel, and on to the Tower of the Hundred. Then we
continued on to the Sheep Gate and stopped at the Guard Gate.

The two choirs that were giving thanks then proceeded to the Temple
of God, where they took their places. So did I, together with the group of
leaders who were with me. We went together with the trumpet-playing
priests—Eliakim, Maaseiah, Miniamin, Micaiah, Elioenai, Zechariah, and
Hananiah—and the singers—Maaseiah, Shemaiah, Eleazar, Uzzi, Jehohanan, Malkijah, Elam, and Ezer. They played and sang loudly under the
direction of Jezrahiah the choir director.

Many sacrifices were offered on that joyous day, for God had given the
people cause for great joy. The women and children also participated in
the celebration, and the joy of the people of Jerusalem could be heard far
away.

On that day men were appointed to be in charge of the storerooms for
the offerings, the first part of the harvest, and the tithes. They were responsible to collect from the fields outside the towns the portions required by
the Law for the priests and Levites. For all the people of Judah took joy
in the priests and Levites and their work. They performed the service of
their God and the service of purification, as commanded by David and
his son Solomon, and so did the singers and the gatekeepers. The custom

of having choir directors to lead the choirs in hymns of praise and thanksgiving to God began long ago in the days of David and Asaph. So now, in the days of Zerubbabel and of Nehemiah, all Israel brought a daily supply of food for the singers, the gatekeepers, and the Levites. The Levites, in turn, gave a portion of what they received to the priests, the descendants of Aaron.

On that same day, as the Book of Moses was being read to the people, the passage was found that said no Ammonite or Moabite should ever be permitted to enter the assembly of God. For they had not provided the Israelites with food and water in the wilderness. Instead, they hired Balaam to curse them, though our God turned the curse into a blessing. When this passage of the Law was read, all those of foreign descent were immediately excluded from the assembly.

Before this had happened, Eliashib the priest, who had been appointed as supervisor of the storerooms of the Temple of our God and who was also a relative of Tobiah, had converted a large storage room and placed it at Tobiah's disposal. The room had previously been used for storing the grain offerings, the frankincense, various articles for the Temple, and the tithes of grain, new wine, and olive oil (which were prescribed for the Levites, the singers, and the gatekeepers), as well as the offerings for the priests.

I was not in Jerusalem at that time, for I had returned to King Artaxerxes of Babylon in the thirty-second year of his reign, though I later asked his permission to return. When I arrived back in Jerusalem, I learned about Eliashib's evil deed in providing Tobiah with a room in the courtyards of the Temple of God. I became very upset and threw all of Tobiah's belongings out of the room. Then I demanded that the rooms be purified, and I brought back the articles for God's Temple, the grain offerings, and the frankincense.

I also discovered that the Levites had not been given their prescribed portions of food, so they and the singers who were to conduct the worship services had all returned to work their fields. I immediately confronted the leaders and demanded, "Why has the Temple of God been neglected?" Then I called all the Levites back again and restored them to their proper duties. And once more all the people of Judah began bringing their tithes of grain, new wine, and olive oil to the Temple storerooms.

I assigned supervisors for the storerooms: Shelemiah the priest, Zadok the scribe, and Pedaiah, one of the Levites. And I appointed Hanan son of Zaccur and grandson of Mattaniah as their assistant. These men had an excellent reputation, and it was their job to make honest distributions to their fellow Levites.

Remember this good deed, O my God, and do not forget all that I have faithfully done for the Temple of my God and its services.

In those days I saw men of Judah treading out their winepresses on the Sabbath. They were also bringing in grain, loading it on donkeys, and bringing their wine, grapes, figs, and all sorts of produce to Jerusalem to sell on the Sabbath. So I rebuked them for selling their produce on that day. Some men from Tyre, who lived in Jerusalem, were bringing in fish and all kinds of merchandise. They were selling it on the Sabbath to the people of Judah—and in Jerusalem at that!

So I confronted the nobles of Judah. "Why are you profaning the Sabbath in this evil way?" I asked. "Wasn't it just this sort of thing that your ancestors did that caused our God to bring all this trouble upon us and our city? Now you are bringing even more wrath upon Israel by permitting the Sabbath to be desecrated in this way!"

Then I commanded that the gates of Jerusalem should be shut as darkness fell every Friday evening, not to be opened until the Sabbath ended. I sent some of my own servants to guard the gates so that no merchandise could be brought in on the Sabbath day. The merchants and tradesmen with a variety of wares camped outside Jerusalem once or twice. But I spoke sharply to them and said, "What are you doing out here, camping around the wall? If you do this again, I will arrest you!" And that was the last time they came on the Sabbath. Then I commanded the Levites to purify themselves and to guard the gates in order to preserve the holiness of the Sabbath.

Remember this good deed also, O my God! Have compassion on me according to your great and unfailing love.

About the same time I realized that some of the men of Judah had married women from Ashdod, Ammon, and Moab. Furthermore, half their children spoke the language of Ashdod or of some other people and could not speak the language of Judah at all. So I confronted them and called down curses on them. I beat some of them and pulled out their hair. I made them swear in the name of God that they would not let their children intermarry with the pagan people of the land.

"Wasn't this exactly what led King Solomon of Israel into sin?" I demanded. "There was no king from any nation who could compare to him, and God loved him and made him king over all Israel. But even he was led into sin by his foreign wives. How could you even think of committing this sinful deed and acting unfaithfully toward God by marrying foreign women?"

One of the sons of Joiada son of Eliashib the high priest had married a daughter of Sanballat the Horonite, so I banished him from my presence.

Remember them, O my God, for they have defiled the priesthood and the solemn vows of the priests and Levites.

So I purged out everything foreign and assigned tasks to the priests and Levites, making certain that each knew his work. I also made sure that the supply of wood for the altar and the first portions of the harvest were brought at the proper times.

Remember this in my favor, O my God.

IMMERSED IN ESTHER

AS THE HEBREW BIBLE WAS GROWING, several small books were grouped together and named *The Five Scrolls*. These five books—Song of Songs, Ruth, Lamentations, Ecclesiastes, and Esther—were each assigned to be read at a different Jewish festival or special day of observance. The last book, Esther, was read at the festival known as Purim.

After Israel's exile in Babylon, the Jewish people made a concerted effort to renew their commitment to God and to his instructions given in the Law of Moses. Part of this commitment included faithfully observing the festivals and special days prescribed therein. However, in this postexilic period the Jews began to celebrate a brand-new festival called Purim. But what is Purim? And how could a new festival be added to those already given in the Law? The book of Esther answers these questions by telling the intriguing, fast-paced story that lies behind the celebration.

The account is set in the period of the Persian Empire (550–330 BC). Some Jews have returned to the land of Israel and are trying to rebuild a Jewish society there after the Exile. But others have remained abroad and face the challenge of crafting a distinctive identity and way of life as God's people while living in a foreign land.

The book of Esther tells the story of two courageous exiles: a beautiful young woman named Esther and Mordecai, the devout uncle who raised her after her parents' deaths. At great personal risk and aided by God's providential intervention, Esther and Mordecai stop a plot to destroy all the Jews in the Persian Empire. They turn the weapons of their enemies against them and save the Jewish people.

The whole Jewish community agreed that this was a deliverance to "be remembered and kept from generation to generation and celebrated by every family throughout the provinces and cities of the empire." Purim became a particularly joyous festival of feasting and gift-giving, highlighting the continuing gifts of life and protection. And so, the book of Esther explains, another festival was established to be kept "at the appointed time each year."

This book also gives us important insight into how biblical storytelling came to function in the community of God's people. The story of Esther contains six references to banquets: two at the beginning, two in the middle, and the two at the end that celebrate the Jewish victory. The book was very likely read during the feasting that was a regular part of the Purim festivities. So each new generation of Jews comes to relive the story as they are put right into the action.

By following this pattern of reading and rereading the Scriptures today, the ancient stories can become our stories. Through regular feasting on God's word—especially during our own festivals and celebrations of God's work in history—we can enter the drama of the Bible ourselves. We tell and retell the stories in the Bible in order to be shaped into people who play our parts well in the ongoing story of redemption.

From Esther, we learn that we too must sometimes take bold actions for the sake of others. We too must be courageous, trusting that God is providentially working, and we must be willing to confront the dominant powers of our world in creative ways. And each generation can rightly celebrate the good gifts of community and life that we receive from God.

ESTHER

———— ✠ ————

These events happened in the days of King Xerxes, who reigned over 127 provinces stretching from India to Ethiopia. At that time Xerxes ruled his empire from his royal throne at the fortress of Susa. In the third year of his reign, he gave a banquet for all his nobles and officials. He invited all the military officers of Persia and Media as well as the princes and nobles of the provinces. The celebration lasted 180 days—a tremendous display of the opulent wealth of his empire and the pomp and splendor of his majesty.

When it was all over, the king gave a banquet for all the people, from the greatest to the least, who were in the fortress of Susa. It lasted for seven days and was held in the courtyard of the palace garden. The courtyard was beautifully decorated with white cotton curtains and blue hangings, which were fastened with white linen cords and purple ribbons to silver rings embedded in marble pillars. Gold and silver couches stood on a mosaic pavement of porphyry, marble, mother-of-pearl, and other costly stones.

Drinks were served in gold goblets of many designs, and there was an abundance of royal wine, reflecting the king's generosity. By edict of the king, no limits were placed on the drinking, for the king had instructed all his palace officials to serve each man as much as he wanted.

At the same time, Queen Vashti gave a banquet for the women in the royal palace of King Xerxes.

On the seventh day of the feast, when King Xerxes was in high spirits because of the wine, he told the seven eunuchs who attended him— Mehuman, Biztha, Harbona, Bigtha, Abagtha, Zethar, and Carcas—to bring Queen Vashti to him with the royal crown on her head. He wanted the nobles and all the other men to gaze on her beauty, for she was a very beautiful woman. But when they conveyed the king's order to Queen Vashti, she refused to come. This made the king furious, and he burned with anger.

He immediately consulted with his wise advisers, who knew all the Persian laws and customs, for he always asked their advice. The names of these men were Carshena, Shethar, Admatha, Tarshish, Meres, Marsena, and Memucan—seven nobles of Persia and Media. They met with the king regularly and held the highest positions in the empire.

"What must be done to Queen Vashti?" the king demanded. "What penalty does the law provide for a queen who refuses to obey the king's orders, properly sent through his eunuchs?"

Memucan answered the king and his nobles, "Queen Vashti has wronged not only the king but also every noble and citizen throughout your empire. Women everywhere will begin to despise their husbands when they learn that Queen Vashti has refused to appear before the king. Before this day is out, the wives of all the king's nobles throughout Persia and Media will hear what the queen did and will start treating their husbands the same way. There will be no end to their contempt and anger.

"So if it please the king, we suggest that you issue a written decree, a law of the Persians and Medes that cannot be revoked. It should order that Queen Vashti be forever banished from the presence of King Xerxes, and that the king should choose another queen more worthy than she. When this decree is published throughout the king's vast empire, husbands everywhere, whatever their rank, will receive proper respect from their wives!"

The king and his nobles thought this made good sense, so he followed Memucan's counsel. He sent letters to all parts of the empire, to each province in its own script and language, proclaiming that every man should be the ruler of his own home and should say whatever he pleases.

But after Xerxes' anger had subsided, he began thinking about Vashti and what she had done and the decree he had made. So his personal attendants suggested, "Let us search the empire to find beautiful young virgins for the king. Let the king appoint agents in each province to bring these beautiful young women into the royal harem at the fortress of Susa. Hegai, the king's eunuch in charge of the harem, will see that they are all given beauty treatments. After that, the young woman who most pleases the king will be made queen instead of Vashti." This advice was very appealing to the king, so he put the plan into effect.

At that time there was a Jewish man in the fortress of Susa whose name was Mordecai son of Jair. He was from the tribe of Benjamin and was a descendant of Kish and Shimei. His family had been among those who, with King Jehoiachin of Judah, had been exiled from Jerusalem to Babylon by King Nebuchadnezzar. This man had a very beautiful and lovely young cousin, Hadassah, who was also called Esther. When her father and mother died, Mordecai adopted her into his family and raised her as his own daughter.

As a result of the king's decree, Esther, along with many other young women, was brought to the king's harem at the fortress of Susa and placed in Hegai's care. Hegai was very impressed with Esther and treated her kindly. He quickly ordered a special menu for her and provided her with beauty treatments. He also assigned her seven maids specially chosen from the king's palace, and he moved her and her maids into the best place in the harem.

Esther had not told anyone of her nationality and family background, because Mordecai had directed her not to do so. Every day Mordecai would take a walk near the courtyard of the harem to find out about Esther and what was happening to her.

Before each young woman was taken to the king's bed, she was given the prescribed twelve months of beauty treatments—six months with oil of myrrh, followed by six months with special perfumes and ointments. When it was time for her to go to the king's palace, she was given her choice of whatever clothing or jewelry she wanted to take from the harem. That evening she was taken to the king's private rooms, and the next morning she was brought to the second harem, where the king's wives lived. There she would be under the care of Shaashgaz, the king's eunuch in charge of the concubines. She would never go to the king again unless he had especially enjoyed her and requested her by name.

Esther was the daughter of Abihail, who was Mordecai's uncle. (Mordecai had adopted his younger cousin Esther.) When it was Esther's turn to go to the king, she accepted the advice of Hegai, the eunuch in charge of the harem. She asked for nothing except what he suggested, and she was admired by everyone who saw her.

Esther was taken to King Xerxes at the royal palace in early winter of the seventh year of his reign. And the king loved Esther more than any of the other young women. He was so delighted with her that he set the royal crown on her head and declared her queen instead of Vashti. To celebrate the occasion, he gave a great banquet in Esther's honor for all his nobles and officials, declaring a public holiday for the provinces and giving generous gifts to everyone.

Even after all the young women had been transferred to the second harem and Mordecai had become a palace official, Esther continued to keep her family background and nationality a secret. She was still following Mordecai's directions, just as she did when she lived in his home.

One day as Mordecai was on duty at the king's gate, two of the king's eunuchs, Bigthana and Teresh—who were guards at the door of the king's private quarters—became angry at King Xerxes and plotted to assassinate him. But Mordecai heard about the plot and gave the information to Queen Esther. She then told the king about it and gave Mordecai credit for the report. When an investigation was made and Mordecai's story was found to be true, the two men were impaled on a sharpened pole. This was all recorded in *The Book of the History of King Xerxes' Reign.*

+

Some time later King Xerxes promoted Haman son of Hammedatha the Agagite over all the other nobles, making him the most powerful official in the empire. All the king's officials would bow down before Haman to show him respect whenever he passed by, for so the king had commanded. But Mordecai refused to bow down or show him respect.

Then the palace officials at the king's gate asked Mordecai, "Why are you disobeying the king's command?" They spoke to him day after day, but still he refused to comply with the order. So they spoke to Haman about this to see if he would tolerate Mordecai's conduct, since Mordecai had told them he was a Jew.

When Haman saw that Mordecai would not bow down or show him respect, he was filled with rage. He had learned of Mordecai's nationality, so he decided it was not enough to lay hands on Mordecai alone. Instead, he looked for a way to destroy all the Jews throughout the entire empire of Xerxes.

So in the month of April, during the twelfth year of King Xerxes' reign, lots were cast in Haman's presence (the lots were called *purim*) to determine the best day and month to take action. And the day selected was March 7, nearly a year later.

Then Haman approached King Xerxes and said, "There is a certain race of people scattered through all the provinces of your empire who keep themselves separate from everyone else. Their laws are different from those of any other people, and they refuse to obey the laws of the king. So it is not in the king's interest to let them live. If it please the king, issue a decree that they be destroyed, and I will give 10,000 large sacks of silver to the government administrators to be deposited in the royal treasury."

The king agreed, confirming his decision by removing his signet ring from his finger and giving it to Haman son of Hammedatha the Agagite, the enemy of the Jews. The king said, "The money and the people are both yours to do with as you see fit."

So on April 17 the king's secretaries were summoned, and a decree was written exactly as Haman dictated. It was sent to the king's highest officers, the governors of the respective provinces, and the nobles of each province in their own scripts and languages. The decree was written in the name of King Xerxes and sealed with the king's signet ring. Dispatches were sent by swift messengers into all the provinces of the empire, giving the order that all Jews—young and old, including women and children—must be killed, slaughtered, and annihilated on a single day. This was scheduled to happen on March 7 of the next year. The property of the Jews would be given to those who killed them.

A copy of this decree was to be issued as law in every province and proclaimed to all peoples, so that they would be ready to do their duty on the appointed day. At the king's command, the decree went out by swift messengers, and it was also proclaimed in the fortress of Susa. Then the king and Haman sat down to drink, but the city of Susa fell into confusion.

When Mordecai learned about all that had been done, he tore his clothes, put on burlap and ashes, and went out into the city, crying with a loud and bitter wail. He went as far as the gate of the palace, for no one was allowed to enter the palace gate while wearing clothes of mourning. And as news of the king's decree reached all the provinces, there was great mourning among the Jews. They fasted, wept, and wailed, and many people lay in burlap and ashes.

When Queen Esther's maids and eunuchs came and told her about Mordecai, she was deeply distressed. She sent clothing to him to replace the burlap, but he refused it. Then Esther sent for Hathach, one of the king's eunuchs who had been appointed as her attendant. She ordered him to go to Mordecai and find out what was troubling him and why he was in mourning. So Hathach went out to Mordecai in the square in front of the palace gate.

Mordecai told him the whole story, including the exact amount of money Haman had promised to pay into the royal treasury for the destruction of the Jews. Mordecai gave Hathach a copy of the decree issued in Susa that called for the death of all Jews. He asked Hathach to show it to Esther and explain the situation to her. He also asked Hathach to direct her to go to the king to beg for mercy and plead for her people. So Hathach returned to Esther with Mordecai's message.

Then Esther told Hathach to go back and relay this message to Mordecai: "All the king's officials and even the people in the provinces know that anyone who appears before the king in his inner court without being invited is doomed to die unless the king holds out his gold scepter. And the king has not called for me to come to him for thirty days." So Hathach gave Esther's message to Mordecai.

Mordecai sent this reply to Esther: "Don't think for a moment that because you're in the palace you will escape when all other Jews are killed. If you keep quiet at a time like this, deliverance and relief for the Jews will arise from some other place, but you and your relatives will die. Who knows if perhaps you were made queen for just such a time as this?"

Then Esther sent this reply to Mordecai: "Go and gather together all the Jews of Susa and fast for me. Do not eat or drink for three days, night or day. My maids and I will do the same. And then, though it is against the law, I will go in to see the king. If I must die, I must die." So Mordecai went away and did everything as Esther had ordered him.

On the third day of the fast, Esther put on her royal robes and entered the inner court of the palace, just across from the king's hall. The king was sitting on his royal throne, facing the entrance. When he saw Queen Esther standing there in the inner court, he welcomed her and held out the gold scepter to her. So Esther approached and touched the end of the scepter.

Then the king asked her, "What do you want, Queen Esther? What is your request? I will give it to you, even if it is half the kingdom!"

And Esther replied, "If it please the king, let the king and Haman come today to a banquet I have prepared for the king."

The king turned to his attendants and said, "Tell Haman to come quickly to a banquet, as Esther has requested." So the king and Haman went to Esther's banquet.

And while they were drinking wine, the king said to Esther, "Now tell me what you really want. What is your request? I will give it to you, even if it is half the kingdom!"

Esther replied, "This is my request and deepest wish. If I have found favor with the king, and if it pleases the king to grant my request and do what I ask, please come with Haman tomorrow to the banquet I will prepare for you. Then I will explain what this is all about."

Haman was a happy man as he left the banquet! But when he saw Mordecai sitting at the palace gate, not standing up or trembling nervously before him, Haman became furious. However, he restrained himself and went on home.

Then Haman gathered together his friends and Zeresh, his wife, and boasted to them about his great wealth and his many children. He bragged about the honors the king had given him and how he had been promoted over all the other nobles and officials.

Then Haman added, "And that's not all! Queen Esther invited only me and the king himself to the banquet she prepared for us. And she has invited me to dine with her and the king again tomorrow!" Then he added, "But this is all worth nothing as long as I see Mordecai the Jew just sitting there at the palace gate."

So Haman's wife, Zeresh, and all his friends suggested, "Set up a sharpened pole that stands seventy-five feet tall, and in the morning ask the king to impale Mordecai on it. When this is done, you can go on your merry way to the banquet with the king." This pleased Haman, and he ordered the pole set up.

That night the king had trouble sleeping, so he ordered an attendant to bring the book of the history of his reign so it could be read to him. In those records he discovered an account of how Mordecai had exposed the plot of Bigthana and Teresh, two of the eunuchs who guarded the door to the king's private quarters. They had plotted to assassinate King Xerxes.

"What reward or recognition did we ever give Mordecai for this?" the king asked.

His attendants replied, "Nothing has been done for him."

"Who is that in the outer court?" the king inquired. As it happened, Haman had just arrived in the outer court of the palace to ask the king to impale Mordecai on the pole he had prepared.

So the attendants replied to the king, "Haman is out in the court."

"Bring him in," the king ordered. So Haman came in, and the king said, "What should I do to honor a man who truly pleases me?"

Haman thought to himself, "Whom would the king wish to honor more than me?" So he replied, "If the king wishes to honor someone, he should bring out one of the king's own royal robes, as well as a horse that the king himself has ridden—one with a royal emblem on its head. Let the robes and the horse be handed over to one of the king's most noble officials. And let him see that the man whom the king wishes to honor is dressed in the king's robes and led through the city square on the king's horse. Have the official shout as they go, 'This is what the king does for someone he wishes to honor!'"

"Excellent!" the king said to Haman. "Quick! Take the robes and my horse, and do just as you have said for Mordecai the Jew, who sits at the gate of the palace. Leave out nothing you have suggested!"

So Haman took the robes and put them on Mordecai, placed him on the king's own horse, and led him through the city square, shouting, "This is what the king does for someone he wishes to honor!" Afterward Mordecai returned to the palace gate, but Haman hurried home dejected and completely humiliated.

When Haman told his wife, Zeresh, and all his friends what had happened, his wise advisers and his wife said, "Since Mordecai—this man who has humiliated you—is of Jewish birth, you will never succeed in your plans against him. It will be fatal to continue opposing him."

While they were still talking, the king's eunuchs arrived and quickly took Haman to the banquet Esther had prepared.

So the king and Haman went to Queen Esther's banquet. On this second occasion, while they were drinking wine, the king again said to Esther, "Tell me what you want, Queen Esther. What is your request? I will give it to you, even if it is half the kingdom!"

Queen Esther replied, "If I have found favor with the king, and if it pleases the king to grant my request, I ask that my life and the lives of my people will be spared. For my people and I have been sold to those who would kill, slaughter, and annihilate us. If we had merely been sold as slaves, I could remain quiet, for that would be too trivial a matter to warrant disturbing the king."

"Who would do such a thing?" King Xerxes demanded. "Who would be so presumptuous as to touch you?"

Esther replied, "This wicked Haman is our adversary and our enemy." Haman grew pale with fright before the king and queen. Then the king jumped to his feet in a rage and went out into the palace garden.

Haman, however, stayed behind to plead for his life with Queen Esther, for he knew that the king intended to kill him. In despair he fell on the couch where Queen Esther was reclining, just as the king was returning from the palace garden.

The king exclaimed, "Will he even assault the queen right here in the palace, before my very eyes?" And as soon as the king spoke, his attendants covered Haman's face, signaling his doom.

Then Harbona, one of the king's eunuchs, said, "Haman has set up a sharpened pole that stands seventy-five feet tall in his own courtyard. He intended to use it to impale Mordecai, the man who saved the king from assassination."

"Then impale Haman on it!" the king ordered. So they impaled Haman on the pole he had set up for Mordecai, and the king's anger subsided.

On that same day King Xerxes gave the property of Haman, the enemy of the Jews, to Queen Esther. Then Mordecai was brought before the king, for Esther had told the king how they were related. The king took off his signet ring—which he had taken back from Haman—and gave it to Mordecai. And Esther appointed Mordecai to be in charge of Haman's property.

Then Esther went again before the king, falling down at his feet and begging him with tears to stop the evil plot devised by Haman the Agagite against the Jews. Again the king held out the gold scepter to Esther. So she rose and stood before him.

Esther said, "If it please the king, and if I have found favor with him, and if he thinks it is right, and if I am pleasing to him, let there be a decree that reverses the orders of Haman son of Hammedatha the Agagite, who ordered that Jews throughout all the king's provinces should be destroyed. For how can I endure to see my people and my family slaughtered and destroyed?"

Then King Xerxes said to Queen Esther and Mordecai the Jew, "I have given Esther the property of Haman, and he has been impaled on a pole because he tried to destroy the Jews. Now go ahead and send a message to the Jews in the king's name, telling them whatever you want, and seal it with the king's signet ring. But remember that whatever has already been written in the king's name and sealed with his signet ring can never be revoked."

So on June 25 the king's secretaries were summoned, and a decree was written exactly as Mordecai dictated. It was sent to the Jews and to the highest officers, the governors, and the nobles of all the 127 provinces stretching from India to Ethiopia. The decree was written in the scripts and languages of all the peoples of the empire, including that of the Jews. The decree was written in the name of King Xerxes and sealed with the king's signet ring. Mordecai sent the dispatches by swift messengers, who rode fast horses especially bred for the king's service.

The king's decree gave the Jews in every city authority to unite to defend their lives. They were allowed to kill, slaughter, and annihilate anyone of any nationality or province who might attack them or their children and wives, and to take the property of their enemies. The day chosen for this event throughout all the provinces of King Xerxes was March 7 of the next year.

A copy of this decree was to be issued as law in every province and proclaimed to all peoples, so that the Jews would be ready to take revenge on their enemies on the appointed day. So urged on by the king's command, the messengers rode out swiftly on fast horses bred for the king's service. The same decree was also proclaimed in the fortress of Susa.

Then Mordecai left the king's presence, wearing the royal robe of blue and white, the great crown of gold, and an outer cloak of fine linen and purple. And the people of Susa celebrated the new decree. The Jews were filled with joy and gladness and were honored everywhere. In every province and city, wherever the king's decree arrived, the Jews rejoiced and had a great celebration and declared a public festival and holiday. And many of the people of the land became Jews themselves, for they feared what the Jews might do to them.

So on March 7 the two decrees of the king were put into effect. On that day, the enemies of the Jews had hoped to overpower them, but quite the opposite happened. It was the Jews who overpowered their enemies. The Jews gathered in their cities throughout all the king's provinces to attack anyone who tried to harm them. But no one could make a stand against them, for everyone was afraid of them. And all the nobles of the provinces, the highest officers, the governors, and the royal officials helped the Jews for fear of Mordecai. For Mordecai had been promoted in the king's palace, and his fame spread throughout all the provinces as he became more and more powerful.

So the Jews went ahead on the appointed day and struck down their enemies with the sword. They killed and annihilated their enemies and did as they pleased with those who hated them. In the fortress of Susa itself, the Jews killed 500 men. They also killed Parshandatha, Dalphon, Aspatha, Poratha, Adalia, Aridatha, Parmashta, Arisai, Aridai, and Vaizatha—the ten sons of Haman son of Hammedatha, the enemy of the Jews. But they did not take any plunder.

That very day, when the king was informed of the number of people killed in the fortress of Susa, he called for Queen Esther. He said, "The Jews have killed 500 men in the fortress of Susa alone, as well as Haman's ten sons. If they have done that here, what has happened in the rest of the provinces? But now, what more do you want? It will be granted to you; tell me and I will do it."

Esther responded, "If it please the king, give the Jews in Susa permission to do again tomorrow as they have done today, and let the bodies of Haman's ten sons be impaled on a pole."

So the king agreed, and the decree was announced in Susa. And they impaled the bodies of Haman's ten sons. Then the Jews at Susa gathered together on March 8 and killed 300 more men, and again they took no plunder.

Meanwhile, the other Jews throughout the king's provinces had gathered together to defend their lives. They gained relief from all their enemies, killing 75,000 of those who hated them. But they did not take any plunder. This was done throughout the provinces on March 7, and on March 8 they rested, celebrating their victory with a day of feasting and gladness. (The Jews at Susa killed their enemies on March 7 and again on March 8, then rested on March 9, making that their day of feasting and gladness.) So to this day, rural Jews living in remote villages celebrate an annual festival and holiday on the appointed day in late winter, when they rejoice and send gifts of food to each other.

Mordecai recorded these events and sent letters to the Jews near and far, throughout all the provinces of King Xerxes, calling on them to celebrate an annual festival on these two days. He told them to celebrate these days with feasting and gladness and by giving gifts of food to each other and presents to the poor. This would commemorate a time when the Jews gained relief from their enemies, when their sorrow was turned into gladness and their mourning into joy.

So the Jews accepted Mordecai's proposal and adopted this annual custom. Haman son of Hammedatha the Agagite, the enemy of the Jews, had plotted to crush and destroy them on the date determined by casting lots (the lots were called *purim*). But when Esther came before the king, he issued a decree causing Haman's evil plot to backfire, and Haman and his sons were impaled on a sharpened pole. That is why this celebration is called Purim, because it is the ancient word for casting lots.

So because of Mordecai's letter and because of what they had experienced, the Jews throughout the realm agreed to inaugurate this tradition and to pass it on to their descendants and to all who became Jews. They declared they would never fail to celebrate these two prescribed days at the appointed time each year. These days would be remembered and kept from generation to generation and celebrated by every family throughout the provinces and cities of the empire. This Festival of Purim would never cease to be celebrated among the Jews, nor would the memory of what happened ever die out among their descendants.

Then Queen Esther, the daughter of Abihail, along with Mordecai the Jew, wrote another letter putting the queen's full authority behind Mordecai's letter to establish the Festival of Purim. Letters wishing peace and security were sent to the Jews throughout the 127 provinces of the empire of Xerxes. These letters established the Festival of Purim—an annual celebration of these days at the appointed time, decreed by both Mordecai the Jew and Queen Esther. (The people decided to observe this festival, just as they had decided for themselves and their descendants to establish the times of fasting and mourning.) So the command of Esther confirmed the practices of Purim, and it was all written down in the records.

+

King Xerxes imposed a tribute throughout his empire, even to the distant coastlands. His great achievements and the full account of the greatness of Mordecai, whom the king had promoted, are recorded in *The Book of the History of the Kings of Media and Persia*. Mordecai the Jew became the prime minister, with authority next to that of King Xerxes himself. He was very great among the Jews, who held him in high esteem, because he continued to work for the good of his people and to speak up for the welfare of all their descendants.

IMMERSED IN DANIEL

IN THE FEW CENTURIES BEFORE the birth of Jesus the Messiah, the nation of Israel faced increasing pressure as they lived under the rule of hostile empires. This meant dealing with not only the possibility of religious contamination but also the threat of extinction. The book of Esther records the courage of faithful Jews when threatened under Persian rule. The book of Daniel shows their steadfastness under the rule of several powerful empires—first under the Babylonians and Persians, and then in association with the Greek Seleucids.

The book of Daniel is divided into two main parts: a collection of stories and a collection of apocalyptic visions. The six stories in the first part are of two different types: interpretation stories and deliverance stories. In the interpretation stories, a mystery arises that the king's own wise men can't interpret or resolve, but the Most High God of Israel reveals the meaning to Daniel. In the deliverance stories, the king demands that the Jews compromise their worship of God (by worshiping an idol or by abandoning regular times of prayer to God) and attempts to execute them when they refuse. But God powerfully intervenes to rescue his people from danger. Both story types emphasize that Israel's God is the one true Creator and King over all things.

These stories center on four young Judeans—Daniel, Shadrach, Meshach, and Abednego—who were taken into exile by the Babylonians. Their stories are among the most memorable and inspiring in the Bible. These humble captives are lifted up after they refuse to compromise their faith, while a proud king is brought low until he acknowledges that "the Most High rules over the kingdoms of the world and gives them to anyone he chooses."

After these stories, the book presents four visions filled with vivid and intricate symbolism. These visions closely follow the conventions of a particular type of writing known as *apocalypse*, which often features heavenly visitors, symbols representing historical periods, and a command to seal up the book, among other elements. Apocalyptic literature developed as a genre late in the First Testament period. In the face of suffering and uncertainty, the Jewish people needed stories that would reveal the cosmic realities behind their experience and give them hope in the battle against the rulers of this world.

As the visions themselves depict, the Babylonian Empire fell to the Persians, who were conquered in turn by the Greeks under Alexander the Great. The Greek Empire was divided up after Alexander's death, and the Seleucids, who ruled one part, eventually carved out an empire of their own that was nearly as large as Alexander's and included Judea. After Antiochus IV Epiphanes became emperor, he desecrated the Temple in Jerusalem and tried to force all the Jews to worship Greek gods. But under the leadership of the Maccabees, the Jews fought back. After great suffering and sacrifice and with God's help, they temporarily won their freedom.

The stories and visions in the book of Daniel work together to strengthen God's people as they struggle to maintain their distinctive identity as a people loyal to God alone. They reveal that God is truly working, even when it looks like evil is triumphing. The pride of even the greatest human rulers is shown to be empty and weak when the Most High God acts to save his people.

The book of Daniel became one of Israel's most popular books in the first century AD, the time of Jesus. God's people were still suffering greatly under the oppression of foreign Roman rulers, and they were longing for the arrival of God's promised redeemer. Daniel gave them hope that God would bring a change in the future: "Then the sovereignty, power, and greatness of all the kingdoms under heaven will be given to the holy people of the Most High. His kingdom will last forever, and all rulers will serve and obey him."

DANIEL

✝

During the third year of King Jehoiakim's reign in Judah, King Nebuchadnezzar of Babylon came to Jerusalem and besieged it. The Lord gave him victory over King Jehoiakim of Judah and permitted him to take some of the sacred objects from the Temple of God. So Nebuchadnezzar took them back to the land of Babylonia and placed them in the treasure-house of his god.

Then the king ordered Ashpenaz, his chief of staff, to bring to the palace some of the young men of Judah's royal family and other noble families, who had been brought to Babylon as captives. "Select only strong, healthy, and good-looking young men," he said. "Make sure they are well versed in every branch of learning, are gifted with knowledge and good judgment, and are suited to serve in the royal palace. Train these young men in the language and literature of Babylon." The king assigned them a daily ration of food and wine from his own kitchens. They were to be trained for three years, and then they would enter the royal service.

Daniel, Hananiah, Mishael, and Azariah were four of the young men chosen, all from the tribe of Judah. The chief of staff renamed them with these Babylonian names:

Daniel was called Belteshazzar.
Hananiah was called Shadrach.
Mishael was called Meshach.
Azariah was called Abednego.

But Daniel was determined not to defile himself by eating the food and wine given to them by the king. He asked the chief of staff for permission not to eat these unacceptable foods. Now God had given the chief of staff both respect and affection for Daniel. But he responded, "I am afraid of my lord the king, who has ordered that you eat this food and wine. If you become pale and thin compared to the other youths your age, I am afraid the king will have me beheaded."

Daniel spoke with the attendant who had been appointed by the chief of staff to look after Daniel, Hananiah, Mishael, and Azariah. "Please test us for ten days on a diet of vegetables and water," Daniel said. "At the end of the ten days, see how we look compared to the other young men who are eating the king's food. Then make your decision in light of what you see." The attendant agreed to Daniel's suggestion and tested them for ten days.

At the end of the ten days, Daniel and his three friends looked healthier and better nourished than the young men who had been eating the food assigned by the king. So after that, the attendant fed them only vegetables instead of the food and wine provided for the others.

God gave these four young men an unusual aptitude for understanding every aspect of literature and wisdom. And God gave Daniel the special ability to interpret the meanings of visions and dreams.

When the training period ordered by the king was completed, the chief of staff brought all the young men to King Nebuchadnezzar. The king talked with them, and no one impressed him as much as Daniel, Hananiah, Mishael, and Azariah. So they entered the royal service. Whenever the king consulted them in any matter requiring wisdom and balanced judgment, he found them ten times more capable than any of the magicians and enchanters in his entire kingdom.

Daniel remained in the royal service until the first year of the reign of King Cyrus.

+

One night during the second year of his reign, Nebuchadnezzar had such disturbing dreams that he couldn't sleep. He called in his magicians, enchanters, sorcerers, and astrologers, and he demanded that they tell him what he had dreamed. As they stood before the king, he said, "I have had a dream that deeply troubles me, and I must know what it means."

Then the astrologers answered the king in Aramaic, "Long live the king! Tell us the dream, and we will tell you what it means."

But the king said to the astrologers, "I am serious about this. If you don't tell me what my dream was and what it means, you will be torn limb from limb, and your houses will be turned into heaps of rubble! But if you tell me what I dreamed and what the dream means, I will give you many wonderful gifts and honors. Just tell me the dream and what it means!"

They said again, "Please, Your Majesty. Tell us the dream, and we will tell you what it means."

The king replied, "I know what you are doing! You're stalling for time because you know I am serious when I say, 'If you don't tell me the dream, you are doomed.' So you have conspired to tell me lies, hoping I will change my mind. But tell me the dream, and then I'll know that you can tell me what it means."

The astrologers replied to the king, "No one on earth can tell the king his dream! And no king, however great and powerful, has ever asked such a thing of any magician, enchanter, or astrologer! The king's demand is impossible. No one except the gods can tell you your dream, and they do not live here among people."

The king was furious when he heard this, and he ordered that all the wise men of Babylon be executed. And because of the king's decree, men were sent to find and kill Daniel and his friends.

When Arioch, the commander of the king's guard, came to kill them, Daniel handled the situation with wisdom and discretion. He asked Arioch, "Why has the king issued such a harsh decree?" So Arioch told him all that had happened. Daniel went at once to see the king and requested more time to tell the king what the dream meant.

Then Daniel went home and told his friends Hananiah, Mishael, and Azariah what had happened. He urged them to ask the God of heaven to show them his mercy by telling them the secret, so they would not be executed along with the other wise men of Babylon. That night the secret was revealed to Daniel in a vision. Then Daniel praised the God of heaven. He said,

> "Praise the name of God forever and ever,
>   for he has all wisdom and power.
> He controls the course of world events;
>   he removes kings and sets up other kings.
> He gives wisdom to the wise
>   and knowledge to the scholars.
> He reveals deep and mysterious things
>   and knows what lies hidden in darkness,
>   though he is surrounded by light.
> I thank and praise you, God of my ancestors,
>   for you have given me wisdom and strength.
> You have told me what we asked of you
>   and revealed to us what the king demanded."

Then Daniel went in to see Arioch, whom the king had ordered to execute the wise men of Babylon. Daniel said to him, "Don't kill the wise men. Take me to the king, and I will tell him the meaning of his dream."

Arioch quickly took Daniel to the king and said, "I have found one of the captives from Judah who will tell the king the meaning of his dream!"

The king said to Daniel (also known as Belteshazzar), "Is this true? Can you tell me what my dream was and what it means?"

Daniel replied, "There are no wise men, enchanters, magicians, or fortune-tellers who can reveal the king's secret. But there is a God in heaven who reveals secrets, and he has shown King Nebuchadnezzar what will happen in the future. Now I will tell you your dream and the visions you saw as you lay on your bed.

"While Your Majesty was sleeping, you dreamed about coming events. He who reveals secrets has shown you what is going to happen. And it is not because I am wiser than anyone else that I know the secret of your dream, but because God wants you to understand what was in your heart.

"In your vision, Your Majesty, you saw standing before you a huge, shining statue of a man. It was a frightening sight. The head of the statue was made of fine gold. Its chest and arms were silver, its belly and thighs were bronze, its legs were iron, and its feet were a combination of iron and baked clay. As you watched, a rock was cut from a mountain, but not by human hands. It struck the feet of iron and clay, smashing them to bits. The whole statue was crushed into small pieces of iron, clay, bronze, silver, and gold. Then the wind blew them away without a trace, like chaff on a threshing floor. But the rock that knocked the statue down became a great mountain that covered the whole earth.

"That was the dream. Now we will tell the king what it means. Your Majesty, you are the greatest of kings. The God of heaven has given you sovereignty, power, strength, and honor. He has made you the ruler over all the inhabited world and has put even the wild animals and birds under your control. You are the head of gold.

"But after your kingdom comes to an end, another kingdom, inferior to yours, will rise to take your place. After that kingdom has fallen, yet a third kingdom, represented by bronze, will rise to rule the world. Following that kingdom, there will be a fourth one, as strong as iron. That kingdom will smash and crush all previous empires, just as iron smashes and crushes everything it strikes. The feet and toes you saw were a combination of iron and baked clay, showing that this kingdom will be divided. Like iron mixed with clay, it will have some of the strength of iron. But while some parts of it will be as strong as iron, other parts will be as weak as clay. This mixture of iron and clay also shows that these kingdoms will try to strengthen themselves by forming alliances with each other through intermarriage. But they will not hold together, just as iron and clay do not mix.

"During the reigns of those kings, the God of heaven will set up a kingdom that will never be destroyed or conquered. It will crush all these kingdoms into nothingness, and it will stand forever. That is the meaning of the rock cut from the mountain, though not by human hands, that crushed to pieces the statue of iron, bronze, clay, silver, and gold. The great God was showing the king what will happen in the future. The dream is true, and its meaning is certain."

Then King Nebuchadnezzar threw himself down before Daniel and worshiped him, and he commanded his people to offer sacrifices and burn sweet incense before him. The king said to Daniel, "Truly, your God is the greatest of gods, the Lord over kings, a revealer of mysteries, for you have been able to reveal this secret."

Then the king appointed Daniel to a high position and gave him many valuable gifts. He made Daniel ruler over the whole province of Babylon, as well as chief over all his wise men. At Daniel's request, the king appointed Shadrach, Meshach, and Abednego to be in charge of all the affairs of the province of Babylon, while Daniel remained in the king's court.

+

King Nebuchadnezzar made a gold statue ninety feet tall and nine feet wide and set it up on the plain of Dura in the province of Babylon. Then he sent messages to the high officers, officials, governors, advisers, treasurers, judges, magistrates, and all the provincial officials to come to the dedication of the statue he had set up. So all these officials came and stood before the statue King Nebuchadnezzar had set up.

Then a herald shouted out, "People of all races and nations and languages, listen to the king's command! When you hear the sound of the horn, flute, zither, lyre, harp, pipes, and other musical instruments, bow to the ground to worship King Nebuchadnezzar's gold statue. Anyone who refuses to obey will immediately be thrown into a blazing furnace."

So at the sound of the musical instruments, all the people, whatever their race or nation or language, bowed to the ground and worshiped the gold statue that King Nebuchadnezzar had set up.

But some of the astrologers went to the king and informed on the Jews. They said to King Nebuchadnezzar, "Long live the king! You issued a decree requiring all the people to bow down and worship the gold statue when they hear the sound of the horn, flute, zither, lyre, harp, pipes, and other musical instruments. That decree also states that those who refuse to obey must be thrown into a blazing furnace. But there are some Jews—Shadrach, Meshach, and Abednego—whom you have put in charge of the province of Babylon. They pay no attention to you, Your Majesty. They refuse to serve your gods and do not worship the gold statue you have set up."

Then Nebuchadnezzar flew into a rage and ordered that Shadrach, Meshach, and Abednego be brought before him. When they were brought in, Nebuchadnezzar said to them, "Is it true, Shadrach, Meshach, and Abednego, that you refuse to serve my gods or to worship the gold statue I have set up? I will give you one more chance to bow down and worship the statue I have made when you hear the sound of the musical instruments. But if you refuse, you will be thrown immediately into the blazing furnace. And then what god will be able to rescue you from my power?"

Shadrach, Meshach, and Abednego replied, "O Nebuchadnezzar, we do not need to defend ourselves before you. If we are thrown into the blazing furnace, the God whom we serve is able to save us. He will rescue us from your power, Your Majesty. But even if he doesn't, we want to make it clear to you, Your Majesty, that we will never serve your gods or worship the gold statue you have set up."

Nebuchadnezzar was so furious with Shadrach, Meshach, and Abednego that his face became distorted with rage. He commanded that the furnace be heated seven times hotter than usual. Then he ordered some of the strongest men of his army to bind Shadrach, Meshach, and Abednego and throw them into the blazing furnace. So they tied them up and threw them into the furnace, fully dressed in their pants, turbans, robes, and other garments. And because the king, in his anger, had demanded such a hot fire in the furnace, the flames killed the soldiers as they threw the three men in. So Shadrach, Meshach, and Abednego, securely tied, fell into the roaring flames.

But suddenly, Nebuchadnezzar jumped up in amazement and exclaimed to his advisers, "Didn't we tie up three men and throw them into the furnace?"

"Yes, Your Majesty, we certainly did," they replied.

"Look!" Nebuchadnezzar shouted. "I see four men, unbound, walking around in the fire unharmed! And the fourth looks like a god!"

Then Nebuchadnezzar came as close as he could to the door of the flaming furnace and shouted: "Shadrach, Meshach, and Abednego, servants of the Most High God, come out! Come here!"

So Shadrach, Meshach, and Abednego stepped out of the fire. Then the high officers, officials, governors, and advisers crowded around them and saw that the fire had not touched them. Not a hair on their heads was singed, and their clothing was not scorched. They didn't even smell of smoke!

Then Nebuchadnezzar said, "Praise to the God of Shadrach, Meshach, and Abednego! He sent his angel to rescue his servants who trusted in him. They defied the king's command and were willing to die rather than serve or worship any god except their own God. Therefore, I make this decree: If any people, whatever their race or nation or language, speak a word against the God of Shadrach, Meshach, and Abednego, they will be torn limb from limb, and their houses will be turned into heaps of rubble. There is no other god who can rescue like this!"

Then the king promoted Shadrach, Meshach, and Abednego to even higher positions in the province of Babylon.

+

King Nebuchadnezzar sent this message to the people of every race and nation and language throughout the world:

"Peace and prosperity to you!

"I want you all to know about the miraculous signs and wonders the Most High God has performed for me.

How great are his signs,
how powerful his wonders!
His kingdom will last forever,
his rule through all generations.

"I, Nebuchadnezzar, was living in my palace in comfort and prosperity. But one night I had a dream that frightened me; I saw visions that terrified me as I lay in my bed. So I issued an order calling in all the wise men of Babylon, so they could tell me what my dream meant. When all the magicians, enchanters, astrologers, and fortune-tellers came in, I told them the dream, but they could not tell me what it meant. At last Daniel came in before me, and I told him the dream. (He was named Belteshazzar after my god, and the spirit of the holy gods is in him.)

"I said to him, 'Belteshazzar, chief of the magicians, I know that the spirit of the holy gods is in you and that no mystery is too great for you to solve. Now tell me what my dream means.

"'While I was lying in my bed, this is what I dreamed. I saw a large tree in the middle of the earth. The tree grew very tall and strong, reaching high into the heavens for all the world to see. It had fresh green leaves, and it was loaded with fruit for all to eat. Wild animals lived in its shade, and birds nested in its branches. All the world was fed from this tree.

"'Then as I lay there dreaming, I saw a messenger, a holy one, coming down from heaven. The messenger shouted,

"Cut down the tree and lop off its branches!
Shake off its leaves and scatter its fruit!
Chase the wild animals from its shade
and the birds from its branches.
But leave the stump and the roots in the ground,
bound with a band of iron and bronze
and surrounded by tender grass.
Now let him be drenched with the dew of heaven,
and let him live with the wild animals among the plants
of the field.

For seven periods of time,
    let him have the mind of a wild animal
    instead of the mind of a human.
For this has been decreed by the messengers;
    it is commanded by the holy ones,
so that everyone may know
    that the Most High rules over the kingdoms of the world.
He gives them to anyone he chooses—
    even to the lowliest of people.'

"'Belteshazzar, that was the dream that I, King Nebuchadnezzar, had. Now tell me what it means, for none of the wise men of my kingdom can do so. But you can tell me because the spirit of the holy gods is in you.'

"Upon hearing this, Daniel (also known as Belteshazzar) was overcome for a time, frightened by the meaning of the dream. Then the king said to him, 'Belteshazzar, don't be alarmed by the dream and what it means.'

"Belteshazzar replied, 'I wish the events foreshadowed in this dream would happen to your enemies, my lord, and not to you! The tree you saw was growing very tall and strong, reaching high into the heavens for all the world to see. It had fresh green leaves and was loaded with fruit for all to eat. Wild animals lived in its shade, and birds nested in its branches. That tree, Your Majesty, is you. For you have grown strong and great; your greatness reaches up to heaven, and your rule to the ends of the earth.

"'Then you saw a messenger, a holy one, coming down from heaven and saying, "Cut down the tree and destroy it. But leave the stump and the roots in the ground, bound with a band of iron and bronze and surrounded by tender grass. Let him be drenched with the dew of heaven. Let him live with the animals of the field for seven periods of time."

"'This is what the dream means, Your Majesty, and what the Most High has declared will happen to my lord the king. You will be driven from human society, and you will live in the fields with the wild animals. You will eat grass like a cow, and you will be drenched with the dew of heaven. Seven periods of time will pass while you live this way, until you learn that the Most High rules over the kingdoms of the world and gives them to anyone he chooses. But the stump and roots of the tree were left in the ground. This means that you will receive your kingdom back again when you have learned that heaven rules.

"'King Nebuchadnezzar, please accept my advice. Stop sinning and do what is right. Break from your wicked past and be merciful to the poor. Perhaps then you will continue to prosper.'

"But all these things did happen to King Nebuchadnezzar. Twelve months later he was taking a walk on the flat roof of the royal palace in Babylon. As he looked out across the city, he said, 'Look at this great city of Babylon! By my own mighty power, I have built this beautiful city as my royal residence to display my majestic splendor.'

"While these words were still in his mouth, a voice called down from heaven, 'O King Nebuchadnezzar, this message is for you! You are no longer ruler of this kingdom. You will be driven from human society. You will live in the fields with the wild animals, and you will eat grass like a cow. Seven periods of time will pass while you live this way, until you learn that the Most High rules over the kingdoms of the world and gives them to anyone he chooses.'

"That same hour the judgment was fulfilled, and Nebuchadnezzar was driven from human society. He ate grass like a cow, and he was drenched with the dew of heaven. He lived this way until his hair was as long as eagles' feathers and his nails were like birds' claws.

"After this time had passed, I, Nebuchadnezzar, looked up to heaven. My sanity returned, and I praised and worshiped the Most High and honored the one who lives forever.

His rule is everlasting,
　　and his kingdom is eternal.
All the people of the earth
　　are nothing compared to him.
He does as he pleases
　　among the angels of heaven
　　and among the people of the earth.
No one can stop him or say to him,
　　'What do you mean by doing these things?'

"When my sanity returned to me, so did my honor and glory and kingdom. My advisers and nobles sought me out, and I was restored as head of my kingdom, with even greater honor than before.

"Now I, Nebuchadnezzar, praise and glorify and honor the King of heaven. All his acts are just and true, and he is able to humble the proud."

+

Many years later King Belshazzar gave a great feast for 1,000 of his nobles, and he drank wine with them. While Belshazzar was drinking the wine, he gave orders to bring in the gold and silver cups that his predecessor, Nebuchadnezzar, had taken from the Temple in Jerusalem. He wanted to drink from them with his nobles, his wives, and his concubines. So they brought these gold cups taken from the Temple, the house of God in Jerusalem, and the king and his nobles, his wives, and his concubines drank from them. While they drank from them they praised their idols made of gold, silver, bronze, iron, wood, and stone.

Suddenly, they saw the fingers of a human hand writing on the plaster wall of the king's palace, near the lampstand. The king himself saw the hand as it wrote, and his face turned pale with fright. His knees knocked together in fear and his legs gave way beneath him.

The king shouted for the enchanters, astrologers, and fortune-tellers to be brought before him. He said to these wise men of Babylon, "Whoever can read this writing and tell me what it means will be dressed in purple robes of royal honor and will have a gold chain placed around his neck. He will become the third highest ruler in the kingdom!"

But when all the king's wise men had come in, none of them could read the writing or tell him what it meant. So the king grew even more alarmed, and his face turned pale. His nobles, too, were shaken.

But when the queen mother heard what was happening, she hurried to the banquet hall. She said to Belshazzar, "Long live the king! Don't be so pale and frightened. There is a man in your kingdom who has within him the spirit of the holy gods. During Nebuchadnezzar's reign, this man was found to have insight, understanding, and wisdom like that of the gods. Your predecessor, the king—your predecessor King Nebuchadnezzar—made him chief over all the magicians, enchanters, astrologers, and fortune-tellers of Babylon. This man Daniel, whom the king named Belteshazzar, has exceptional ability and is filled with divine knowledge and understanding. He can interpret dreams, explain riddles, and solve difficult problems. Call for Daniel, and he will tell you what the writing means."

So Daniel was brought in before the king. The king asked him, "Are you Daniel, one of the exiles brought from Judah by my predecessor, King Nebuchadnezzar? I have heard that you have the spirit of the gods within you and that you are filled with insight, understanding, and wisdom. My wise men and enchanters have tried to read the words on the wall and tell me their meaning, but they cannot do it. I am told that you can give interpretations and solve difficult problems. If you can read these words and tell me their meaning, you will be clothed in purple robes of royal honor, and you will have a gold chain placed around your neck. You will become the third highest ruler in the kingdom."

Daniel answered the king, "Keep your gifts or give them to someone else, but I will tell you what the writing means. Your Majesty, the Most High God gave sovereignty, majesty, glory, and honor to your predecessor, Nebuchadnezzar. He made him so great that people of all races and nations and languages trembled before him in fear. He killed those he wanted to kill and spared those he wanted to spare. He honored those he wanted to honor and disgraced those he wanted to disgrace. But when his heart and mind were puffed up with arrogance, he was brought down from his royal throne and stripped of his glory. He was driven from human society. He was given the mind of a wild animal, and he lived among the wild donkeys. He ate grass like a cow, and he was drenched with the dew of heaven, until he learned that the Most High God rules over the kingdoms of the world and appoints anyone he desires to rule over them.

"You are his successor, O Belshazzar, and you knew all this, yet you have not humbled yourself. For you have proudly defied the Lord of heaven and have had these cups from his Temple brought before you. You and your nobles and your wives and concubines have been drinking wine from them while praising gods of silver, gold, bronze, iron, wood, and stone—gods that neither see nor hear nor know anything at all. But you have not honored the God who gives you the breath of life and controls your destiny! So God has sent this hand to write this message.

"This is the message that was written: MENE, MENE, TEKEL, and PARSIN. This is what these words mean:

Mene means 'numbered'—God has numbered the days of your reign and has brought it to an end.
Tekel means 'weighed'—you have been weighed on the balances and have not measured up.
Parsin means 'divided'—your kingdom has been divided and given to the Medes and Persians."

Then at Belshazzar's command, Daniel was dressed in purple robes, a gold chain was hung around his neck, and he was proclaimed the third highest ruler in the kingdom.

That very night Belshazzar, the Babylonian king, was killed.

And Darius the Mede took over the kingdom at the age of sixty-two.

+

Darius the Mede decided to divide the kingdom into 120 provinces, and he appointed a high officer to rule over each province. The king also chose Daniel and two others as administrators to supervise the high officers and protect the king's interests. Daniel soon proved himself more capable than all the other administrators and high officers. Because of Daniel's great ability, the king made plans to place him over the entire empire.

Then the other administrators and high officers began searching for some fault in the way Daniel was handling government affairs, but they couldn't find anything to criticize or condemn. He was faithful, always responsible, and completely trustworthy. So they concluded, "Our only chance of finding grounds for accusing Daniel will be in connection with the rules of his religion."

So the administrators and high officers went to the king and said, "Long live King Darius! We are all in agreement—we administrators, officials, high officers, advisers, and governors—that the king should make a law that will be strictly enforced. Give orders that for the next thirty days any person who prays to anyone, divine or human—except to you, Your Majesty—will be thrown into the den of lions. And now, Your Majesty, issue and sign this law so it cannot be changed, an official law of the Medes and Persians that cannot be revoked." So King Darius signed the law.

But when Daniel learned that the law had been signed, he went home and knelt down as usual in his upstairs room, with its windows open toward Jerusalem. He prayed three times a day, just as he had always done, giving thanks to his God. Then the officials went together to Daniel's house and found him praying and asking for God's help. So they went straight to the king and reminded him about his law. "Did you not sign a law that for the next thirty days any person who prays to anyone, divine or human—except to you, Your Majesty—will be thrown into the den of lions?"

"Yes," the king replied, "that decision stands; it is an official law of the Medes and Persians that cannot be revoked."

Then they told the king, "That man Daniel, one of the captives from Judah, is ignoring you and your law. He still prays to his God three times a day."

Hearing this, the king was deeply troubled, and he tried to think of a way to save Daniel. He spent the rest of the day looking for a way to get Daniel out of this predicament.

In the evening the men went together to the king and said, "Your Majesty, you know that according to the law of the Medes and the Persians, no law that the king signs can be changed."

So at last the king gave orders for Daniel to be arrested and thrown into the den of lions. The king said to him, "May your God, whom you serve so faithfully, rescue you."

A stone was brought and placed over the mouth of the den. The king sealed the stone with his own royal seal and the seals of his nobles, so that no one could rescue Daniel. Then the king returned to his palace and spent the night fasting. He refused his usual entertainment and couldn't sleep at all that night.

Very early the next morning, the king got up and hurried out to the lions' den. When he got there, he called out in anguish, "Daniel, servant of the living God! Was your God, whom you serve so faithfully, able to rescue you from the lions?"

Daniel answered, "Long live the king! My God sent his angel to shut the lions' mouths so that they would not hurt me, for I have been found innocent in his sight. And I have not wronged you, Your Majesty."

The king was overjoyed and ordered that Daniel be lifted from the den. Not a scratch was found on him, for he had trusted in his God.

Then the king gave orders to arrest the men who had maliciously accused Daniel. He had them thrown into the lions' den, along with their wives and children. The lions leaped on them and tore them apart before they even hit the floor of the den.

Then King Darius sent this message to the people of every race and nation and language throughout the world:

"Peace and prosperity to you!

"I decree that everyone throughout my kingdom should tremble with fear before the God of Daniel.

For he is the living God,
  and he will endure forever.
His kingdom will never be destroyed,
  and his rule will never end.
He rescues and saves his people;
  he performs miraculous signs and wonders
  in the heavens and on earth.
He has rescued Daniel
  from the power of the lions."

So Daniel prospered during the reign of Darius and the reign of Cyrus the Persian.

✛ ✛ ✛

Earlier, during the first year of King Belshazzar's reign in Babylon, Daniel had a dream and saw visions as he lay in his bed. He wrote down the dream, and this is what he saw.

In my vision that night, I, Daniel, saw a great storm churning the surface of a great sea, with strong winds blowing from every direction. Then four huge beasts came up out of the water, each different from the others.

The first beast was like a lion with eagles' wings. As I watched, its wings were pulled off, and it was left standing with its two hind feet on the ground, like a human being. And it was given a human mind.

Then I saw a second beast, and it looked like a bear. It was rearing up on one side, and it had three ribs in its mouth between its teeth. And I heard a voice saying to it, "Get up! Devour the flesh of many people!"

Then the third of these strange beasts appeared, and it looked like a leopard. It had four bird's wings on its back, and it had four heads. Great authority was given to this beast.

Then in my vision that night, I saw a fourth beast—terrifying, dreadful, and very strong. It devoured and crushed its victims with huge iron teeth and trampled their remains beneath its feet. It was different from any of the other beasts, and it had ten horns.

As I was looking at the horns, suddenly another small horn appeared among them. Three of the first horns were torn out by the roots to make room for it. This little horn had eyes like human eyes and a mouth that was boasting arrogantly.

> I watched as thrones were put in place
>   and the Ancient One sat down to judge.
> His clothing was as white as snow,
>   his hair like purest wool.
> He sat on a fiery throne
>   with wheels of blazing fire,
> and a river of fire was pouring out,
>   flowing from his presence.
> Millions of angels ministered to him;
>   many millions stood to attend him.
> Then the court began its session,
>   and the books were opened.

I continued to watch because I could hear the little horn's boastful speech. I kept watching until the fourth beast was killed and its body was destroyed by fire. The other three beasts had their authority taken from them, but they were allowed to live a while longer.

As my vision continued that night, I saw someone like a son of man coming with the clouds of heaven. He approached the Ancient One and was led into his presence. He was given authority, honor, and sovereignty over all the nations of the world, so that people of every race and nation and language would obey him. His rule is eternal—it will never end. His kingdom will never be destroyed.

I, Daniel, was troubled by all I had seen, and my visions terrified me. So I approached one of those standing beside the throne and asked him what it all meant. He explained it to me like this: "These four huge beasts represent four kingdoms that will arise from the earth. But in the end, the holy people of the Most High will be given the kingdom, and they will rule forever and ever."

Then I wanted to know the true meaning of the fourth beast, the one so different from the others and so terrifying. It had devoured and crushed its victims with iron teeth and bronze claws, trampling their remains beneath its feet. I also asked about the ten horns on the fourth beast's head and the little horn that came up afterward and destroyed three of the other horns. This horn had seemed greater than the others, and it had human eyes and a mouth that was boasting arrogantly. As I watched, this horn was waging war against God's holy people and was defeating them, until the Ancient One—the Most High—came and judged in favor of his holy people. Then the time arrived for the holy people to take over the kingdom.

Then he said to me, "This fourth beast is the fourth world power that will rule the earth. It will be different from all the others. It will devour the whole world, trampling and crushing everything in its path. Its ten horns are ten kings who will rule that empire. Then another king will arise, different from the other ten, who will subdue three of them. He will defy the Most High and oppress the holy people of the Most High. He will try to change their sacred festivals and laws, and they will be placed under his control for a time, times, and half a time.

"But then the court will pass judgment, and all his power will be taken away and completely destroyed. Then the sovereignty, power, and greatness of all the kingdoms under heaven will be given to the holy people of the Most High. His kingdom will last forever, and all rulers will serve and obey him."

That was the end of the vision. I, Daniel, was terrified by my thoughts and my face was pale with fear, but I kept these things to myself.

+

During the third year of King Belshazzar's reign, I, Daniel, saw another vision, following the one that had already appeared to me. In this vision I was at the fortress of Susa, in the province of Elam, standing beside the Ulai River.

As I looked up, I saw a ram with two long horns standing beside the river. One of the horns was longer than the other, even though it had grown later than the other one. The ram butted everything out of his way to the west, to the north, and to the south, and no one could stand against him or help his victims. He did as he pleased and became very great.

While I was watching, suddenly a male goat appeared from the west, crossing the land so swiftly that he didn't even touch the ground. This goat, which had one very large horn between its eyes, headed toward the two-horned ram that I had seen standing beside the river, rushing at him in a rage. The goat charged furiously at the ram and struck him, breaking off both his horns. Now the ram was helpless, and the goat knocked him down and trampled him. No one could rescue the ram from the goat's power.

The goat became very powerful. But at the height of his power, his large horn was broken off. In the large horn's place grew four prominent horns pointing in the four directions of the earth. Then from one of the prominent horns came a small horn whose power grew very great. It extended toward the south and the east and toward the glorious land of Israel. Its power reached to the heavens, where it attacked the heavenly army, throwing some of the heavenly beings and some of the stars to the ground and trampling them. It even challenged the Commander of heaven's army by canceling the daily sacrifices offered to him and by destroying his Temple. The army of heaven was restrained from responding to this rebellion. So the daily sacrifice was halted, and truth was overthrown. The horn succeeded in everything it did.

Then I heard two holy ones talking to each other. One of them asked, "How long will the events of this vision last? How long will the rebellion that causes desecration stop the daily sacrifices? How long will the Temple and heaven's army be trampled on?"

The other replied, "It will take 2,300 evenings and mornings; then the Temple will be made right again."

As I, Daniel, was trying to understand the meaning of this vision, someone who looked like a man stood in front of me. And I heard a human voice calling out from the Ulai River, "Gabriel, tell this man the meaning of his vision."

As Gabriel approached the place where I was standing, I became so terrified that I fell with my face to the ground. "Son of man," he said, "you must understand that the events you have seen in your vision relate to the time of the end."

While he was speaking, I fainted and lay there with my face to the ground. But Gabriel roused me with a touch and helped me to my feet.

Then he said, "I am here to tell you what will happen later in the time of wrath. What you have seen pertains to the very end of time. The two-horned ram represents the kings of Media and Persia. The shaggy male goat represents the king of Greece, and the large horn between his eyes represents the first king of the Greek Empire. The four prominent horns that replaced the one large horn show that the Greek Empire will break into four kingdoms, but none as great as the first.

"At the end of their rule, when their sin is at its height, a fierce king, a master of intrigue, will rise to power. He will become very strong, but not by his own power. He will cause a shocking amount of destruction and succeed in everything he does. He will destroy powerful leaders and devastate the holy people. He will be a master of deception and will become arrogant; he will destroy many without warning. He will even take on the Prince of princes in battle, but he will be broken, though not by human power.

"This vision about the 2,300 evenings and mornings is true. But none of these things will happen for a long time, so keep this vision a secret."

Then I, Daniel, was overcome and lay sick for several days. Afterward I got up and performed my duties for the king, but I was greatly troubled by the vision and could not understand it.

✝

It was the first year of the reign of Darius the Mede, the son of Ahasuerus, who became king of the Babylonians. During the first year of his reign, I, Daniel, learned from reading the word of the LORD, as revealed to Jeremiah the prophet, that Jerusalem must lie desolate for seventy years. So I turned to the Lord God and pleaded with him in prayer and fasting. I also wore rough burlap and sprinkled myself with ashes.

I prayed to the LORD my God and confessed:

"O Lord, you are a great and awesome God! You always fulfill your covenant and keep your promises of unfailing love to those who love you and obey your commands. But we have sinned and done wrong. We have rebelled against you and scorned your commands and regulations. We have refused to listen to your servants the prophets, who spoke on your authority to our kings and princes and ancestors and to all the people of the land.

"Lord, you are in the right; but as you see, our faces are covered with shame. This is true of all of us, including the people of Judah and Jerusalem and all Israel, scattered near and far, wherever you have driven us because of our disloyalty to you. O LORD, we and our kings, princes, and ancestors are covered with shame because we have sinned against you. But the Lord our God is merciful and forgiving, even though we have rebelled against him. We have not obeyed the LORD our God, for we have not followed the instructions he gave us through his servants the prophets. All Israel has disobeyed your instruction and turned away, refusing to listen to your voice.

"So now the solemn curses and judgments written in the Law of Moses, the servant of God, have been poured down on us because of our sin. You have kept your word and done to us and our rulers exactly as you warned. Never has there been such a disaster as happened in Jerusalem. Every curse written against us in the Law of Moses has come true. Yet we have refused to seek mercy from the LORD our God by turning from our sins and recognizing his truth. Therefore, the LORD has brought upon us the disaster he prepared. The LORD our God was right to do all of these things, for we did not obey him.

"O Lord our God, you brought lasting honor to your name by rescuing your people from Egypt in a great display of power. But we have sinned and are full of wickedness. In view of all your faithful mercies, Lord, please turn your furious anger away from your city Jerusalem, your holy mountain. All the neighboring nations mock Jerusalem and your people because of our sins and the sins of our ancestors.

"O our God, hear your servant's prayer! Listen as I plead. For your own sake, Lord, smile again on your desolate sanctuary.

"O my God, lean down and listen to me. Open your eyes and see our despair. See how your city—the city that bears your name—lies in ruins. We make this plea, not because we deserve help, but because of your mercy.

"O Lord, hear. O Lord, forgive. O Lord, listen and act! For your own sake, do not delay, O my God, for your people and your city bear your name."

I went on praying and confessing my sin and the sin of my people, pleading with the LORD my God for Jerusalem, his holy mountain. As I was praying, Gabriel, whom I had seen in the earlier vision, came swiftly to me at the time of the evening sacrifice. He explained to me, "Daniel, I have come here to give you insight and understanding. The moment you began praying, a command was given. And now I am here to tell you what it was, for you are very precious to God. Listen carefully so that you can understand the meaning of your vision.

"A period of seventy sets of seven has been decreed for your people and your holy city to finish their rebellion, to put an end to their sin, to atone for their guilt, to bring in everlasting righteousness, to confirm the prophetic vision, and to anoint the Most Holy Place. Now listen and understand! Seven sets of seven plus sixty-two sets of seven will pass from the time the command is given to rebuild Jerusalem until a ruler—the Anointed One—comes. Jerusalem will be rebuilt with streets and strong defenses, despite the perilous times.

"After this period of sixty-two sets of seven, the Anointed One will be killed, appearing to have accomplished nothing, and a ruler will arise whose armies will destroy the city and the Temple. The end will come with a flood, and war and its miseries are decreed from that time to the very end. The ruler will make a treaty with the people for a period of one set of seven, but after half this time, he will put an end to the sacrifices and offerings. And as a climax to all his terrible deeds, he will set up a sacrilegious object that causes desecration, until the fate decreed for this defiler is finally poured out on him."

+

In the third year of the reign of King Cyrus of Persia, Daniel (also known as Belteshazzar) had another vision. He understood that the vision concerned events certain to happen in the future—times of war and great hardship.

When this vision came to me, I, Daniel, had been in mourning for three whole weeks. All that time I had eaten no rich food. No meat or wine crossed my lips, and I used no fragrant lotions until those three weeks had passed.

On April 23, as I was standing on the bank of the great Tigris River, I looked up and saw a man dressed in linen clothing, with a belt of pure gold around his waist. His body looked like a precious gem. His face flashed like lightning, and his eyes flamed like torches. His arms and feet shone like polished bronze, and his voice roared like a vast multitude of people.

Only I, Daniel, saw this vision. The men with me saw nothing, but they were suddenly terrified and ran away to hide. So I was left there all alone to see this amazing vision. My strength left me, my face grew deathly pale, and I felt very weak. Then I heard the man speak, and when I heard the sound of his voice, I fainted and lay there with my face to the ground.

Just then a hand touched me and lifted me, still trembling, to my hands and knees. And the man said to me, "Daniel, you are very precious to God, so listen carefully to what I have to say to you. Stand up, for I have been sent to you." When he said this to me, I stood up, still trembling.

Then he said, "Don't be afraid, Daniel. Since the first day you began to pray for understanding and to humble yourself before your God, your request has been heard in heaven. I have come in answer to your prayer. But for twenty-one days the spirit prince of the kingdom of Persia blocked my way. Then Michael, one of the archangels, came to help me, and I left him there with the spirit prince of the kingdom of Persia. Now I am here to explain what will happen to your people in the future, for this vision concerns a time yet to come."

While he was speaking to me, I looked down at the ground, unable to say a word. Then the one who looked like a man touched my lips, and I opened my mouth and began to speak. I said to the one standing in front of me, "I am filled with anguish because of the vision I have seen, my lord, and I am very weak. How can someone like me, your servant, talk to you, my lord? My strength is gone, and I can hardly breathe."

Then the one who looked like a man touched me again, and I felt my strength returning. "Don't be afraid," he said, "for you are very precious to God. Peace! Be encouraged! Be strong!"

As he spoke these words to me, I suddenly felt stronger and said to him, "Please speak to me, my lord, for you have strengthened me."

He replied, "Do you know why I have come? Soon I must return to fight against the spirit prince of the kingdom of Persia, and after that the spirit prince of the kingdom of Greece will come. Meanwhile, I will tell you what is written in the Book of Truth. (No one helps me against these spirit princes except Michael, your spirit prince. I have been standing beside Michael to support and strengthen him since the first year of the reign of Darius the Mede.)

"Now then, I will reveal the truth to you. Three more Persian kings will reign, to be succeeded by a fourth, far richer than the others. He will use his wealth to stir up everyone to fight against the kingdom of Greece.

"Then a mighty king will rise to power who will rule with great authority and accomplish everything he sets out to do. But at the height of his power, his kingdom will be broken apart and divided into four parts. It will not be ruled by the king's descendants, nor will the kingdom hold the authority it once had. For his empire will be uprooted and given to others.

"The king of the south will increase in power, but one of his own officials will become more powerful than he and will rule his kingdom with great strength.

"Some years later an alliance will be formed between the king of the north and the king of the south. The daughter of the king of the south will be given in marriage to the king of the north to secure the alliance, but she will lose her influence over him, and so will her father. She will be abandoned along with her supporters. But when one of her relatives becomes king of the south, he will raise an army and enter the fortress of the king of the north and defeat him. When he returns to Egypt, he will carry back their idols with him, along with priceless articles of gold and silver. For some years afterward he will leave the king of the north alone.

"Later the king of the north will invade the realm of the king of the south but will soon return to his own land. However, the sons of the king of the north will assemble a mighty army that will advance like a flood and carry the battle as far as the enemy's fortress.

"Then, in a rage, the king of the south will rally against the vast forces assembled by the king of the north and will defeat them. After the enemy army is swept away, the king of the south will be filled with pride and will execute many thousands of his enemies. But his success will be short lived.

"A few years later the king of the north will return with a fully equipped army far greater than before. At that time there will be a general uprising against the king of the south. Violent men among your own people will join them in fulfillment of this vision, but they will not succeed. Then the king of the north will come and lay siege to a fortified city and capture it. The best troops of the south will not be able to stand in the face of the onslaught.

"The king of the north will march onward unopposed; none will be able to stop him. He will pause in the glorious land of Israel, intent on destroying it. He will make plans to come with the might of his entire kingdom and will form an alliance with the king of the south. He will give him a daughter in marriage in order to overthrow the kingdom from within, but his plan will fail.

"After this, he will turn his attention to the coastland and conquer many cities. But a commander from another land will put an end to his insolence and cause him to retreat in shame. He will take refuge in his own fortresses but will stumble and fall and be seen no more.

"His successor will send out a tax collector to maintain the royal splendor. But after a very brief reign, he will die, though not from anger or in battle.

"The next to come to power will be a despicable man who is not in line for royal succession. He will slip in when least expected and take over the kingdom by flattery and intrigue. Before him great armies will be swept away, including a covenant prince. With deceitful promises, he will make various alliances. He will become strong despite having only a handful of followers. Without warning he will enter the richest areas of the land. Then he will distribute among his followers the plunder and wealth of the rich—something his predecessors had never done. He will plot the overthrow of strongholds, but this will last for only a short while.

"Then he will stir up his courage and raise a great army against the king of the south. The king of the south will go to battle with a mighty army, but to no avail, for there will be plots against him. His own household will cause his downfall. His army will be swept away, and many will be killed. Seeking nothing but each other's harm, these kings will plot against each other at the conference table, attempting to deceive each other. But it will make no difference, for the end will come at the appointed time.

"The king of the north will then return home with great riches. On the way he will set himself against the people of the holy covenant, doing much damage before continuing his journey.

"Then at the appointed time he will once again invade the south, but this time the result will be different. For warships from western coastlands will scare him off, and he will withdraw and return home. But he will vent his anger against the people of the holy covenant and reward those who forsake the covenant.

"His army will take over the Temple fortress, pollute the sanctuary, put a stop to the daily sacrifices, and set up the sacrilegious object that causes desecration. He will flatter and win over those who have violated the covenant. But the people who know their God will be strong and will resist him.

"Wise leaders will give instruction to many, but these teachers will die by fire and sword, or they will be jailed and robbed. During these persecutions, little help will arrive, and many who join them will not be sincere. And some of the wise will fall victim to persecution. In this way, they will be refined and cleansed and made pure until the time of the end, for the appointed time is still to come.

"The king will do as he pleases, exalting himself and claiming to be greater than every god, even blaspheming the God of gods. He will succeed, but only until the time of wrath is completed. For what has been determined will surely take place. He will have no respect for the gods of his ancestors, or for the god loved by women, or for any other god, for he will boast that he is greater than them all. Instead of these, he will worship the god of fortresses—a god his ancestors never knew—and lavish on him gold, silver, precious stones, and expensive gifts. Claiming this foreign god's help, he will attack the strongest fortresses. He will honor those who submit to him, appointing them to positions of authority and dividing the land among them as their reward.

"Then at the time of the end, the king of the south will attack the king of the north. The king of the north will storm out with chariots, charioteers, and a vast navy. He will invade various lands and sweep through them like a flood. He will enter the glorious land of Israel, and many nations will fall, but Moab, Edom, and the best part of Ammon will escape. He will conquer many countries, and even Egypt will not escape. He will gain control over the gold, silver, and treasures of Egypt, and the Libyans and Ethiopians will be his servants.

"But then news from the east and the north will alarm him, and he will set out in great anger to destroy and obliterate many. He will stop between the glorious holy mountain and the sea and will pitch his royal tents. But while he is there, his time will suddenly run out, and no one will help him.

"At that time Michael, the archangel who stands guard over your nation, will arise. Then there will be a time of anguish greater than any since nations first came into existence. But at that time every one of your people whose name is written in the book will be rescued. Many of those whose bodies lie dead and buried will rise up, some to everlasting life and some to shame and everlasting disgrace. Those who are wise will shine as bright as the sky, and those who lead many to righteousness will shine like the stars forever. But you, Daniel, keep this prophecy a secret; seal up the book until the time of the end, when many will rush here and there, and knowledge will increase."

Then I, Daniel, looked and saw two others standing on opposite banks of the river. One of them asked the man dressed in linen, who was now standing above the river, "How long will it be until these shocking events are over?"

The man dressed in linen, who was standing above the river, raised both his hands toward heaven and took a solemn oath by the One who lives forever, saying, "It will go on for a time, times, and half a time. When the shattering of the holy people has finally come to an end, all these things will have happened."

I heard what he said, but I did not understand what he meant. So I asked, "How will all this finally end, my lord?"

But he said, "Go now, Daniel, for what I have said is kept secret and sealed until the time of the end. Many will be purified, cleansed, and refined by these trials. But the wicked will continue in their wickedness, and none of them will understand. Only those who are wise will know what it means.

"From the time the daily sacrifice is stopped and the sacrilegious object that causes desecration is set up to be worshiped, there will be 1,290 days. And blessed are those who wait and remain until the end of the 1,335 days!

"As for you, go your way until the end. You will rest, and then at the end of the days, you will rise again to receive the inheritance set aside for you."

THE STORIES AND THE STORY
How the Bible Works

The Bible is a gift. The Creator of all things has entered into our human story, and he has spoken. Working through all the authors of the Bible's various writings, God brings wisdom into our lives and light to our path. But his biggest intention for the Bible is to invite us into its Story. What God wants from us, more than anything else, is to make the Bible's great drama of restoration and new life the story of our lives too.

The appropriate way to receive a gift like this is to come to know the Bible deeply, to lose ourselves in it precisely so that we can find ourselves in it. In other words, the best thing we can do with the Bible is to immerse ourselves in it.

The first step on this journey of immersion is to become intimately familiar with the Bible's individual books—the songs and stories, the visions and letters. These books reflect different kinds of writing, and each book with its various parts must first be read and understood on its own terms. Your *Immerse Bible* is designed to help you easily see what kind of writing is found in each book. This will foster a better reading experience that leads to reading more and to reading in context.

But there is an even bigger goal than understanding the individual books. At its heart, the Bible is God's grand narrative of the world and his intentions for it. By reading whole books and then reading them as a collection of writings, we discover how the Bible presents God's big story—*the* Story. The true destination of Bible reading is for us to inhabit the Story. All the smaller parts of the Bible—Gospels and histories, proverbs and prophecies—take their rightful places in revealing the saving drama of God.

As we begin our journey deep into the heart of the Bible, we come across many stories. The plots and subplots of these stories fit together to tell the Bible's big Story. All the characters, communities, and covenants play a part in bringing the overall Story to its fitting conclusion. That is, they are related to each other and work together to reveal God's bigger purposes for the world.

But how are they related?

The following overview of the main stories that make up the Story will help you understand the overall flow of the Bible. It will reveal how the major stories in the Bible are really subplots of the big Story. As each new subplot is introduced, we will see how it serves the bigger narrative, particularly the story that immediately precedes it.

The Bible is a connected, multi-layered story, and Jesus the Messiah is directly at the center of it all. Sent by the Father and empowered by the Spirit, he is the One who ultimately brings resolution to all the stories. He is the thread—the beginning and the end—that ties the Scriptures together. Jesus the Messiah makes the Story's good ending possible, enabling the completion of God's one, big, saving purpose for all things.

1. The Story of God and His World

In the beginning God made everything and said it was all very good. It is evident from the rich variety of interconnected living things in his created order that God delights in flourishing life. This thriving, teeming world brings God glory and reveals his power.

When we read the Bible in its ancient Near Eastern context, something else also becomes clear. The opening song of creation shows us that God intends for the entire cosmos to be his temple, the place where he makes his home. When the Bible says God "rested" on the seventh day, it doesn't simply mean he stopped working. In the ancient world, a deity "rested" in order to take up residence within a temple. So the new world God made becomes his creation-temple, and he rules over it, bringing peace and life.

This is the Bible's first account, and it forms the frame for everything else that happens. God's creation is the stage for all the acts of the Story going forward. And the role of others in the drama will determine whether or not the Creator's plan for flourishing life will be realized.

2. The Story of Humanity

Humans come into the creation story in a special way. They are portrayed as being formed from the earth itself, establishing their permanent connection with the rest of the creation. Yet they are set apart from the beginning with a unique calling: stewardship. Out of all the creatures, only humans are made in the image of God himself and are to bring God's intentions for his creation to fruition. Their job is to rule over all things, helping life to flourish. Humanity is God's plan for managing his world. As priests in the temple of God's creation, humans—more than any other creature—will determine the success or failure of God's purposes for the world.

However, there are also other forces at work. Evil powers exist and are in a position to influence humans, drawing them away from God and interfering with his aims. God's people are lured into self-assertion and rebellion. This disrupts not only their relationship with God but also the way they function in the world. Because of humanity's bond with the rest of creation and their special vocation within it, great tragedy comes into the world. As their own humanity is twisted out of shape, guilt, pain, violence, and death begin to wreak havoc throughout God's good creation. Human beings are made for worship, created to bring glory to the Creator. But when humans direct their worship elsewhere, the damage reverberates throughout the world.

You'd think this would be enough to make God reject humans completely. But instead, God makes a promise to Adam and Eve that he will continue to work in and through human beings. In fact, it will be an offspring of the woman who will defeat the powers of evil. God will overcome the moral chaos of the world, and he will do it in partnership with humanity. In the Bible's Story, the fate of humanity and the rest of creation are irrevocably bound together.

But the question then becomes: How will God do this?

3. The Story of Abraham and His Family

The book of Genesis reveals a surprising answer: God is going to mend the world and bring his blessing to all the families on earth through one man and his descendants. God calls Abram (his name is later changed to Abraham) to leave his home and go to a new land and a new future. God narrows his focus to one family for a time as the means for bringing restoration to all the world's families.

From this point on, the big stories of humanity and of creation will hinge on what happens in the smaller story of Abraham's descendants. God intends for this family to be an agent for the renewal of the world. This plan begins with God's making promises to Abraham—to bless him, to make his family into a great nation, and to bring blessing to all nations. Over time, God makes a series of these promises, or covenantal agreements, with Abraham's family. Each new covenant moves the story forward and makes God's ultimate intentions more clear.

Early in the narrative, Abraham's descendants go down to Egypt and are eventually enslaved there. But God comes down to set them free and bring them into their own land, an event known as the Exodus. This great act of liberation becomes the template, or pattern, for all the acts of deliverance that God will bring in the future. (The nation that comes from Abraham's descendants becomes known as Israel, named after Abraham's grandson.)

As part of the Exodus, God gives his Law to the people through the great leader Moses, and this Law becomes an important part of his covenantal agreement with Israel. In revealing his mandates to Israel, God expects Israel to become a light to the nations. God wants his people to show the rest of the world what it looks like to live well under God's rule.

Another critical event in the Exodus occurs when God's personal presence comes down and inhabits the Tabernacle (a great tent set up at the center of Israel's camp). This Tabernacle becomes God's house in the midst of his people and is filled with symbols of the earth and sky. It is thus a miniature picture of the cosmos, revealing God's desire to cleanse and renew the whole creation and to make his home with us here once again.

God is present with his people in their new land, keeping the promises he made through Moses. But Israel struggles to honor its covenantal obligations. Throughout the story of Israel, the nation turns away from God again and again. This breakdown threatens the covenant itself. God is committed to working through his people. So if they fail, then his restoration project cannot move forward.

But this story is full of God's surprises. Along the way, God establishes a further covenant with Israel's king David. God assures David of a dynasty of kings on which the promises and hopes of Israel will be concentrated. The destiny of Israel as the beginning of God's new humanity is now focused here.

However, the people of Israel persist in rejecting God's covenant—worshiping idols, inflicting injustice on the poor, and looking out only for themselves. In anger and frustration, God finally intervenes. He exiles his people from their own land and withdraws his presence from them. Others now rule over Abraham's family, and Israel's role in the divine drama seems to have disappeared. A key biblical truth is revealed here: There can be no renewal, for Israel or the wider world, until evil and wrongdoing are dealt with. Judgment is part of setting things right.

The failure of Israel is critical for the overall Story. Israel was called to be the means by which God saves the world, but now the rescue party itself needs rescuing. Everything God intended for his people—indeed, for the entire creation—now seems in doubt.

God sees everything that has gone wrong. But wrongdoing, violence, and death will not get the last word—not in God's Story. He has another promise. Through his prophets, God brings a vision of a new future, one aligned with his founding purpose. He will establish a new covenant, one that completes and surpasses all the covenants that came before. God himself will return to his people and restore them. They will be the light they were always meant to be. So the people wait—praying, worshiping, longing—for one more promise to come true.

4. The Story of Messiah Jesus

By the first century AD, Israel had been suffering under foreign rule for centuries. Now subjugated by the Roman Empire, God's people are divided about what to do. Zealous factions advocate violent rebellion. Many teachers and other religious leaders are urging people to get more serious about following Israel's distinctive way of life under God's law. And those running the Temple in Jerusalem survive by making compromises with their Roman overlords.

Israel's ancient prophet Isaiah had foretold a time when a messenger would come to Jerusalem proclaiming the good news that God is returning at last, that his people are being saved. But Rome had its own version of the good news, and it wasn't about Israel's God. The empire's gospel was about the great blessings brought by their own powerful leader, Caesar Augustus. He is, they said, "a savior for us and those who come after us, to make war to cease, to create order everywhere. The birthday of the god Augustus was the beginning for the world of the good tidings that have come to men through him" (from the Priene Calendar Inscription in Asia Minor, ca. 9 BC).

Into this world a child is born in Israel. He is a descendant of King David, but he comes from a humble family. An angel speaks to his mother, Mary, before he is born. He tells her that this child will be the long-promised and long-awaited Messiah, Israel's King, the One who will fulfill their history. Remarkably, Scripture's account of the ministry of Jesus echoes particulars of Israel's history.

Before Israel's Exodus, Pharaoh killed many Israelite babies, but Israel's deliverer, Moses, escaped; King Herod also kills many Israelite babies in trying to kill Jesus, but Jesus also escapes. The family of Israel went to Egypt to survive a deadly famine; the family of Jesus also survives by going to Egypt. Israel passed through the Jordan River to enter the Promised Land; Jesus is baptized in the Jordan River before beginning his ministry in Israel. Israel spent forty years in the wilderness, where they struggled with temptation; Jesus spends forty days fasting in the wilderness and is tempted by the devil. And as Israel had twelve sons who fathered twelve tribes, Jesus chooses twelve men to be his closest followers. In all of this, Jesus is reliving aspects of the ancient narrative of Israel, but now with a different outcome. Jesus is refreshing Israel's story and renewing Israel itself—through himself.

In his opening message to the people of Israel, Jesus calls them to be the light they were always meant to be, announcing the Good News that something unprecedented is happening in Israel's story. He demonstrates in powerful words and miraculous deeds what it looks like when God comes as King—teaching, correcting, and healing. Jesus is widely recognized as a rabbi and a mighty prophet in Israel, but the current religious leaders see him as a dangerous new problem. Jesus critiques their leadership, thus threatening their positions of power.

This tension between Jesus and the Jewish religious leaders rises until Jesus travels to Jerusalem for a final confrontation. His twelve disciples now recognize him as the Son of David, the Messiah, but they still don't understand his mission. They assume Jesus is going to fight his enemies and claim the throne. But Jesus talks about fighting a different kind of battle. He says his struggle is against the powers of darkness and the spiritual ruler of this world.

Then during Israel's annual celebration of the Exodus, Jesus shares a final Passover meal with his disciples. He tells them that his death will inaugurate the new covenant promised by the prophets. He is arrested by the religious leaders and handed over to the Romans for execution. He is nailed to a cross, with a mocking sign posted above his head that reads "The King of the Jews." It certainly looks as though Jesus has lost, that he is no king after all. But three days later, Jesus is raised from the dead and appears to his disciples.

It turns out that Jesus willingly went to his death as a sacrifice for the sins of his people. Through his sacrifice, he wins a surprising victory over the spiritual powers of darkness. He takes on sin and death directly—ironically, through death—emptying them of their power over humanity, and he rises from the dead to confirm his triumph. This unexpected story of Israel's Messiah reveals God's long-term plan. All the earlier covenants were leading to this one. The life and ministry of Jesus brings all the narrative threads in the Scriptures together into a single, coherent Story.

5. All the Stories in One

So we see that the story of Jesus does not simply stand alone. The Bible presents his narrative as intimately tied to all the plots and subplots that came before him. Jesus, crucified and raised, is God's answer to Israel's previous failure, humanity's wrongdoing and death, and the curse on all creation.

Jesus fulfills Israel's story and successfully plays the role of rescuer given to Abraham's family. He is Abraham's faithful descendant and David's powerful son, the Messiah. He is the light the nations have been longing for. People from every tribe, nation, and community can now join Abraham's family through belief in Jesus the Messiah. As the true Israelite, Jesus is also a new Adam, a fresh start for the human race. He has defeated our archenemies sin and death, restoring our relationship with God and ushering us into the life that is truly life. The new covenant in Jesus introduces a new world.

Jesus opens the doorway to the true worship of God, and we recover our God-given vocation to be his image-bearers through our stewardship of the world. As the new Adam, Jesus brings flourishing life back into the world. He embodies the new creation in his resurrection, blazing a path of future renewal for everything in heaven and on earth.

Jesus also launches a new community of God's people—the church—creating the renewed humanity that God envisioned from the beginning. This community is the focus of God's work on the way to a completely restored and healed creation. The book of Acts and the letters of the New Testament record how the earliest churches continued the ministry of God's coming reign that Jesus had begun. The context of this ministry changes over time and in location, but the ministry itself remains the same for God's new family: to embody and proclaim the Good News of God's victory through the Messiah.

In the end, the discovery of the narrative unity we find in the Scriptures is not merely for the purpose of information. The Bible is an invitation. It calls us to join the Story and take up our own role in God's ongoing redemptive drama. We read the Bible deeply and well in order to learn the true story of our lives within God's bigger Story of the world. We read the Bible to grasp the cosmic scope and meaning of Jesus' victory. And we read the Bible to know what it means to follow Jesus ourselves. The path of the cross—selfless love and sacrifice—is the path for us, too. But that path also ends in our own resurrection when the Messiah returns.

> Yet what we suffer now is nothing compared to the glory he will reveal to us later. For all creation is waiting eagerly for that future day when God will reveal who his children really are. Against its will, all creation was subjected to God's curse. But with eager hope, the creation looks forward to the day when it will join God's children in glorious freedom from death and decay. For we know that all creation has been groaning as in the pains of childbirth right up to the present time. And we believers also groan, even though we have the Holy Spirit within us as a foretaste of future glory, for we long for our bodies to be released from sin and suffering. We, too, wait with eager hope for the day when God will give us our full rights as his adopted children, including the new bodies he has promised us. We were given this hope when we were saved.
>
> From Paul's letter to the Romans

The final theme of the biblical chronicle is life, the same theme that began the Story. Through the power of the Spirit and the action of the Son, the Father's intention will be realized in a new heaven and a new earth.

I M M E R S E
The Reading Bible

Many people feel discouraged in their Bible reading. The size and scope (not to mention the tiny fonts and the thin pages) intimidate new and seasoned readers alike, keeping them from diving into and immersing themselves in the word of God. The Bible itself is not the problem; how the Bible has been presented to readers for generations is.

Our Bibles currently look like reference books—a resource to put on the shelf and consult only when needed. So we read it like a reference book: infrequently and in small pieces. But the Bible is a collection of good writings that invite us to good reading—and it's God's word! There is an urgent need today for Christians to know the word of God, and the best way to do so is by reading the Bible. However, we need to understand the Bible on its own terms. We need to become deeply acquainted with whole books by reading them at length. And we can learn how to read the Bible well by altering a few of our current Bible reading habits.

First, we need to think about the Bible as a collection of writings written in various literary forms known as *genres*. Each literary form, or genre, used in the Bible—such as a poem, story, or letter—was chosen because, along with the words, it works to communicate truths about God to real people. (See "The Literary Forms of the Bible," p. 195, for a further explanation of some of these genres.) A complete book can be composed in a single genre, or the author may use several genres to tell one story. And even when books of the Bible are made up of several different compositions, as in the book of Psalms, those components are drawn together in such a way as to give each book an overall unity as a distinct work in itself.

Second, recognizing that the Bible is made up of whole books that tell a complete story, we should seek to understand the Bible's teaching and live out its story. To help readers better understand and read the Bible as whole books, we've removed any additives from the Bible text. Those additions, while inserted with good intentions, have accumulated over the centuries, changing how people view the Bible and, therefore, what they think they're supposed to do with it.

Chapters and verses aren't the original units of the Bible. The latest books of the Bible were written in the first century AD; however, chapter divisions were added in the thirteenth century, and the verse divisions we use today appeared in the middle of the sixteenth century. So for the majority of its history, the Bible had no chapters or verses. They were introduced so that reference works like commentaries and concordances could be created. But if we rely on these later additions to guide our reading of the Bible, we often miss the original, natural structure. This also puts us at risk of missing the message and meaning of the Bible. For this reason, we have removed the chapter and verse markers from the text. (We do, however, include a verse range at the top of each page, allowing for easy reference.)

This edition also removes the section headings that are found in most Bibles. These are also not original but the work of modern publishers. These headings create the impression that the Bible is made up of short, encyclopedic sections. So, like chapters and verses, they can encourage us to treat the Bible as a kind of reference work rather than a collection of good writings that invite good reading. Many headings may also spoil the suspense that the inspired storytellers sought to create and use to such good effect. (For example, a heading that often appears in the book of Acts announces in advance "Peter's Miraculous Escape from Prison.")

So, in place of section headings, *Immerse: The Reading Bible* uses line spacing and graphic markers to simply and elegantly reflect the natural structures of the Bible's books. For example, in the letter known as 1 Corinthians, Paul addresses twelve issues in the life of the community in Corinth. In this edition, double line breaks and a single cross mark off the teaching Paul offers for each issue. Single line breaks separate different phases of the longer arguments Paul makes to support his teaching. And triple line breaks with three crosses set off the opening and closing of the letter from the main body. By contrast, the section headings in a typical Bible divide 1 Corinthians into nearly thirty parts. These divisions give no indication of which parts speak together to the same issue or where the letter's main body begins and ends.

Modern Bibles also include hundreds of footnotes and often include cross-references throughout the text. While these features provide information that can be helpful in certain settings, there's a danger that they, too, can encourage us to treat the Bible as a reference work. Constantly going back and forth between the text and the notes doesn't really qualify as being immersed in reading the Bible.

Third, the order in which the books appear is another important factor in reading the Bible well and at length. For the majority of the Bible's history, its books were not arranged in any fixed order. Instead, they were placed in a great variety of orders, depending on the needs and goals of each presentation. In some cases, books from the same time period were put together. In other cases, similar kinds of writing were set side by side. And often the Bible's books were organized according to the way the community used them in worship.

The order of books that we know today didn't become fixed until near the time of the invention of the printing press in the fifteenth century. This ordering has many drawbacks. For example, it presents Paul's letters in order of length (longest to shortest) rather than in the order in which he wrote them. Also, in this order, the books of the prophets are divided into groups by size, and the smaller books are then organized based on phrases they share. This arrangement puts them out of historical order and sends the reader swinging back and forth between centuries. And there are many other similar concerns in what we know as the traditional order.

This edition returns to the church's longstanding tradition of arranging the Bible's books to best meet the goals of a given presentation. To help readers delve deeper into the Story of the Bible, it places Paul's letters in their likely historical order. The books of the prophets are arranged in similar fashion. Furthermore, the collection of prophetic books is placed immediately after the story of Israel because the prophets were God's messengers to the people during the unfolding of that story. The remaining books of the First Testament, known traditionally as the "Writings," are placed after the prophets and arranged by type of writing. The introductions to the various groups of books in this Bible will explain more about how they are arranged and why.

Finally, some complete books of the Bible were broken into parts over time. The books of Samuel and Kings originally made up one long book, but they were separated into four parts so they would fit conveniently on ancient papyrus scrolls. The books of Chronicles, Ezra, and Nehemiah are similarly the divided parts of an originally unified composition. In this edition, both of these two longer works are put back together as Samuel–Kings and Chronicles–Ezra–Nehemiah. Luke and Acts were written as a unified story of the life of Jesus and the birth of the community of his followers. These two volumes had been separated so that Luke could be placed with the other Gospels. But since the two parts were meant to be read together, they have been reunited here as Luke–Acts.

All of this is presented in a clean, single-column format, allowing each of the Bible's basic units to be read like the books they are. The lines of Hebrew poetry can easily be seen, and stories, proverbs, letters, and other genres can readily be identified. In short, *Immerse: The Reading Bible* takes full advantage of good visual design to provide a more authentic encounter with God's sacred words.

It is our prayer that the combined effect of these changes to the visual layout of the Bible will enhance your reading experience. We believe these changes serve the Scriptures well and will allow you to receive these books on their own terms. The goal, after all, is to let the Bible be the book that God inspired so it can do its powerful work in our lives.

THE LITERARY FORMS OF THE BIBLE

Just as God's word uses existing human language, the inspired authors also employ existing human literary forms that enable words to be arranged in meaningful ways. These different types of writing are called *genres*.

Today most of us are probably more familiar with the concept of genre from watching movies. By watching the opening scene, we can identify whether it's a Western, a science fiction thriller, a romantic comedy, or a documentary. Once we know what kind of film it is, we know what expectations we should have about what can or can't happen, how things are likely to develop, and how we should interpret what is being shown. These expectations, created by previous films and respected by filmmakers, are like an agreement with the audience about how its message will be communicated and should be interpreted.

Likewise, the Bible's authors and editors, through God's inspiration, used and respected the genres of their day. We may be able to recognize some of them as similar to genres we know today, but others may be less familiar.

Since understanding genres is critical to reading the Bible well, we will describe the key types below. The compositions that reflect these genres make up either whole Bible books or smaller sections of larger books, so some Bible books are written partly in one genre and partly in another. (Many of the genres introduced here will be further explained in the introductions to books or sections of the Bible.) As indicated below, the specific genres employed in the Bible can be divided into two general categories of writing: prose and poetry.

PROSE GENRES

- *Stories.* Narrative—or stories—weave together events in a way that shows they have a larger meaning. Typically, a story situates the reader in a place and time and then introduces a conflict. This conflict intensifies until it reaches a climax, which is followed by a resolution.

  Narrative is the most common genre used in the Bible, emphasizing that God primarily makes himself known through his words and actions in specific historical events. The Bible doesn't teach about God merely in the abstract; its historical narratives are intentionally shaped to highlight key points about God and how he relates to people and the world.

The Bible features two special types of stories-within-stories. Sometimes a person will tell a story to illustrate a point about the larger narrative that person is in. These stories are called *parables* and were a favorite teaching tool of Jesus. They usually describe real-life situations but sometimes can be fanciful, like Jotham's parable in the book of Judges, which uses talking trees as the characters. People in a story may also relate *dreams* and *visions* that they've had. In this case they're not making up a story but reporting one they've seen. This subset of narrative speaks in pictures and uses symbols to represent realities.

- *Apocalypse.* Meaning "unveiling," apocalypse is an ancient genre structured as a narrative but composed entirely of *visions* employing vivid symbols which a heavenly visitor reveals to a person. These visions disclose the secrets of the spiritual world and, often, the future. The book of Revelation is a complete apocalypse, while the book of Daniel is split between narrative and apocalypse. Elements of apocalypse also appear in Isaiah, Ezekiel, and Zechariah.

- *Letters.* About one-third of the Bible's books are letters that were originally written by one person to another person or to a group. Letters in the Bible, following the form of ancient letters, have three parts: the opening, the main body, and the closing. In the opening, writers typically give their name, say who they're writing to, and offer a word of thanksgiving or prayer. The main body deals with the business of the letter. In the closing, the writer extends greetings, shares prayer requests, and offers a prayer for God to bless the recipients. Letters in the Bible are typically used by leaders to present their authoritative teaching to a community when they aren't physically present.

- *Laws.* Also known as commands, these are instructions for what to do in specific situations in order to live as God intends. Less frequently, laws are statements of general principles to follow. Many biblical laws have been gathered into large collections, but sometimes they are placed within narratives as part of the resolution after a conflict. God's instructions are most often presented in the Bible as part of his covenantal agreements with his people, contributing to his larger saving purposes.

- *Sermons.* These are public addresses to groups that have gathered for worship or for the celebration of a special occasion. They typically explain the meaning of earlier parts of the Bible's story for people living in a later part of that story. Most sermons in the Bible are found within narratives, but the book of Hebrews comprises four sermons that were collected and then sent out in the same letter.

The book of Deuteronomy is a series of sermons by Moses to the people of Israel as they were about to enter the Promised Land. Parts of it take the form of a *treaty* that high kings would make with the kings who served them. The Ten Commandments are a miniature version of that kind of treaty.

- **Prayers.** These are addressed to God and are usually offered in a public setting in the Bible, though sometimes they are private. They can include praise, thanksgiving, confession, and requests.

- **Lists.** Many kinds of lists are found in the Bible. One of the most common types, *genealogy*, is a record of a person's ancestors or descendants. The Bible also includes lists of things like offerings, building materials, assigned territories, stops along journeys, court officials, population counts, and so on. Lists in the Bible are not merely informative but usually make a theological point or provide verification of someone's connection to God's people.

POETRY GENRES

Hebrew poetry is based not on the repetition of sound (rhyme) but on the repetition of meaning. Its essential unit, the couplet, features a form of parallelism. One line states something, and the next line repeats, contrasts, or elaborates on the first line, intensifying its meaning. This feature is sometimes expanded to a triplet (three-line unit) for greater emphasis.

Poetry frequently uses metaphors and other figurative language to communicate messages with greater strength and emotion.

- **Proverbs.** These are short sayings, typically two lines in length (though sometimes longer), that teach practical lessons for life in God's world. Proverbs are not necessarily promises about how things will work out; mainly they are descriptions of wise ways to live.

- **Songs.** Poetry set to music. In the Bible, songs are used primarily for celebration or for mourning (in which case they are called *laments*). They are often found within narratives, but some books of the Bible are whole collections of songs.

  Psalms are songs used by people gathered for worship. These songs are most often addressed to God as prayers set to music.

- **Oracles.** These are messages from God delivered by prophets. In the Bible, oracles are most often recorded in poetry; originally, they may have been sung. Some oracles are in prose, but even those often use symbolic language similar to dreams and visions. Most biblical oracles are found within larger collections from the same prophet; however, the book of Obadiah consists of a single oracle.

- *Poetic dialogue.* Utilized in a number of ancient writings, poetic dialogue is a conversation in which each participant speaks in a form of poetry. In the Bible, this genre is found only in the book of Job.

Reading the Bible well starts with recognizing and then honoring each book's genre. Following this practice will help prevent mistakes in interpretation and allow us to discover the meaning that the Bible's creators originally intended.

NLT: A NOTE TO READERS

The *Holy Bible*, New Living Translation, was first published in 1996. It quickly became one of the most popular Bible translations in the English-speaking world. While the NLT's influence was rapidly growing, the Bible Translation Committee determined that an additional investment in scholarly review and text refinement could make it even better. So shortly after its initial publication, the committee began an eight-year process with the purpose of increasing the level of the NLT's precision without sacrificing its easy-to-understand quality. This second-generation text was completed in 2004, with minor changes subsequently introduced in 2007, 2013, and 2015.

The goal of any Bible translation is to convey the meaning and content of the ancient Hebrew, Aramaic, and Greek texts as accurately as possible to contemporary readers. The challenge for our translators was to create a text that would communicate as clearly and powerfully to today's readers as the original texts did to readers and listeners in the ancient biblical world. The resulting translation is easy to read and understand, while also accurately communicating the meaning and content of the original biblical texts. The NLT is a general-purpose text especially good for study, devotional reading, and reading aloud in worship services.

We believe that the New Living Translation—which combines the latest biblical scholarship with a clear, dynamic writing style—will communicate God's word powerfully to all who read it. We publish it with the prayer that God will use it to speak his timeless truth to the church and the world in a fresh, new way.

The Publishers

A full introduction to the NLT can be found at:
http://newlivingtranslation.com/05discoverthenlt/nltintro.asp

A complete list of the translators can be found at:
http://newlivingtranslation.com/05discoverthenlt/meetthescholars.asp

UNITED AND DIVIDED KINGDOMS

UNITED KINGDOM OF ISRAEL

DIVIDED KINGDOM

① Kingdom of Saul
② David's Expansion
③ Solomon's Expansion

COPYRIGHT © 2017 TYNDALE HOUSE PUBLISHERS, INC.

EXILE AND RETURN
UNDER ASSYRIA AND BABYLON

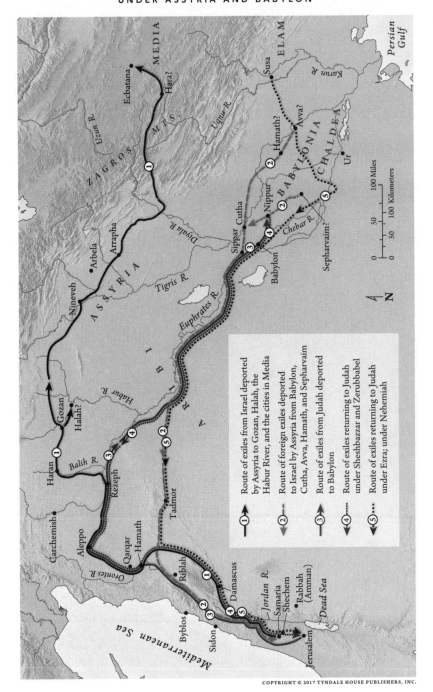

Route of exiles from Israel deported by Assyria to Gozan, Halah, the Habur River, and the cities in Media

Route of foreign exiles deported to Israel by Assyria from Babylon, Cutha, Avva, Hamath, and Sepharvaim

Route of exiles from Judah deported to Babylon

Route of exiles returning to Judah under Sheshbazzar and Zerubbabel

Route of exiles returning to Judah under Ezra; under Nehemiah

THE IMMERSE BIBLE SERIES

IMMERSE: THE READING BIBLE comes in six volumes and presents each Bible book without the distractions of chapter and verse numbers, subject headers, or footnotes. It's designed for reading—especially for reading with others. By committing to just two eight-week sessions per year (spring and fall), you can read through the entire Bible in three years. And online video and audio support tools make it easy to read together in groups. Step into this three-year Immerse Bible reading cycle with your friends; then do it again—and again—for a lifetime of life-giving, life-changing Bible engagement!

Immerse: Beginnings includes the first five books of the Bible, known as the *Torah* (meaning "instruction"). These books describe the origins of God's creation, the human rebellion, and the family of Israel—the people God chose to be a light to all peoples. We follow the covenant community from its earliest ancestors to the time it is about to enter the Promised Land.

Immerse: Kingdoms tells the story of Israel from the time of its conquest of Canaan (Joshua) through its struggle to settle the land (Judges, Ruth) and the establishment of Israel's kingdom, which ends in a forced exile (Samuel–Kings). The nation of Israel, commissioned to be God's light to the nations, falls to division and then foreign conquest for rejecting God's rule.

Immerse: Prophets presents the First Testament prophets in groupings that generally represent four historical periods: before the fall of Israel's northern kingdom (Amos, Hosea, Micah, Isaiah), before the fall of the southern kingdom (Zephaniah, Nahum, Habakkuk), around the time of Jerusalem's destruction (Jeremiah, Obadiah, Ezekiel), and after the return from exile (Haggai, Zechariah, Malachi, Joel, Jonah).

Immerse: Poets presents the poetical books of the First Testament in two groupings, dividing the books between songs (Psalms, Lamentations, Song of Songs) and wisdom writings (Proverbs, Ecclesiastes, Job). These writings all reflect the daily, down-to-earth faith of God's people as they live out their covenant relationship with him in worship and wise living.

Immerse: Chronicles contains the remaining First Testament books: Chronicles–Ezra–Nehemiah, Esther, and Daniel. These works were all written after the Jewish people fell under the control of foreign empires and were scattered among the nations. They remind God's chastened people of their identity and calling to faithfully represent God to the nations and that there is still hope for the struggling dynasty of David.

Immerse: Messiah provides a unique guided journey through the entire New Testament. Each major section is anchored by one of the Gospels, highlighting the richness of Scripture's fourfold witness to Jesus the Messiah. This creates a fresh reading of the New Testament centered on Christ.